BOOM, BUST AND CRISIS

BOOM, BUST AND CRISIS

LABOUR, CORPORATE POWER AND POLITICS IN CANADA

EDITED BY
JOHN PETERS

FERNWOOD PUBLISHING • HALIFAX & WINNIPEG

Editing: Brenda Conroy
Cover design: John van der Woude
Printed and bound in Canada by Marquis imprimeur

Published in Canada by Fernwood Publishing
32 Oceanvista Lane, Black Point, Nova Scotia, B0J 1B0
and 748 Broadway Avenue, Winnipeg, Manitoba, R3G 0X3
www.fernwoodpublishing.ca

Fernwood Publishing Company Limited gratefully acknowledges the financial support
of the Government of Canada through the Canada Book Fund and the Canada Council
for the Arts, the Nova Scotia Department of Communities, Culture and Heritage,
the Manitoba Department of Culture, Heritage and Tourism under the
Manitoba Publishers Marketing Assistance Program and the Province of Manitoba,
through the Book Publishing Tax Credit, for our publishing program.

Library and Archives Canada Cataloguing in Publication

Boom, bust and crisis : labour, corporate power and
politics in Canada / edited by John Peters.

Includes bibliographical references.

ISBN 978-1-55266-518-3

1. Industrial relations--Canada. 2. Business and
politics--Canada. 3. Employee rights--Canada. 4. Labor
policy--Canada. 5. Canada--Economic conditions--21st
century. I. Peters, John, 1963-

HD8106.5.B65 2012   331.0971'09051   C2012-903150-X

CONTENTS

LABOUR IN CANADA SERIES

This volume is part of the Labour in Canada Series, which focuses on assessing how global and national political economic changes have affected Canada's labour movement and labour force as well as how working people have responded. The series offers a unique Canadian perspective to parallel international debates on work and labour in the United States, Great Britain and Western Europe.

Authors seek to understand the impact of governments and markets on working people. They examine the role of governments in shaping economic restructuring and the loss of unionized jobs, as well as how governments promote the growth of low-wage work. They also analyze the impacts of economic globalization on women, minorities and immigrants.

Contributors provide insight on how unions have responded to global labour market deregulation and globalization. They present accessible new research on how Canadian unions function in both the private and public sectors, how they organize and how their political strategies work. The books document recent success stories (and failures) of union renewal and explore the new opportunities emerging as the labour movement attempts to rebuild the economy on sound environmental principles.

Over the past thirty years, the union movement has increasingly been put on the defensive as its traditional tactics of economic and political engagement have failed to protect wages, maintain membership and advance progressive agendas. Yet there has been far too little discussion of how the terrain of Canadian politics has shifted and how this has, in turn, affected the Canadian labour movement. There has also been far too little acknowledgment of working people's attempts to develop new strategies to regain political and economic influence. This series aims to fill these major gaps in public debate.

The volumes are resources that can help unions successfully confront new dilemmas. They also serve to promote discussion and support labour education programs within unions and postsecondary education programs. It is our hope that the series informs debate on the policies and institutions that Canadians need to improve jobs, create better workplaces and build a more egalitarian society.

Series editors
John Peters and Reuben Roth

Labour in Canada series editorial committee:
Marjorie Griffin Cohen, Julie Guard,
Grace-Edward Galabuzi, Joel Harden, Wayne Lewchuk,
Stephanie Ross, Larry Savage, Mercedes Steedman and Erin Weir

BOOM, BUST AND CRISIS IN TWENTY-FIRST-CENTURY CANADA

John Peters

Since the late 1990s, Canada's economy, politics and labour movement have been transformed — and the changes have not been for the better. First, an economic boom in natural resources, finance and housing provided new means for the wealthiest income earners to further increase their wealth, in both relative and absolute terms. Then, as resource exports exploded and the dollar rose, manufacturing industries throughout Canada restructured their operations, laid off workers and hired more temporary and contract workers, or simply closed operations and opened them elsewhere, for example, the southern United States or Mexico. For Canadians, what should have been an era of prosperity, the twenty-first century, was one of worsening jobs, declining incomes and more insecurity about their future.

In 2008–09, the boom gave way to a bust, with even more destructive consequences for average Canadians. Global credit markets dried up, and the world was thrown into an economic crisis not seen since the Great Depression of the 1930s. With a worldwide financial crisis leading to bank closures and company bankruptcies, unemployment numbers skyrocketed by more than 400,000 in Canada, eight million in the United States and thirty-four million worldwide. Major manufacturing companies like General Motors and Chrysler closed plants, laid off workers and forced major concessions on their workforces. Smaller manufacturing and forestry companies throughout Canada similarly closed the doors, which, combined with corporate restructuring efforts, led to the loss of further manufacturing jobs throughout Canada.

Even if Canada has avoided the worst of the recession, the main effect of the last decade of boom, bust and crisis has been only to worsen and reinforce tendencies long underway: the increasing power and wealth imbalance favouring business and top income earners, the declining power of Canada's labour movement and the worsening of jobs and incomes for the majority of Canadian workers.

Boom, Bust and Crisis attempts to provide some answers to how and why these developments have occurred. The second volume in a series on work and labour relations in Canada, this collection examines issues ranging from the supply-side economic policies of federal and provincial governments to the impacts of tax and investment policy on income inequality. We take stock of economic and financial changes in three of Canada's most important industrial export sectors — auto, steel and resources — where businesses have done everything possible to lower labour costs through economic restructuring and concession bargaining. We also examine key policies of labour market deregulation, their impacts on organized labour and unions' responses. Finally, we tackle one of the more troubling developments of the past decade: the fact that only a minority of Canadian workers have benefited from Canada's resource boom, while the vast majority were bypassed.

PEACE, ORDER AND INEQUALITY

Contributors to this volume cite strong evidence that government is doing little to reduce inequality through taxing the income and benefits at the very top of the income ladder and even less to ensure good, stable, long-term jobs for the rest of us. Taking a bird's-eye view of developments over the last ten years, Part One focuses on the changing structures of Canada's political and economic landscape. John Peters, Sean Cadigan, Diana Gibson and Regan Boychuk examine how natural resources and real estate have been major drivers of Canada's economy over the past decade — often to the benefit of only a few. As governments have given greater tax breaks to corporations, deregulated financial markets and reshaped labour laws in order to boost natural resource and real estate prices, so too have they made significant efforts to reconstruct markets in order to assist the privileged. The boom in Canada's energy and mining industries, along with a dizzying rise in residential and commercial building construction and sales, has made Canada into a resource powerhouse.

Yet even if resource industries driven by large transnational corporations have created new jobs in the construction, mining and oil and gas industries, the vast majority of the benefits from this growth has gone into the pockets of the richest 10 percent. At the same time, much of this new growth has come with a heavy price: a serious decline in manufacturing across the country and the growth of low-wage jobs and precarious employment. As Stephen Arnold and John Peters show, the steel and auto industries have gone into long-term decline, in part because of globalization and the international integration of manufacturing industries, but also because of how the change in the terms of trade have increased costs and led businesses to shed unionized jobs in the thousands.

Economic globalization has increased competition and forced many businesses to significantly restructure operations. This has hurt unionized workers and worsened jobs through layoffs, wage and benefit concessions and a rise in part-time and temporary employment. In manufacturing and mining, for example, new dollars in foreign direct investment (FDI) have meant finance-fuelled mergers and acquisitions that in turn have led to industrial job loss and widespread union decline. Just as common, for big business, "survival of the fittest" has meant job cuts and wage and benefit concessions. Today, it is regular business practice to contract out work formerly done by union labour and for corporations and small enterprises to expand their non-unionized workforce.

Canada's steel industry has probably been the hardest hit. But so too has the auto industry undergone massive changes as free trade agreements have allowed American companies to restructure and close Canadian facilities in the wake of the rising dollar, only to open new plants in the non-union south or overseas. In 2010, Canadian manufacturing's share of the country's total employment has fallen to 10 percent, down from 15 percent in 2000, and is the lowest among all the advanced industrial economies. At the same time, the growth of construction and services supporting the oil and gas industries has triggered a vast expansion of a non-union workforce. Today, new facilities are non-union, and throughout the country, new foreign companies have remained resolutely anti-union and have defeated — time and again — efforts by unions like the Canadian Auto Workers (CAW), the United Steel Workers (USW) and the Communications Energy and Paper Workers (CEP) to organize new workers or simply defend existing collective agreements.

But across the country, as Sean Cadigan, Diana Gibson and Regan Boychuk demonstrate, Canada's workers are feeling the effects of a "re-source curse": the heavy local impacts associated with a country having an abundance of natural resources. These impacts include a rising dollar, which undermines a competitive manufacturing industry, the contraction of other non-resource sectors, ever-widening trade imbalances, poverty and the growth of finance, real estate and service industries that depend on a low-wage labour force. Through these and a host of other negative impacts, workers have paid the price of Canada's resource boom.

Part Two focuses on how government policy has grown much more generous towards the fortunate, resulting in skyrocketing inequality. Instead of offsetting this rise, government taxes and benefits have worsened it. And when we look at the less visible redistribution that occurs through government regulation of union certification, minimum wages, employment standards, pensions and benefits, the situation is even worse. As Peter Graefe, David Fairey and Tom Sandborn reveal, in a range of areas from labour law to employment standards to foreign investment regulation, public policy has reshaped the economy to favour those at the top and remade the labour market to lower labour costs and make jobs more "flexible" for employers.

Such transformations in Canada's public policy have been especially hard on Canada's labour movement — another central theme throughout the volume.

In the wake of the global economic crisis, the central focus of Canada's federal and provincial governments, as elsewhere, has been to impose austerity measures: the reduction of taxes and government spending alongside restrictions on the rights of workers — in order to make labour markets more flexible and the economy more "productive." Many provincial governments are more concerned with the pace of resource extraction and attracting foreign investment than with managing resources in the public interest or ensuring good jobs. Led by centre-right provincial governments, the new policy emphasis is on "freeing labour markets" — i.e., labour market deregulation policies that weaken the bargaining power, protections, work conditions and institutions that have traditionally provided income and job security for Canadians.

In British Columbia, as Fairey, Sandborn and Peters highlight, the most notable trend of the past decade has been governments' tendency to legislate public-sector unions back to work, freeze wages, force workers to accept privatization of public infrastructure and public jobs, arbitrarily extend contracts and give mandatory unpaid days off. This has followed the wider trends of provincial governments from Newfoundland to B.C., which have threatened public-sector unions with further draconian actions such as essential service legislation, which removes the right to strike, and B.C.'s Bill 29 and Saskatchewan's Bill 5, which removed the right to unionize for thousands of workers. Meanwhile, at the municipal level, local governments have pointed to the state of the economy to justify major concessions in collective agreements and the privatization of services.

In Quebec — long the province with the highest rates of union density, ongoing participation in policy-making through representation in economic and social development boards and commissions, leadership in improving industrial relations legislation (e.g., an anti-scab law) and the social wage (e.g., childcare, social housing, family benefits —the Québec Liberal Party (2003–present) is rolling back many of the key policies that supported labour and enacting economic and financial legislation that makes other labour-friendly laws out of date. As Peter Graefe shows, through the changes to finance and industry regulation, labour reform and social spending, the Quebec labour force is becoming divided between "insiders," with good jobs and often union collective bargaining protection, and "outsiders," with poor and insecure employment.

Now, despite significant economic growth and reduced unemployment, a third of Quebec's labour force is stuck in non-standard employment, wages are stagnant, and a retreat in union strength has only been masked by the fact that unionized construction jobs have grown. As elsewhere, the boom years in Quebec have been years of feast for the rich and stagnation and continued insecurity for the rest. More and more, jobs for Quebecers are part-time, temporary or self-employed. At the same time, Quebec workers are seeing manufacturing jobs disappear.

Adding to these problems for Quebec and the rest of Canadian workers alike are the basic facts that provincial labour board elections and certification procedures do not work well for unions, and none are being updated in ways that protect work, unions or working conditions. Typically, card-check certification in the largest provinces (except Quebec) has given managers access to workers to urge employees to vote against representation (USW 2004). But as labour boards have been redesigned and restaffed and have seen their budgets either frozen or cut, employers have seized the opportunity to keep unions out of their workplaces, and few boards have imposed anything like adequate remedies, penalties or enforcement capabilities to temper such behaviour. When bargaining a first contract, employers have taken advantage of the limited resources of provincial labour boards and sought to delay certification, close facilities and decertify unions — all with no or limited penalties. Outside of Manitoba, which has automatic procedures that unions can use to generate a first contract, all other provinces have much more stringent requirements for first contract arbitration. There are few instances of governments imposing contracts on employers as penalties for seeking to avoid signing collective agreements (Fairey, Peters and Sandborn Forthcoming). This too has played in favour of aggressive employers seeking to avoid a unionized labour force. And even when — as in Quebec — the labour board imposed a contract on Walmart, the company simply closed the store, throwing more than two hundred people out of work.

Finally, in Part Three, we consider the implications of a declining and embattled labour movement, growing corporate power and government policies of labour market deregulation. In the 1960s and 1970s, when Canada's labour movement was strong, unions did more than simply bargain better deals for unionized workers. They set the wage and benefit trends that non-unionized employers had to match, and they pushed for health and safety systems that protected all workers — union and non-union alike. Organized labour brought workers into politics, often for the first time, through education, strikes and election mobilization. Unions helped members identify common issues of concern, informed members about politics and policy and pressed members' demands in political debates, while helping the NDP and the PQ to victory in the Prairie Provinces and Quebec.

But since the late 1980s, organized labour in Canada has lost ground in the face of the unprecedented mobilization of business and government to deregulate labour markets and create a more "flexible" labour force. Over the past ten years, organized labour has slipped even further, even as many workers continued to voice strong public support for unions and their goals. Now unions have shifted from confident involvement in politics to embattled defence of their ever smaller protected pocket of the workforce.

Rather than engage in wide campaigns for the majority of workers, unions are increasingly unwilling or unable to play their role as champions of the broad middle class. Desperate to regain membership, many unions are simply focusing on maintaining key elements of their collective agreements and lobbying for partnership deals with governments that exchange contract concessions for job and pension security for an ever-shrinking few. As is shown in later chapters, these limited and constrained strategies are affecting everything from organizing to workers' health and safety.

The results are a largely lopsided and unequal Canadian economy driven largely by resource-based investment, which has worsened jobs and left organized labour in a weakened state. Today, not only are unions unable to effectively influence public policy, but as Yale Belanger, Wayne Lewchuk, Marlea Clarke and Alice de Wolff demonstrate, unions lack the organizational muscle and political clout to organize in new sectors (e.g., First Nations casinos) or make even minor changes to health and safety policies that would improve the workplace conditions for the growing millions of part-time and temporary workers in Ontario.

Across Canada, the gaming industry over the past ten or more years has become a multi-billion dollar industry, with thousands of workers and nearly ten thousand First Nations workers. As Belanger shows, First Nations workers have tried numerous times in Saskatchewan and Ontario to organize casinos but without success. Faced with First Nations leaders vehemently opposed to unionization for reasons of profit as much as claims to the Aboriginal right to self-government and full control over labour law, unions have not been able to develop the community support or the political campaigns that would win basic union rights for casino workers.

Part-time, temporary and contract workers are also more at risk than ever before. In Ontario, for example, the Workers Compensation Board has accepted over 5,000 workplace fatality claims since 2000, well over one per day on average. During the 1990s, fatality claims accepted by the board had declined by about 10 percent, but beginning in 2000, these claims began to rise and remained above 500 per year until 2008. To make matters worse, few Ontario workers are receiving health and safety training, and even fewer are being informed about the risks associated with the materials they are using.

In the 1970s, the creation of provincial internal responsibility systems (IRSs) for health and safety, as in Ontario, was the product of demands by organized workers in Canadian mines and factories for better protection from workplace hazards. Though the system fell well short of labour demands, injury and illness rates fell significantly at workplaces where workers were represented by strong unions and even where non-unionized full-time workers could establish internal health and safety committees. But over the past fifteen years, as Lewchuk, Clarke and de Wolf highlight, the ability of workers to use IRSs to protect their health and safety has declined. With waning labour power to influence governments and the widespread growth of precarious employment, more and more workers are being placed at risk — another key feature of the boom, bust and crisis pattern of the past decade.

Part I

THE SHIFTING POLITICAL AND ECONOMIC LANDSCAPE

1. FREE MARKETS AND THE DECLINE
OF UNIONS AND GOOD JOBS

John Peters

Since early 2011, economists and the federal Conservative government have been emphatically asserting that Canada has weathered the financial storm. Canada, it is claimed, with its sound economic fundamentals, stable banking system and highly profitable resource sectors, has provided Canadian businesses with economic advantages that will allow them to compete and export to the rapidly growing developing-world economies. This argument is built on the assumption of policy-makers and economists that unfettered markets promote economic growth and prosperity for all. The much-touted "New Economy" — which began in the late 1990s with liberalized trade and finance, international corporate champions and ever-greater levels of foreign direct investment (FDI) — is supposed to ensure better jobs for Canadians. Exporting Canada's natural resources is also an integral part of this economic plan: ever increasing exports are seen as essential to creating and sustaining an economic boom in a rapidly expanding global economy. If this combination of the New Economy and intensified natural resources exports policy does not prevent the occasional economic downturn in Canada, mainstream economists and Conservative pundits argue, it will at least moderate them.

The reality, however, has proved far different from the rhetoric. Reports of Canada's good economic shape during the recent recession neglected to mention the federal government's bank bailout, totalling $120 billion in bad mortgages and unsellable financial products. Positive reports of Canada's weathering the economic storm also overlooked the impact on working Canadians: by the end of the recession in late 2010, over a half a million more Canadians were unemployed. The financial crisis — the worst downturn since the 1930s Great Depression — shattered the illusion of free and unfettered markets providing economic prosperity for all.

Moreover, in contrast to the boom for business, the lived reality for many Canadians is now an economy that is largely a "bust," particularly as it slid into crisis over the past few years. Most Canadians' experience of the New Economy over the last decade or more has been one of income stagnation. Many people saw job prospects worsen. More worked at low-paying, part-time and temporary jobs. More fell into poverty and became part of what is termed the "working poor." Across Canada, income inequality rose. Yet even in the aftermath of a severe economic crisis, the notion that markets unfettered by governments and enhanced resource exploitation can ensure economic prosperity for all remains virtually unchallenged. Instead, the federal and provincial governments continue to support those who have profited from market fundamentalism. The illusion of widespread prosperity through a resource-based New Economy endures.

This chapter provides a sharp counterpoint to such economic illusions. It examines some of the fundamental changes to Canada's political economy that "freed" enterprise, liberalized finance and globalized resource industries. Counter to standard economic interpretations, this chapter argues that while corporations and the wealthy few did very well out of Canada's booming financial, resource and construction sectors over the last decade, the majority of Canadians did not. The chapter traces how Canadian workers and the trade unions who represent them were under constant pressure, if not open attack, to give up wages, benefits and good working conditions during Canada's boom years, in large part because of the demands of finance and the growing economic might of corporations.

The case is also made that many Canadian workers experienced job loss because of the pressures of the "resource curse": Canada's reliance on natural resource exports and the subsequent rise in the currency exchange rate, which has resulted in the decline in manufacturing exports and the loss of good manufacturing jobs. The recent financial crisis has only worsened these trends, and it has given the federal and provincial governments the pretext to reduce public-sector services and employment, while bowing to companies' demands for more concessions from workers or standing by as companies close Canadian unionized operations to re-open non-union plants in the United States.

Driving all these changes is one fundamental political fact — since the late 1990s the power structure of Canada's society has fundamentally shifted to favour the affluent and the corporate elite. As detailed below, one of the primary reasons for Canada's boom and bust economy was the growing political power of business and the affluent. Through enhanced lobbying efforts, intensified policy development via corporate-sponsored think-tanks and augmented donations to mainstream political parties supportive of free market fundamentalism, business has come to dominate government agendas across the country. With centre-right party success at the federal and the provincial levels, political leaders have been especially receptive to this shift in the political terrain. Most notably, public officials have enacted what may be best characterized as a "second wave" of neoliberal policies, directed at liberalizing finance, exporting even greater amounts of natural resources, boosting consumption through debt and lowering labour costs through "flexibility" policies, which have expanded atypical employment and done nothing to protect good full-time jobs with benefits and adequate wages. Not only have such policies helped ensure economic growth, this shift in political power and public policy has also guaranteed that the economic rewards have continued to flow to those at the top of income ladder.

The other key political reason for Canada's boom and bust economy has been the decline of organized labour and its waning influence on business, government and policy. In the 1960s and 1970s, organized labour in Canada constituted a workers' movement that mobilized the energies of workers to fight for health care, health and safety standards and gender equality. But over the past fifteen years, besieged by business and governments alike, unions have shifted from confident involvement in workplaces and politics to the embattled defence of their ever smaller protected pockets of the workforce.

As argued in the second part of the chapter, there has been no movement of working people to match the rise of business power. Indeed, the labour market has been increasingly segmented between those with good jobs and those in precarious work. These ever growing numbers of labour market "outsiders," in atypical, non-unionized jobs, are increasingly resentful of workers with union protection and secure employment. Now unions are not only smaller and more isolated in relatively advantaged enclaves, they lack the political muscle and the institutional clout to influence employers or government policy.

THE INEQUALITY BOOM

The past two decades have been miserable ones for most Canadians—and even worse for the lowest income Canadians. Despite the economic upturn in the 2000s, in the eight years between 2000 and 2008, after adjusting for inflation, the incomes of the average household rose by only 5.6 percent, or by less than 0.8 percent per year (see Figure 1.1). In 2000, median family income was $50,000. Nine years later, it had risen only to $54,000—primarily because the majority of households were working an additional 336 hours a year (Marshall 2009). Without these additional hours, household income would have fallen.

Economic growth and globalization were supposed to bring a rising tide that lifted all boats and made living standards better for everyone. But as shown in Figure 1.2, the Gini Index, the standard measure of inequality, rose dramatically in the 1990s, fell slightly in the early 2000s, then rose again after 2005. Over the past forty years, since the data have been collected,

Canadians have never seen higher levels of inequality than right now. Canada is unfortunately unique in this trend: among advanced industrial countries, only the United States regularly experiences higher levels of inequality. And from 1990–2009, the rise in inequality in Canada was twice that of the United States (OECD 2011a).

Why has inequality increased so dramatically? The concentration of wealth in Canada provides part of the response. As Figure 1.1 shows, most of the gains over the last decade went to the top 10 percent of income earners, and especially to the top 1 percent and richest 0.01 percent of households (Yalnizyan 2010). While the growth in the incomes of the majority of households was flat, the incomes of the richest 0.01 percent grew by more than 145 percent over the 1990 to 2010 period. In 1990, the richest 1 percent had incomes eleven times larger than the average household; in 2008, the incomes of the rich were thirty-three times greater.

Figure 1.1 The Unequal Growth of Canadian Family Incomes, 1990–2009 (Dollars)

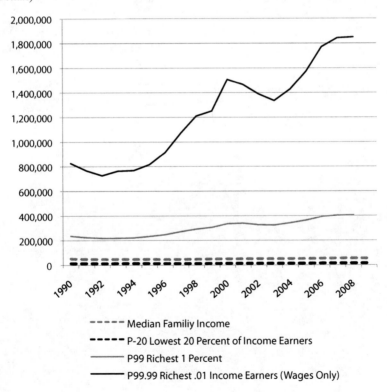

Source: Statistics Canada CANSIM Tables 2020411 and 2020703; Veall 2010.

Yet these stark numbers may underestimate growing Canadian inequality. These trends are based on Statistics Canada data, but these data are limited because the wealthiest Canadians are not reached by census surveys, which treat all incomes over $1 million as $1 million, ostensibly to protect confidentiality. Census data therefore provide a good picture of what is happening at the bottom 95 percent of incomes, but obscures trends at the very top.

For a clearer picture of top income earners, economists Hugh Mackenzie and Michael Veall analyzed tax returns and corporate executive compensation figures (bonuses, stock options and pension packages). Their results show that the average corporate compensation of Canada's CEO Elite 100 — the hundred highest-paid CEOs of companies listed in the Toronto Stock Exchange (TSX) Index — reached $8.38 million in 2010, more than 189 times larger than the pay of the average worker (Mackenzie 2012). The growth of these benefits is even more astonishing. Since 1998, CEOs' compensation has grown by nearly 90 percent. If we factor in the ongoing reductions in top marginal and corporate tax rates, it is clear the top 1 percent have gained the most from economic growth over the past few years. In fact, as of 2007, the top 1 percent had captured more than thirty-one percent of all recent income growth (Yalnizyan 2010: Chart 2).

What accounts for this rapid rise in the income of the very rich? Why has income become so unequally distributed? Why have most of the gains

Figure 1.2 Rising Inequality in Canada

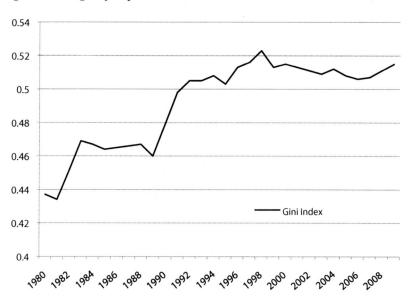

of economic growth gone to the top 1 percent and especially to the highest reaches of the top 1 percent? There are several dimensions to the rise of business and the wealthy to pre-eminence over the last few decades, but the dominance of the Liberal and Conservative parties and the power of business and finance have been key in making public policies that have grown more generous towards those at the top.

EXPLAINING RISING INEQUALITY: THE CENTRE-RIGHT AND NEOLIBERALISM

Canada's political system and its political parties have played a critical part in adopting the public policies that have facilitated business and the affluent in boosting their power and income. In first-past-the-post electoral systems like those in Canada and the United States, two- and three-party systems have always narrowed the expression of political demands, favouring centre-right parties and often excluding left parties and "outsider" political groups (Amable 2003). Indeed, in examining how electoral systems determine the partisan colour of government in the rich democracies over the past century, scholars found that systems of proportional representation have been heavily biased towards centre-left governments, while majoritarian systems are as biased towards the centre-right, so much so that three-quarters of government years in first-past-the-post electoral systems have been centre-right (Iversen and Soskice 2008). The same is true of Canada, where centre-right parties have dominated the federal and provincial governments over the postwar period, winning all federal elections and more than 93 percent of provincial elections since 1940, even with the exceptions of Saskatchewan and Manitoba, where the New Democratic Party (NDP) has been far more successful (Carroll and Ratner 2005).

In the 1960s and 1970s, organized labour and the NDP and Parti Quebecois (PQ) were able to partially overcome these disadvantages in the system and the dominance of business-friendly governments by organizing strikes and national "days of action" and successfully pushing for moderately progressive tax systems and redistributive social programs. The political spectrum in Canada was also moved to the left by the provincial electoral victories of the NDP in British Columbia, Saskatchewan and Manitoba and of the PQ in Quebec in the early to mid-1970s (Bernard and Schenk 1992; Bruce 1988). Consequently, Canada's political leaders occasionally listened to labour, and, however much many governments sought to restrain their activity, public officials saw unions as an unavoidable and often a necessary force in moving the country forward. The importance of unions was acknowledged at the highest levels of politics with, for example, Prime Ministers Lester Pearson and Pierre Trudeau both recognizing the necessity for unions having a secure place in the economy and society (Arthurs 1969; Trudeau 1962).

The tenor of the debate, however, began to shift in the late 1970s in response to economic stagnation and inflation and the subsequent political counter-attack of capital. Business began more actively to seek public policies that would dramatically improve profitability, create new opportunities for investment and speculation and seriously weaken the labour movement in order to lower labour costs. In Canada, Liberal and Conservative federal and provincial governments heard these demands and sought ways to restore employer authority and improve economic growth (Mcbride and Shields 2004). Tight monetary policy and fiscal austerity were imposed federally and provincially in the name of defeating inflation (Osberg and Fortin 1998). Governments unwound much of the detailed government intervention in particular sectors and markets through privatization and contracting out (McBride 2005). And by the mid-1990s, with financial markets making deficit reduction a priority, public officials decreed spending reductions and tax cuts as key policies in the attempt to restore financial orthodoxy to public-sector financing (Yalnizyan 2004). Through such measures, the federal and provincial governments sought to cut deficits and thereby lower interest rates to spur borrowing and investment by companies facing international competition and falling profit margins.

In the 1990s, centre-right governments (most notably at the provincial level in Canada) were also instrumental in enacting policies that "deregulated" labour markets and made workers more "flexible" (Panitch and Swartz 2003; Stanford 2000; Western 1997). Business and international organizations like the Organization for Economic Cooperation and Development (OECD) championed the case for labour market deregulation and pushed for comprehensive structural reforms to reduce "labour market rigidities" in order to lower wage and benefit costs (Freeman 2008). Governments in countries with high unemployment, as in Canada, also made reforms to a range of labour market policies, regulations and institutions in the attempt create more "active" workers, willing to be employed at lower wages in poorer jobs. These changes included restricting unemployment and other benefit systems, changing tax credits for low-income earners, weakening minimum wages and cutting back basic employment standards covering hours of work and rates of overtime pay (Vosko 2006b). Equally common were reforms to regulations covering temporary workers and the expansion of temporary foreign worker programs, again with the goal of expanding of the supply of low-wage labour (Fairey, Peters and Sandborn, this volume).

Canada's governing parties similarly took the lead in pushing for free trade and financial liberalization in the 1990s, as they sought to expand new opportunities for companies and new foreign direct investment in Canada, as well as create the economic conditions that allowed companies to make productivity gains by shedding high-wage labour (Clarkson 2008). In doing so, public officials made the flow of capital easier between Canada, the United

States and Mexico, helping Canadian and American companies expand and integrate their operations throughout North America (Stanford 2010). At the same time, the financial liberalization of stock markets and equity and money markets allowed foreign firms to buy up Canadian companies and invest in new building and facilities, easing the logistics of integrating operations across borders and giving the firms the opportunities to restructure their workplaces to employ more non-unionized labour, more part-time and temporary workers and more contractors across Canada, the United States and Mexico.

The NDP and PQ also changed with the times. Neither party converted to tax and program cuts as eagerly as the Liberals and Conservatives. But struggling mightily to compete with their better-financed rivals and coping with rising deficits and the recession of the 1990s, provincial NDP and PQ governments alike embarked on deficit reduction and welfare reforms ostensibly to lower interest rates and create more "active" labour markets (Stanford 2001). Under electoral pressure to adapt, NDP and PQ governments of the 1990s were increasingly keen to show their friendliness to business, and in the face of strenuous union opposition, they went forward with public-sector program cuts, back-to-work legislation, wage freezes and corporate as well as income tax cuts (Carroll and Ratner 2005; Savage 2010).

By the early 1990s, low inflation, quiescent industrial relations, freedom for capital to chase profitable opportunities without restraint and the domination of market-based solutions had become familiar features of Canada's political landscape. The current permissiveness to capital was rooted in this earlier incarnation of neoliberalism. Led by business-friendly political parties and with limited push-back from increasingly timid social democratic parties, Canada's federal and provincial governments effectively eliminated many of the policies that would ensure full employment and good jobs. They also ensured that economic policy was firmly directed to lowering costs for business and improving its competitiveness.

But with the exception of a more profitable financial sector, global competition, falling prices and corporate restructuring spelled trouble for many businesses in the early 1990s (Stanford 2001). Profits fell precipitously in manufacturing, oil and gas and mining throughout the 1990s (Penner 2010). And even despite the sharp rise in productivity and the as sharp decline in wages, corporate profitability in Canada mirrored trends elsewhere in the late 1990s: weakening bottom lines for corporations, declining economic growth with the rise of global production and global over-production and government austerity measures that weakened economic demand (Brenner 2006). The financial collapse of the late 1990s worsened all these trends. Consequently, Canada's public officials and centre-right governments were unable to fully resolve the problems of business or create an economic system that redistributed income upwards at a rate that met the needs of the affluent. Seeing an opportunity to win even greater gains, business went on the offensive, spearheading new campaigns for even more "market friendly" policies and even more restrictions on organized labour.

Rather than rely on the old Keynesian formula based on public deficits, new expansion in the twenty-first century would be secured through rising stock and housing markets and made possible by boosting natural resource development and exports by global corporations. For business, this would result not only in greater wealth through the rise of equity and debt, but the stimulus to finance and resources would function to put even more of the gains of economic growth into the hands of the wealthy. The role of political parties in forwarding neoliberal policy was just the first step in securing better profits and ensuring rising inequality in Canada. The other essential factor in recent shifts to Canada's political economic landscape was how business organized to influence elections and government policy and ensure that income would continue to flow upward (Duménil and Lévy 2011; Hacker and Pierson 2010).

EXPLAINING RISING INEQUALITY: THE NEW SURGE IN BUSINESS MOBILIZATION

Neoliberalism is most commonly described as a retreat from government intervention and a return to a reliance on market forces. But this often misses the influence of organized business on governments and how the business elite has used lobbying, party financing and even policy development to shape politics in favour of leading economic interests. Over the last twenty years—but most notably over the last decade—organized, well-coordinated business interests have worked to influence the exercise of government in Canada, directing grassroots campaigns, cultivating important figures in leading political parties and shaping political discourse. These efforts have not only resulted in more influence on federal and provincial elections, more importantly, they have profoundly influenced Canadian public policy.

Over the past fifteen years, Canada's most economically powerful interests have increasingly focused their political spending on lobbying in Ottawa and the provincial capitals. In Ottawa, for example, it is estimated that over $300 million is now spent every year on lobbying (Democracy Watch 2011) and this figure has doubled in just a decade. (Note that these estimates may greatly understate actual corporate expenditures to influence policy as there are no financial disclosure laws in Canada, in contrast to the United States, that compel companies and consultants to disclose their lobbying related income and expenditures). The number of lobbyists tracks this spending trend. The number of lobbyists in Ottawa grew to more than 5,000 between 2000 and 2010 (Vongdouangchanh 2011). The provinces have seen a similar expansion of lobbyists. In 2000, in Ontario, for example,

914 lobbyists were registered, and only 150 firms directly lobbied Queen's Park (Ontario 2001). By 2010, there were over 1900 lobbyists, and individual businesses had doubled their in-house lobbying representatives to more than 300 (Ontario 2011).

Beyond direct lobbying, employers have also learned how to work together to achieve shared political goals (Brownlee 2005). As members of coalitions, private free-enterprise foundations and advocacy think-tanks, firms have mobilized more proactively and on a much broader front. Through such venues, corporate leaders became advocates not just for the narrow interests of their firms but also for the shared interests of business as a whole. For example, the Canadian Chamber of Commerce has expanded to represent over 420 chambers across the country and more than 192,000 businesses. This overarching body is directly involved in campaigns to reduce tax, cut federal spending, increase competitiveness and privatize government services — all of which it considers "policy wins" (Canadian Chamber of Commerce 2011). Likewise, the Canadian Council of Chief Executives and the revamped Canadian Manufacturers and Exporters is now composed of the hundreds of chief CEOs of the country's leading corporations and have policy committees made up of leading business figures and many former government officials that engage expressly and directly with Canadian economic policy debates.

Major corporations and business associations in Canada have also quickly developed the means to generate mass policy campaigns using the tools of marketing and communications. Through private foundations like the Donner Foundation, the RBC Foundation and Irving Oil Foundation (among the many hundreds established in the past fifteen years), corporate interests have generously funded research institutes with grants to promote research on the benefits of tax competitiveness, free trade and North American integration (Brownlee 2005). Two stark examples are the multi-million dollar operations of the Fraser Institute and the C. D. Howe Institute, the "free market" think-tanks that have flooded newspapers, television and the internet with research reports, opinion editorials and news releases. As business-funded research institutes, they now boast that their media coverage across Canada is cited at a ratio of better than three to one in comparison to progressive think-tanks (Gutstein 2009).

In addition, over the past decade Canadian businesses have poured vast new resources into efforts to shape elections and the promotion of business-friendly politicians and parties. At precisely the time when the costs of campaigns have begun to rise dramatically with the ascendance of television, politicians have worked harder than even before to draw more funds from those with deep pockets. Using new technologies and innovative organizational strategies, Conservative and the most business-oriented, provincial Liberal parties alike have developed new fundraising campaigns to give them a key edge over their opponents.

Federally, up until 2004 and the new political financing law, the Liberal and Conservative Parties drew openly for the majority of their financing from corporate donations (Carroll 2004; Stanbury 2003). With the merger of the Progressive Conservative and Reform parties in 2003, the Conservatives shifted to using the Republican fundraising firm of Odell, Simms and Lynch full-time to support the Conservative Fund Canada, the financial arm of the party (Naumetz 2011). Banned from receiving direct corporate donations, the Conservatives nonetheless quickly outstripped all the opposition parties' efforts at political fundraising in smaller donations, drawing more than half of all the money donated to the five main political parties. By 2008, with more than $21 million in party fundraising, much out of riding associations with significant investment income and a huge database of wealthy donors, they had a financial lead more than double that of the opposition parties (Grenier 2012).

With such a financial edge, the Conservatives have gained a greater share of votes for their preferred candidates in federal elections through voter identification and "get out the vote" programs (Harris 2011). Vast campaign pools have been regularly allocated to critical races where the parties' candidates were evenly matched. Money was spent on advertising, candidate recruitment and training, and subsidized polling and voter targeting. Through these and other means, such as "attack" ads and "robocalls," the Conservatives have targeted and successfully won key elections.

Provincially, where there are far fewer restrictions on party financing (especially outside of election years and leadership and nomination races), the same trends are evident. Business dollars have been as much investments in winning elections as in ensuring ever more accommodating policy. In oil and gas rich provinces such as Alberta and Newfoundland and Labrador, where there are no limits to political contributions, the Conservative parties enjoy an enormous fundraising advantage over all the opposition parties and use this to substantial effect during elections (Elections Newfoundland and Labrador 1996–2010; Sayers and Stewart 2011). In both provinces, the Conservative Party draws more than 50 percent of all annual political donations, and in both provinces, business provides the majority of party finance. Over the past decade, this financial edge has meant that during election campaigns in the oil producing provinces, the Conservative parties regularly outspend all other competing parties combined by at least a two to one margin.

The cumulative effect of the surging policy engagement of business is profound. Over the course of the last twenty years and most notably over the past decade, business has established a formidable organizational network that effectively influences policy. Business and its organizational networks provided platforms for conservative economists to help make the case for business interests. They orchestrated campaigns of op-ed pieces and magazine articles designed to promote tax cuts and criticize government programs. They carefully built up closer relations with important figures in Conservative and Liberal parties alike. In reaction to these efforts, the Conservative, Liberal and even the NDP and PQ have retooled their policies to accommodate the much more assertive and organized business community. More and more, an ever-growing number of elected officials committed themselves to advancing deeper tax cuts and deregulation, particularly to the financial sector.

NEOLIBERALISM 2.0: LIBERATING FINANCE

Deepening tax cuts and shrinking government were one result of the recent surge in business organization. At both the federal and provincial levels, Conservatives slashed corporate and personal income taxes as well as the national sales tax at levels unprecedented in the first neoliberal wave (CCPA 2010). At the federal level alone, over $320 billion in personal and corporate tax cuts have been implemented since 2000 (Yalnizyan 2010). In addition, virtually every province has reduced personal income taxes since the mid-1990s. Now not only are governments continuing to cut taxes and slash public spending, but the political success of the Conservatives has made "taxes" a dirty word and forced both the Liberals and the NDP to stop making proposals that would raise revenues through taxation.

Financial deregulation and major stimulus to stock and housing markets were equally significant measures that Canada's neoliberal governments forwarded at the behest of business lobbying. Governments enacted financial liberalization to increase new foreign investment and drive share prices upward in the expectation this would push the economy ahead and improve corporate returns. Financial deregulation was also viewed as a key policy in making Canada a new energy and natural resource "superpower," with provincial governments openly promoting and underwriting natural resource development and supporting new international financial flows in the tar sands and offshore oil and gas industries to the benefit of multi-national corporations and their shareholders. Governments also supported the growth of new financial assets and the deregulation of bank sectors to boost mortgage markets to unprecedented heights and create a housing boom that would redirect ever-higher capital income flows upwards to banks and financial markets. All such policies were key in structuring private markets to the benefit of business and the wealthy — policies that are perhaps best characterized as a "second wave" of neoliberalism, or "Neoliberalism 2.0."

In market-based economies like Canada, business has long relied upon and actively used high levels of external capital (Amable 2003). There are large and active stock markets, and the financial assets of institutional investors have played critical roles in financial and stock markets. There are shareholder systems with active "outside" markets for corporate profitability and control, and firms often seek to attain short-term profits to increase share prices (Kent Baker et al. 2007). There are also active and competitive corporate governance systems, with takeovers, mergers and acquisitions all part of the routine Canadian and American corporate repertoires to boost profitability and grab market share. But over the past fifteen years, government policy — under the pressure of money and global competition — fundamentally reshaped how financial markets operated and what CEOs earned.

Central to the recent explosion in finance was the deregulation of the industry and the unregulated development of complex new financial products. Financial liberalization and the loosening of restrictions on the international buying and selling of domestic equity spurred foreign investment and drove domestic enterprises to restructure and expand (Carroll 2007). Canada's fragmented securities regulation regime — split between

Figure 1.3 Canada and the Rise of Finance

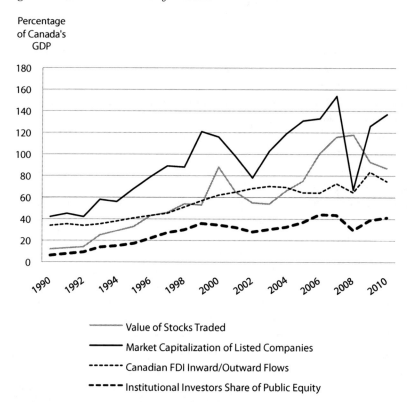

Percentage
of Canada's
GDP

Value of Stocks Traded

Market Capitalization of Listed Companies

Canadian FDI Inward/Outward Flows

Institutional Investors Share of Public Equity

Sources: World Bank Development Indicators; UNCTADstat; OECD Institutional Investor's Assets.

federal and multiple provincial jurisdictions — passed new laws allowing the "securitization" of loans. This gave businesses the opportunity to package loans into bonds that were sold on capital markets to pension and mutual funds (Bank of Canada 2004, 2009).

With these legislative measures in place, financial enterprises and non-financial firms rapidly developed new financial instruments and created new opportunities for incredible profit. Securitization — the buying and selling of corporate and mortgage market debt — was rapidly developed. Companies both large and small also issued thousands of new initial public share offerings (IPOs) on the TSX to raise capital, fend off takeovers and allow executives to "cash in their chips," with compensation totalling hundreds of millions of dollars. So too did the expansion of foreign multi-national corporations (MNCs), federally and in provinces like Ontario, lead to massive inflows of investment into domestic stock markets, especially into the largest hundred companies (the large majority in resource extraction) on the TSX. These now account for more than 80 percent of total market capitalization on the exchange (Nicholls 2006; Peters 2011).

These combined changes resulted in an explosion in new financial wealth, almost all directed to the wealthiest income earners. As Figure 1.3 shows, over the past twenty years, stock trading on the TSX rose to over a trillion dollars annually, even exceeding the entire value of the Canadian economy by 20 percent in 2008, before falling in 2009. Foreign direct investment in oil and natural resources climbed in Toronto and the other "junior" stock exchanges to record levels, making the Toronto stock and venture exchanges among the most natural resource heavy in the world (Cross 2008; Nicholls 2006). Wages and fees in the banking and brokerage industry took off in the late 1990s, skyrocketing throughout the last decade. The size of Canadian listed companies grew by more than $2 trillion. With this rapid growth in finance and the stock market, chief executive officers — all paid in salary, bonuses and stock options — saw earnings skyrocket. Throughout out the past decade not only did executive compensation rise dramatically, but even after the financial collapse, top bank executives continued to annually earn more than $10 million in compensation with the return of rising stock and equity prices (Robertson 2011a, 2011b).

NEOLIBERALISM 2.0: THE NATURAL RESOURCES BOOM

The astronomical growth of finance was paired with a second reason for the sharp rise in inequality and the incomes of the already affluent: over the past decade, Canada experienced an economic boom in natural resource investment and exports. Common sense and economic theory both suggest that countries rich in natural resources should be able to create wealth and jobs. Yet much evidence shows that the opposite is true. Countries depending heavily on oil, gas and mineral exports — like Canada — suffer from a para-doxical "resource curse," marked by uneven economic growth, inequality, immense environmental problems and inflation, as well as rising currency exchange rates that squeeze out manufacturing and good manufacturing jobs (Humphreys, Sachs and Stiglitz 2007; ILO 2011).

This resource curse is afflicting Canada today, as over the past ten years the natural resources boom has redefined the economy. In the 1980s, it seemed that Canada was diversifying its economy, but in recent years, Canada has become increasingly dependent on its resource sector and has seen its manu-facturing sector go into decline. With China now the second largest economy of the world, the resulting rise in global demand for natural resources lifted Canada's trade surplus to near-record levels of exports — above C$45 billion per year for much of the decade. Oil's rise above $100 a barrel also helped spur Canada's export-led growth. Then with the Hibernia development in Newfoundland and the oil sands of northern Alberta, Canada not only started

Figure 1.4 Natural Resource Impact on Canada (Billions of Current Dollars)

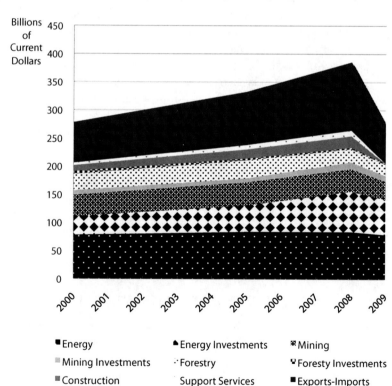

Sources: Natural Resources Canada 2011; Statistics Canada CANSIM Table 379-0023.

to produce record numbers of barrels of oil, it is acknowledged as holding the world's second-biggest oil reserves after Saudi Arabia.

As Figure 1.4 shows, the boom in natural resources was on such a scale that by 2008, the direct and indirect impact of resource output was equivalent to 22 percent of Canada's GDP (Cross 2008). Capital investments in the resource sector rose, as did new investments in construction and support services. Imports of critical resource components necessary for processing and downstream processing similarly increased. But exports by global multi-nationals with extensive value chains and supplier networks increased even faster, to the point that between 2000 and 2008, the annual economic activity tied up in natural resources rose from $275 billion to more than $380 billion. Led by oil, gas and minerals, exports of natural resources increased from $151 billion in 2000 to $253 billion in 2008. Spurred by price increases, natural resources accounted for all of the growth in Canada's export earnings (Cross 2008). The increase was especially pronounced in 2008, reflecting record energy prices.

In this context, earnings from resource exports became a dominant force in the Canadian economy, with dividends to the wealthiest of corporate executives and shareholders skyrocketing. In mining, global corporations regularly made more than 25 percent returns, with PotashCorp of Saskatchewan leading the way, registering annual returns of more than 38 percent for shareholders (Warnock 2011: 21). In oil and gas, gross revenues of the top hundred oil and gas producers exploded to more than $194 billion in 2008, with annual returns of more than 15 percent for operations throughout the decade and cash flow from operations increasing by 25 percent or more each year (Pricewaterhousecoopers 2010c). In 2008, the top multi-national oil and gas companies exceeded even their own expectations, pocketing more than $36 billion in profit. As we shall see below, such rapid changes had serious consequences for the rest of Canada's economy, especially its manufacturing sector and especially for workers in good full-time jobs.

NEOLIBERALISM 2.0: THE HOUSING AND CONSTRUCTION BOOM

The third and final element of Canada's recent boom dynamics and deepening commitment to neoliberalism was the growth in housing and construction — driven by government policies of financial deregulation and attempts to spur economic growth through the creation of ever-higher levels of private debt. As in the United States and across Western Europe, beginning in the mid-1990s, the Canadian government sought to compensate for increasing income inequality and the weakening of broad-based economic demand by stimulating household borrowing and real estate markets (Baker 2009). With annual average earnings of Canadians increasing between 1990 and 2009 by a mere $2900 dollars, from $51,100 to $54,000 (in 2005 constant dollars, adjusted for inflation), the federal government first deregulated mortgage markets to boost housing and consumer spending, then worked with the financial sector to find new ways to generate and sell consumer debt.

Down payment requirements were lowered for homebuyers, and eliminated for those who qualified. Tax breaks were given to property developers. Maximum mortgage amortization terms were extended to forty years. Variable rate mortgages were offered to buyers. Then in 2007, Canada's Housing and Mortgage Corporation (CMHC) not only insured more mortgages, it sold these back into markets in the form of "asset-backed commercial paper" to cover the growing amounts of precarious mortgage debt.

Consequently, in this second-wave neoliberalism, Canadian banks were very accommodating in providing record amounts of credit to Canadian households. Between 2000 and 2008, the value of outstanding mortgages grew from $427 billion to nearly $930 billion. From 1999 to 2005, consumer credit tripled and variable rate mortgages climbed from 2 percent of all residential mortgages to more than 25 percent (CMHC 2009). Between 2002 and 2007, the CMHC insured more than 50 percent of new mortgages,

Figure 1.5 Construction as a Percentage of Total Employment

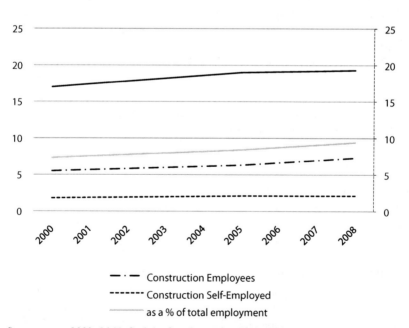

Construction as Percentage
of Total Employment

Construction Employees
Construction Self-Employed
as a % of total employment

Sources: CMHC 2009, 2010; Statistics Canada, CANSIM Tables 282-0008, 282-0012.

reflecting the fact that most individuals were putting down less than 20 percent of the purchase price. Total household debt rose from 95 percent of disposable income to 147 percent in 2009, among the highest in the world (OECD 2010a: 114). In a period of wage stagnation and growing economic inequality, deregulated credit markets were critically important to sustaining consumer demand. Further spurring the "makeover" of Canadian housing markets and Canadian consumer finances were low interest rates. The Bank of Canada responded to the events of 9/11 by pushing the interest rate down to 2.5 percent. The rate bottomed out a few months later but then stayed at historically low rates for the rest of the decade.

With record low interest rates, more Canadian families saved less and borrowed more to support their standard of living. Lower interest rates brought down mortgage rates, which fell to their lowest point in almost fifty years, making it easier for individuals to finance house purchases. With repayment terms eased to thirty-five and forty years, investors bought housing, developers built more stock, and millions of homeowners got out of higher-priced mortgages through refinancing, and bought second homes as investments. These changes fundamentally altered the economy to support housing-fuelled consumption and created the illusion for many Canadians that even though their jobs and wages were declining, their overall wealth was continuing to improve.

By 2008, housing-related spending — a broad category that includes not only home purchases but also repairs, renovations, furniture, appliances and a host of other items — accounted for one-fifth of all economic activity (CMHC 2009: Figure 7). From 2001 to 2006, when Canada led the G7 nations in annual employment growth with a rate of 1.7 percent, construction averaged 4.5 percent growth, nearly triple the rate of overall employment. By 2008, employment in construction — which includes employees and the self-employed working in residential, commercial and infrastructure — rose from 9.2 percent of total employment in 2000 to more than 12 percent (Figure 1.5). Such growth in housing, housing wealth and construction would also set off a number of boom and bust dynamics that would worsen income distribution and jobs.

LABOUR'S BUST

Canada's booming economy, driven by finance, resources and debt-based consumption, directed wealth upwards to the rich. Gains from growth and productivity went to the owners of capital — those who made money from profits, dividends, interest and financial assets. But the concentration of benefits on the wealthy was only one of the boom-time trends: the others were the worsening economic standing of most workers and the loss of political clout by organized labour. Even with solid rates of economic growth, the decline of unions was steady and ongoing. Even with rising global finance and new foreign direct investment, low-wage work continued to flourish. Even with better profits and rising dividends, businesses — both large and small — sought to cut payroll costs and make their labour force work for less in poorer jobs. Governments either actively facilitated these processes or did not intervene to prevent them. Why in the midst of the economic boom did the quality of jobs decline and most working people experience a bust? Why did unionized jobs disappear and organized labour find itself on the defensive? Why did governments across the country side with business at the expense of unions and everyday workers?

In the postwar period, from 1946 to 1980, family incomes grew at all income levels, as wages tracked productivity gains, and a substantial portion of profits were reinvested by firms that hired workers (Brenner 2006). Wages as a proportion of gross domestic product (GDP) increased to approximately 72 percent, employment grew, and family incomes and living standards rose rapidly.

Since the 1990s, these dynamics have gone in reverse. Canadians' real hourly average labour compensation has stagnated, and, for the bottom 70 percent of male full-time workers, wages have declined precipitously (Figure 1.6). Since the recession of the early 1990s, the annual growth rate of real wages for men fell to 1 percent (Sharpe, Arsenault and Harrison 2008) and continued to decline in the 2000s. Even during the boom years of 2005–2007, men and women were unable to obtain wage increases of more than 3

Figure 1.6 Real Earnings Growth for Men and Women Working Full-Time by Decile, 1997–2005 (Average Growth Rate per Year, Percentage)

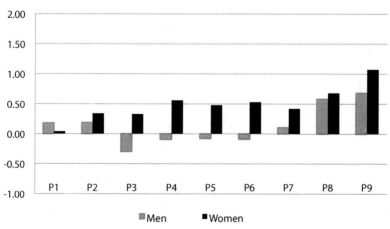

Source: OECD 2008.

percent. As shown in Figure 1.6, women in full-time jobs have done better, at least seeing modest increases in their wages (Marshall 2009). But this increase was generally no more than half a percent per year. Consequently, wages, salaries and supplementary labour income as a percentage of GDP at market prices fell from 55 percent of GDP in 1992 to only 50 percent in 2005 (Osberg 2008).

The basic economic reason for this faltering of workers' incomes is the growth of atypical jobs—part-time, temporary and self-employed—which are typically low paying. Over the past two decades, there have been some good jobs created in education, health care and construction, as well as a small number of very high-paying jobs for a small number of executives and managers in the upper levels of finance and information technology (Peters Forthcoming). But as Table 1.1 demonstrates, the far more common phenomenon was rising non-standard employment and, therefore, low-wage work. Atypical jobs rose three times faster than full-time, full-year jobs. From 1990 to 2008, overall employment rose by more than four million. But of these new jobs, only 21 percent were full-time and full-year (848,000 jobs of the total); the rest of the employment growth was the addition of 3.4 million non-standard jobs.

Table 1.1 The Dualization of the Canadian Labour Market (Millions)

	1990	2000	2005	2008
Total Employed	14.2	15.8	17.29	18.52
Full-time/Full Year	8.75	8.3	9.3	9.6
Part-time	2.2	2.7	2.9	3.16
Temporary	0.9	1.5	1.8	1.77
Self-Employed	1.2	2.4	2.5	2.6

Source: Statistics Canada, CANSIM Tables 2020103, 282-0080; 28200014.

These dynamics have often been obscured by official statistics on low-wage work, which do not include data on atypical employment. Statistics Canada's data classify 24 percent of the workforce as low-wage — the second highest figure among rich democracies after the United States (LaRochelle-Côté and Dionne 2009). But this figure counts only full-time workers, not those in atypical employment. If the window is widened to consider *all* workers, more than 50 percent of Canadians were in low-wage jobs in 2009 (data not shown Statistics Canada Table 2020101).

How families try to deal with the deterioration of income and the rise of low-wage work is often complex. But two trends are evident. First, as discussed above, families take on more debt to cover living expenses. Second, they work more jobs and longer hours (Marshall 2009). Since 1976, the total weekly employment hours of dual-income earning families increased by seven hours to an average of 64.8, nearly an extra day a week. But over this period, more than 50 percent of men have seen their work hours *decline* and their incomes become more unstable with the increasing instability of work hours (Heisz and LaRochelle-Côté 2006). It is women who have worked most of the new hours, attempting to make up for the deterioration of full-time, full-year "good" employment. Fully employed women have seen a rise in their pay and incomes (Jackson 2010). But families overall, given the destabilizing of men's employment, are now more financially stressed and time-poor than ever before.

Consequently, after a decade of economic boom, the Canadian labour market became far more "dualized," with more people finding it increasingly difficult to get by. Instead of a rising tide of financial and resource wealth lifting all boats, the reality of Canada's boom for most workers was one of a receding tide and leaking boats. As we shall see, employer pressure, government negligence and Canada's resource "curse" were each critical in worsening the labour market.

A good deal of existing economic literature argues that what is good for business is good for everyone else. Lower corporate taxes and restrict unions, the argument goes, and employers will hire more, the economy will grow, and workers will see their wages rise. But over the past decade in Canada, the exact opposite occurred. Despite the boom in finance and resources and the return to better profitability for many corporations, businesses in Canada — across all sectors — continued to reduce labour costs through a variety of strategies, including either freezing wages or hiring more workers on temporary or part-time contracts.

Employers in labour intensive sectors like retail, hotel, restaurant, clerical and cleaning were among the worst, readily adopting new production arrangements based on "working time" variations and hiring the majority of their workers on a part-time and temporary basis (Workers' Action Centre 2007; Vosko 2006a). Walmart, for example, led an intensive labour-cost competition among retailers by actively impeding unionization and offering predominantly atypical, low-wage jobs. Construction and low-end manufacturing firms also added to the growth of low-wage work with their extensive use of subcontracting and outsourcing for short-term needs, in part to avoid union contracts, and more generally to make subcontractors compete by lowering wages and benefits (Galabuzi 2006).

One of the main reasons why economists' models are so wrong is that Canadian realities are very different from theories that only explain how the world works for business. Employers operating in Canada were faced with the increased costs of production associated with the "resource boom" (particularly the seven-fold increase in the price of oil and the five-fold or more increase in the prices of minerals and metals), which resulted in rising supply costs. Rocketing natural resource prices, increasing exports and growing numbers of world buyers caused the Canadian dollar to increase in value rapidly, from $0.62 American in 2002 to over $1.03 in 2008 (Cross 2008). This near 50 percent appreciation choked off non-resource extraction industries (Beine, Bos and Coulombe 2009; Sachs and Warner 2001). In a number of industries highly exposed to international trade (including auto, steel, forestry and paper, textile mills, machinery, computer and electronics, plastics and rubber, furniture, paper, printing and transportation equipment), firms shut down or restructured operations to take advantage of the lower labour costs in the American south and midwest (Beine, Bos and Coulombe 2009; Stanford 2010). Full-time manufacturing and unionized job losses resulted, as Figure 1.7 makes clear.

As a result, by September 2008 — even before the recession — manufacturers had shed some 330,000 jobs, more than one in six over the 2004 to 2008 period. In Ontario's "Big 3" auto plants, the Canadian Auto Workers

Figure 1.7 The Rise of the Dollar and Decline of Manufacturing and Unionized Manufacturing

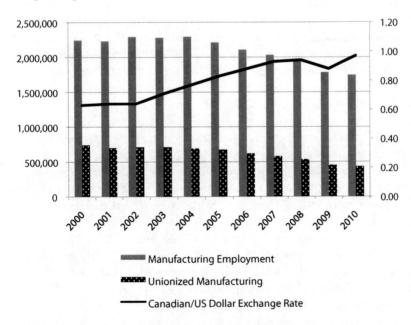

Manufacturing Employment

Unionized Manufacturing

Canadian/US Dollar Exchange Rate

Source: Statistics Canada, CANSIM tables 282-0012; 282-0078; 380-0027; and Bank of Canada.

lost roughly 38 percent of their members in the assembly and parts sectors over the past ten years (Holmes and Hracs 2010). In steel making, centred around Hamilton and Sault Ste. Marie, formerly the home to over 60 percent of Canada's steel manufacturing, job losses of 63,000 totaled more than 40 percent of employment (Livingstone, Smith and Smith 2011). In the forestry, paper and wood industries of British Columbia and Northern Ontario, corporate restructuring and shutdowns led to the loss of thousands of jobs, accounting for a decline of more than 46 percent of total employment in the industries. Then in the aftermath of the financial crisis, manufacturers laid off another 218,000 workers. Manufacturing's share of total employment in Canada has now fallen to 11.5 percent— by far the lowest in Canada's postwar history.

EXPLAINING LABOUR'S BUST:
LABOUR MARKET DEREGULATION AND GOVERNMENT POLICY "DRIFT"

Canada's business-friendly governments and labour policies were the other reasons why most workers experienced a decline in the quality of their jobs and organized labour suffered disproportionately from corporate restructuring and the rise of Canada's dollar. In contrast to the 1960s and early 1970s, when provincial governments introduced new labour legislation and employment standards to better balance the interests of business and workers, over the past decade or more, employer pressures on good jobs were not offset by government policy to protect workers. Instead, the neoliberal shift in Canada's federal and provincial governments led to business-oriented policies that facilitated more "cost effective and flexible" labour markets for business. Or — just as frequently — governments made no policy response at all, and labour law and legislation were simply ignored in tacit support for business interests. This was a case of policy "drift" — governments sitting on their hands in order to allow business to restructure their labour forces as necessary to lower costs.

On the one hand, Canada's governments actively promoted cheap labour through, for example, punitive social assistance policies and restrictive rules on Employment Insurance. These programs were re-designed to restrict access to social benefits and to force benefits recipients into the labour market, often into low-wage, low-security jobs (Handler 2004; Snyder 2006). New training programs were defended as a means to maintain the pool of cheap labour rather than to reduce its size. Similarly, governments promoted reductions in the accessibility to EI as a means to create "active" incentives for workers to return to the labour force and find jobs in other provinces.

Governments also let minimum wages languish and sink with inflation (Murray and Mackenzie 2007). In 2010, Canadian minimum wages ranged from a high of 50 percent of the median wage in Ontario to a low of 39 percent in British Columbia. These figures are even lower than in the United States, the country most commonly believed to have the lowest minimum wage among the advanced industrialized countries (Lucifora and Salverda 2009).

The ongoing promotion of strategic immigration likewise contributed to a larger pool of low-wage workers. In Canada, as in the United States, growing numbers of both skilled and less-skilled immigrants (as well as temporary migrant workers) put downward pressure on wages. Prompted by the introduction of new programs such as the Provincial Nominee Programs (PNP) and the Canadian Experience Class (CEC), as well as the Temporary Foreign Worker (TFW) and Seasonal Agricultural Worker programs, employers have picked up ever-larger amounts of labour at below cost. Over the past decade, the total number of annual TFWs in Canada has increased from 101,259 to 251,235, and they now outnumber newly entering "economic" immigrants by 33 percent (Gates-Gasse 2010).

But on the other hand, many provinces simply failed to enact or to update labour laws and policies, thus allowing business to gain the upper hand. One striking example of official neglect of basic labour rules was federal and provincial governments' failure to respond to employers' breaches of labour law. Over the past decade, employers routinely hired lawyers and consultants during organizing drives and strikes in order to run campaigns that regularly went beyond regulations without consequence (Slinn and Hurd 2009). With the exception of Manitoba, no province imposed adequate remedies or penalties when employers decided to interfere directly with organizing drives, challenge rulings on who is included in the workplace, question the voting procedure itself and then drag out first contract negotiations over a year or more (Slinn 2008). Consequently, when bargaining a first contract, employers regularly took advantage of the limited resources of provincial labour boards and delayed certification, closed facilities and decertified unions — all with no or limited penalties (Murray and Cuillerier 2009; Slinn 2008).

Similarly, over the past decade, many employers began to use the collective bargaining process as an opportunity to rid themselves of unions, and governments did little if anything to halt this. In Ontario over the past few years (2008–12), for example, with agreements about to expire, no fewer than twenty employers in the manufacturing and mining industries demanded major concessions that unions were unable to accept (Ferguson, Benzie and Talaga 2012; OFL 2010; USW 2011; Peters 2010). Forced to strike, or faced with an employer lockout, unions were left at a major disadvantage when employers moved to replace union strikers and continued to operate as "business as usual."

In each of these cases, firms have taken advantage of policy "drift" and increasingly passive labour law to hire replacement workers and run their operations for the duration of the strike or lockout (OFL 2011). Because the hiring of replacement workers always operates to the extreme detriment of a union local, especially as strikes or lockouts drag out for a year or more, employers routinely used the advantage of the law to demand concessions, and when this failed, move operations to non-union jurisdictions. In five of the strikes/lockouts since 2009, firms (e.g., Caterpillar) have simply closed and re-opened in the United States with non-union operations.

Such problematic outcomes, together with the law's general concern with the protection of property rights, have made strikes ever more risky strategies for unions and workers. Powerful corporations now regularly operate despite the presence of a picket line at their facilities (NLFL 2011). To further their advantage, employers obtain injunctions against mass picketing, and they fire strikers who they deem to have engaged in "illegal" activities on the picket line. As a result of these obstacles, many unions discovered that the "voluntarist" nature of Canadian labour law, which was intended to create a rough equality of power between the economic power of employers and that of unions, was increasingly weighted only one way — in favour of companies with deep financial resources and a strong commitment to weaken labour's bargaining power (Slinn 2008).

In these and other ways, Canada's political leaders turned the other way when economic changes benefited the rich and hurt workers. Obsolete rules and regulations that favoured employers were left in place. Deregulation and the retrenchment of social policies made economic insecurity and the fear of losing one's job commonplace. Over the last ten years, this not only hurt workers directly, it also hurt them politically. In an age of rising inequality and globalization, when an organized voice is needed more than ever before, the steady decline of unions has meant a serious lack of resources to counter the ever-rising power and influence of business and the wealthy

ORGANIZED LABOUR'S RESPONSE

Unions attempted to cope with globalization, the opposition of employers, government indifference, inadequate legal protections and new policies hostile to labour rights with a number of tactics. Some unions are using new methods, including partnership arrangements with employers and governments and enhanced worker education. Others are paying greater attention to public advocacy campaigns to increase community support and experimenting with new forms of international cooperation (Fairbrother and Yates 2003; Ross and Savage 2012).

But the general outcomes have been far from ideal. A few labour-led campaigns did protect public services and infrastructure. A few innovative organizing initiatives were successful in certifying previously hard to organize workers. But the far more notable changes to Canada's labour movement have been the macro ones: a slow slide of private-sector unions into irrelevance and the increasing defensiveness of public-sector unions (CAW-CEP 2012). By 2012, instead of a reinvigorated movement, many union officials are openly acknowledging that they are fighting for the very survival of their organizations and engaging in rear-guard actions to uphold the laws that protect collective bargaining (Allemang 2012).

Still, unions fought in a number of ways to protect members' jobs and pensions. Facing job loss in the thousands and fearing that strikes would have little impact and even less public support, private-sector unions have been looking to foster more accommodation and coordination with governments and employers through "partnership oriented" or "pragmatic" relations (Camfield 2011a). The goal is to meet employer demands for flexibility in wages, hours and hiring while seeking contractual guarantees from employers for financing, investment and jobs in return.

In high-wage and high-capital industries such as auto, steel, primary metals, mining and machinery (the sectors hardest hit by competition and corporate restructuring), many locals began to focus on improving the competitive position of the company. Unions gave pension and job concessions while accepting speed-up, job-loading, contracting out, longer hours and two-tier agreements for new hires (Bruno 2005; Peters 2010). In the public sector as well, unions such as the provincial government employees unions and nursing associations in B.C., Ontario and Quebec, attempted to protect jobs and adequate retirement packages in response to government demands for cuts and modernization through "flexicurity," arrangements that expand part-time and temporary employment and provide more opportunities for governments to contract out (Camfield 2011b; Rose 2007).

Organized labour's second noteworthy strategy to counter the rise of low-wage and precarious employment was to launch community outreach organizing campaigns. With the rapid spread of corporations such as Walmart and low-wage work by foreign migrant workers in agriculture, the United Food and Commercial Workers (UFCW), for example, has begun to undertake comprehensive political and community campaigns in their efforts to organize workers and gather community support. To improve the conditions of foreign agricultural workers, most notably in southern Ontario and British Columbia, the UFCW opened outreach offices and provided education, worker aid and organizing support among Canada's agricultural workers. Through provincial advocacy campaigns as well as a series of court challenges, the UFCW was able to force many industrial farmers to provide basic necessities like clean water and bathrooms (Basok 2009; Walchuk 2009). And in 2008, the UFCW launched organizing drives on farms in B.C. and Manitoba and had the first contract for fourteen migrant agricultural workers certified in Manitoba and for another forty workers in B.C. (Sandborn 2008). A similar public battle, with Walmart, has not had as much success, but it has built up wider community support in the UFCW's efforts to organize stores in the global retailer chain (Stout and Pickel 2007).

A third new union approach to employer and government challenges was to work with community groups to leverage wider public support to influence government on issues of broad social value. These public advocacy campaigns have varied from short- to long-term and have been successfully used by unions to oppose legislation as well as to build support for basic democratic principles. The most successful union-community advocacy coalitions have hired coordinators, retained significant organizational strength for more than a year and often pressured politicians during elections and public hearings into proposed legislative reform. CUPE, for example, has worked alongside non-traditional community allies to lobby against lowering labour costs and undermining the public sector through the privatization of services in health care, electricity and pension financing (Camfield 2011a; Tattersall 2010; Swift and Stewart 2005). Similarly, in the early 2000s, the Ontario Health Coalition developed a network of over four hundred community organizations (mostly seniors) and played a key role in labour mobilizations to combat Ontario government plans for the privatization of health care (Tattersall 2010).

In a fourth novel strategy, unions forged international mergers and international framework agreements to counter the power and reach of transnational firms (Bronfenbrenner 2007). Traditionally, in the majority of advanced capitalist countries, large domestic companies generally exported to foreign markets and unions sought to protect domestic jobs and wages. Now, not only do Western firms have global operations, but there are many more foreign transnational companies from the developing world in Canada pushing for wage and benefit concessions. Unions are moving to another level of organizing to deal with this new reality. For example, from 2009 to 2011, the United Steelworkers (USW) used global alliances to coordinate international campaigns publicizing the negative labour and community consequences of the operations of global mining giants Vale and Rio Tinto, as well as U.S. Steel in Hamilton, Ontario (Peters 2010). Emphasizing the importance and impact of strikes and lockouts to U.S. Steel's financial backers, shareholders and customers, the USW attempted to bring financial pressure on the company. And relying on their union allies or NGOs abroad to initiate actions against companies, the USW sought to bring policy-makers into the equation, with the expectation that government officials would pressure the MNCs to return to the bargaining table and offer concessions to labour.

Of course, unions combined these new strategies with traditional methods, such as mobilizing memberships through protests, job actions, bargaining campaigns and lobbying (Camfield Forthcoming; Murnighan and Stanford Forthcoming). In the wake of the financial crisis in 2008, unions undertook dozens of demonstrations and rallies to voice their displeasure and educate members and the general public. They also started education and outreach campaigns to explain current conditions and ongoing strategies. In 2009, the CAW, for example, backed workplace occupations and blockades to demonstrate the union's ability to mobilize members in workplace actions (Rosenfeld 2009). CUPE coordinated province-wide planning meetings for workplace actions in Ontario and British Columbia (Gindin and Hurley 2010). Unions used these opportunities to lobby governments and emphasize the importance of public support for industrial sectors and the benefits of good jobs with stable incomes.

THE LIMITS OF ORGANIZED LABOUR

Even though a number of Canada's unions have used a variety of methods to demonstrate to government and employers alike that they could still resist the harshest demands of neoliberalism and globalization, in the wake of the 2008 economic crisis, many acknowledge that over the past decade they were often unable to hold the line on concessions (Albo, Gindin and Panitch 2010). More and more, union officials concede that their bargaining power has weakened over the last decade and that employers are unilaterally determining investment and employment decisions far more frequently than in the past (Murnighan and Stanford Forthcoming). And despite the efforts of organized labour, it is widely recognized that the balance of power in Canada continues to shift against organized labour and working Canadians and that unions are increasingly overwhelmed by business in terms of organization, money, effectiveness and influence (CAW-CEP 2012).

In the 1970s, unions covered nearly 36 percent of the private workforce in Canada. Pattern agreements often set the standards for wages and benefits that non-unionized employers had to follow. But by 2009, private-sector unionization was in freefall and pattern bargaining was a thing of the past. Officially, Statistics Canada reports that union density has only dropped a quarter, from a high of 36 percent in the 1980s to approximately 30 percent today. However, if we include in that calculation the entire domestic civilian labour force, such as the growing number of workers categorized as "self-employed" and "temporary," as well as those who work as employees but are paid as contractors (currently all these groups are excluded from the official statistics), the fall in union density is much worse. More comprehensive data show a decline of over one-third over the past twenty years, from 33 percent in the 1980s to 25.6 percent in 2008 (Table 1.2). Canada's private-sector unions have faced an even steeper fall. After more than thirty years of decline, by 2009 private-sector union density had fallen to the lowest level since the early decades of the twentieth century, a mere 16 percent. These figures also more closely match the international calculations of the OECD, which has sought to standardize union density calculations (OECD 2011b).

Table 1.2 Union Density in Canada 2000–2009

	2000	2005	2009
Total	27.1	26.6	25.6
Private sector	18.9	17.7	16.2
Manufacturing	30.7	29	24
Construction	15.3	15.6	15.4
Mining, forestry			
Oil, gas, utilities	25.2	23.4	19.6

Note: Includes temporary and self-employed workers, unincorporated with no paid help, in the civilian workforce.
Sources: Statistics Canada CANSIM Tables 2820012, 2820078, 2820074.

This long-term and steep decline in union coverage and union member-ship in much of the private sector had a number of cumulative impacts on organized labour's ability to improve jobs and policy and boost bargaining power and political influence. Above all, deindustrialization and the loss of union members created a harsh new organizing reality for unions: simply put, the fewer the number of union members, the greater the cost per member to organize the vast non-union sector and to support political campaigns. Within private-sector unions, this has proven an insurmountable problem, and as a result, most unions have begun to adopt more cost-conscious and conservative approaches when considering long-term corporate campaigns or organizing low-wage private-service-sector workers (Yates 2007). Some have pursued mergers to boost membership. Others have focused only on large workplaces and continued to rely on the traditional model of "hotshop" organizing. Many have simply ignored new organizing all together. The key outcome has been precipitous declines in new union member certifications (Dickie 2005; Katz-Rosene 2003; OLRB 2009). There are no regular public estimates of new certifications outside of those published by labour boards in some provinces. But it appears that by 2004–2008, unions averaged at best 40,000 new members a year, a figure only roughly a third of the size needed for unions to maintain pace with employment growth.

The upshot has been that unions' bargaining power has gone into de-cline with this decline of organizing. In the postwar period, unions not only affected the wages and jobs of unionized workers, but they also put heavy pressure on non-unionized employers to match union benefits, salaries and jobs — in large measure to head off organizing drives (Jackson 2010; Western and Rosenfeld 2011). Now these processes have gone into reverse. Faltering union influence has meant that employers are under much less pressure to raise wages or improve jobs. And unions are no longer setting pay norms in local labour markets. Expanding their precarious labour force, employers have only made it harder for unions to organize and certify new workplaces (Anderson, Beaton and Laxer 2006).

Now, even where there are union organizers, with high turnover levels and short-term contracts, unions find it extraordinarily difficult to overcome the usual repertoire of managers' union avoidance tactics, which include layoffs, short shifts and termination (Clark and Warskett 2010). Consequently, the fact of a growing non-unionized labour force is turning the dynamics of the labour market around, allowing employers to put even more pressure on unions to accept wage and benefit concessions or face lockouts and layoffs — a situation that further undermines labour's bargaining and economic strength.

The new emphasis on public campaigns, while promising, has proven a poor substitute for historical militancy in educating and mobilizing members. In the past, strikes gave unions the opportunity to involve members in setting priorities, to build workplace unity, to set up and deliver membership communication and action networks, and to undertake public advocacy campaigns that build public support (La Botz 2005; Bronfenbrenner et al. 1998). But with the decline in strikes and the increasing use of advocacy campaigns, unions are finding it far harder to mobilize and educate members, and campaigns often do little to build community links (Peters 2010). Apart from the very successful anti-privatization of health-care campaigns, many union efforts at advocacy campaigning are little more than the distribution of flyers, an afternoon rally and an email distributed to members. Seldom are local leaders and members given extensive education, seldom do many members participate, and seldom do campaigns have the scale, the community "bridge" builders and the coalition structures necessary to influence governments or employers.

Worse, by taking fewer strikes, unions are finding that they have less capacity and fewer members with which to undertake strikes that protect and win contracts. In the 1970s and 1980s, when militancy was at its highest in Canada, unions had no shortage of staff and members with knowledge of how run picket lines, launch community newspapers, undertake province-wide fundraising events and set up women's and community support committees (Gindin 1995; Yates 1990). This is increasingly no longer true. In two of the largest recent strikes, one involving CUPE and the City of Toronto, the other the USW and Vale, the ability of the unions to get members out, communicate their message, and build wider community support was uneven at best (Barnett and Fanelli 2010; Peters 2010). In each case, locals lacked the research, public relations and strategic planning capacities with which to pressure employers, protect jobs and plan long-term wage, job and benefit campaigns that built community support. They also lacked the internal means of member participation to effectively coordinate their efforts against employers and cope with the challenges posed by aggressive employers.

Cross-border corporate and bargaining campaigns as well as union alliances also remain generally undeveloped, with little muscle to protect workers during strikes or in bargaining. The USW, for example, launched international corporate campaigns during their long strike against Vale and the lockout of workers at U.S. Steel in Hamilton (Arnold, this volume). Yet despite having the most global alliances and community networks of any private-sector union in the world, in neither case was the USW able to influence corporate behaviour or public debate. In Sudbury, the USW was forced to accept major concessions on bonuses, layoffs, pensions and bumping rights, and as well saw the loss of over three hundred members (Peters 2010). In Hamilton, the lockout ended with similar job and pension concession, and U.S. Steel laid off all of its 800 employees eleven months later.

Such reversals are part of a larger shift within unions. Leaders and staff are moving from an offensive to defensive posture, focusing less on expanding the frontiers of labour's power in the workplace than to defend what has already been won. When that fails, unions are then resorting to concessions and efforts to protect pensions and severance packages. But the risks of these defensive approaches are far higher than the rewards, because they divide union members and impede new attempts at union renewal.

Above all, the largest new risk that unions are facing is "reverse class warfare" — the public notion that unions are just out for themselves and not for society and that union wages and benefits are out of touch with those of hard-pressed non-unionized workers (Allemang 2012). Rather than aspire to becoming union members, more unorganized workers are coming to envy and resent the relative advantages of unionized workers (Walkom 2010). With no realistic hope of ever becoming union members, labour market "outsiders" are coming to view unionized workers — especially in the public sector — as favoured "insiders," unfairly protected from the pains of globalization and business competition. This public hostility is further marginalizing union status and undermining labour's claims to represent a larger public good.

This resentment has grown in the wake of the economic crisis, because, with the decline of bargaining coverage, Canada's unions have been forced to simply defend the gains of their current membership at the cost of building a larger labour movement. Composed largely of public employees and industrial and resource workers in troubled economic circumstances, the labour movement has found itself without the capacity to gain much in the way of public support. As in the United States, this has meant that the

Canadian labour movement is less able to claim to represent the mass of middle-class workers or the growing low-wage workforce (Dark 2011; Gindin 2011). Unions have not been able to adequately organize or reach out to impoverished workers in any comprehensive manner (Shantz 2009).

Consequently, rather than a "virtuous circle" of strategies and gains, Canadian unions are often finding themselves in a series of "vicious circles" — where government deregulation, job loss and employer opposition is shrinking union capacities and demobilizing the workforce and, in turn, seriously undermining any future possibilities for organizing success and political influence. Absent a strong political constituency like organized labour, business and industry have been largely free to continue exerting their undue influence on Canadian democracy and public policy. Now many unions are not only facing a difficult climate, many more are facing the prospects of following American unions into continuing decline (CAW-CEP 2012) — an organizational crisis made worse by the events of the past few years.

THE 2008 CRISIS AND BEYOND

These troubling trends have only deepened in the aftermath of the financial crisis. In the spring and summer of 2008, global credit markets seized up in response to the growing awareness of massive over-lending in new "financial instruments" and the faltering mortgage markets in the United States. A global economic crisis resulted that is expected to last for years to come, with long-term impacts on Canadian jobs, the labour market and unions: most critically, the financial crisis has provided big businesses in Canada and elsewhere with the opportunity to lay off workers, demand wage concessions and hire more part-time and temporary employees.

Around the world in the wake of the collapse of financial markets, output, investment and employment plummeted, most notably in the United States and Western Europe (Albo, Gindin and Panitch 2010). Staggering declines in GDP were recorded in the final quarter of 2008 and early 2009. At an annualized rate, GDP shrank by 6 percent in the G7 economies. By the end of 2009, the financial crisis had created the worst downturn since the Great Depression. Declines in overall output were dramatic, and even with the return of growth in 2010, underutilized capacity remained at 3 percent in Canada and over 5 percent in the United Kingdom (Figure 1.8).

In Canada, the financial crisis was less severe and shorter than in the other G7 nations, since neither the financial system nor the housing market had been as rapidly deregulated. Nonetheless, the downturn in the U.S. and the world economies had a profound impact on Canadian jobs, income and unemployment. Between the third quarter of 2008 and the second quarter of 2009, real GDP in Canada fell by 3.6 percent. For the year 2009, the decline of 2.9 percent was the second largest since the Great Depression (Cross

2010). Figure 1.8 compares GDP declines in Canada with trends in the U.S. and U.K. to give a sense of the decline.

Canadian and international firms operating in Canada responded to the economic crisis by quickly cutting costs and jobs. Business investment fell a record 14 percent in 2009, and three-quarters of the drop was in mining and manufacturing (Cross 2010). With the sudden decline in commodity prices, mining and oil and gas corporations slashed output and exports. Forestry, which fed the U.S. housing market, went into freefall, with jobs cut by more than a quarter. In the auto industry, after the bankruptcies and bailout of General Motors and Chrysler, output dropped by over 50 percent, plants were closed, and in the wake of worldwide restructuring, jobs in Canadian vehicle assembly and parts manufacturing plunged a further 28 percent in 2010 from 2007 levels.

Data on job losses from late 2008 to November 2009 show that Canadian-based firms laid off over 450,000 full-time workers, the majority in manufacturing and natural resources. The number of unemployed workers (seasonally adjusted) jumped to over 1.5 million (CLC 2009c). The unemployment rate increased faster among men (from 6.8 to 9.8 percent) than among women (from 5.7 to 7.3 percent), reflecting greater job losses in manufacturing and construction, where male workers predominate. But the crisis hit the private and public sectors alike. In the private sector,

Figure 1.8 The Economic Crisis and Declining Output
(Output Gap in Percent of Potential GDP)

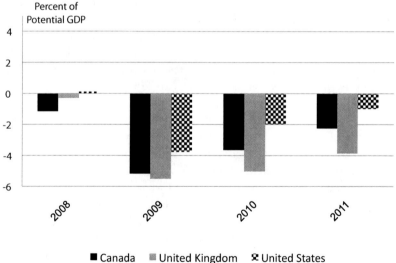

Sources: *OECD Economic Outlook Database; IMF Economic Database.*

employment fell by 450,000, or by 4.1 percent. The percentage decline in full-time private-sector employees was even greater, down by 4.4 percent. In the public sector, the number of employees declined by 55,000, or 1.6 percent (CLC 2009b; CLC 2009c). Young and immigrant workers felt the effects of the financial crisis the hardest. For young workers (age fifteen to twenty-four), who are usually the first to be laid off and the last to be hired, the unemployment rate rose from 12.2 to 15.2 percent, nearly double the overall rate of unemployment (CLC 2009b). Recent immigrants, meanwhile, saw employment fall by 13 percent.

When growth returned in 2010, the labour market was reshaped according to business concerns with profitability. A considerable amount of employment growth in Canada — as elsewhere — over the period 2009–2010 was part-time and temporary (Figure 1.9). Some full-time public-sector jobs were added as governments continued to hire teachers and health-care workers. But overall, employers far preferred to hire more part-time and temporary employees. Part-time employment as a percentage of total employment consequently increased from 18.6 percent to 19.2 percent between 2008 and 2011. Temporary employment also increased, as cash-strapped firms

Figure 1.9 Changes in Canadian Employment, 2007–2010

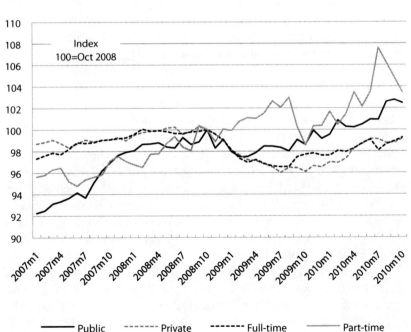

Source: OECD 2010b.

continued to compete largely on the basis of low wages. To cut costs quickly, construction and low-end manufacturing also laid off workers or shifted to part-time hours. And where firms relied on a profusion of temporary contracts for greater "flexibility," the low-skilled, immigrants and young bore the burden of "adjustment" (ILO 2011).

What was the role of the federal and provincial governments in the post-crises Canadian labour market? Like governments around the world, the Canadian government reacted to the economic problems with a range of new monetary and fiscal policies intended to support the financial sector while stabilizing the economy for business and underpinning income for workers. These measures have done little for workers, while doing much for business and the financial sectors. To stabilize jobs and employment, Canadian federal and provincial governments introduced "stimulus" packages that were one part new investment, one part wide-ranging tax cuts and a very small part directed to improving employment insurance for the unemployed. In Canada, as in the United States and the United Kingdom, the vast majority of stimulus came in the form of corporate and personal income tax cuts, business tax credits and to a lesser extent loans to the auto sector.

Between 2009 and 2011, all levels of government in Canada made commitments to spend approximately $13 billion in capital investment. But tax cuts were the key focus of the packages intended to keep individuals spending even if unemployed or working part-time. Together, it was estimated that Canada's governments would spend approximately 2 percent of GDP (55 percent of that in tax cuts) annually for two years to overcome the massive drop in economic output (OECD 2010a: Table Fiscal Stimulus).

But the reality was far more modest. Like many other countries, Canada failed to meet the G20 goal of 2 percent of GDP for fiscal packages, and its public spending was far short of what was needed to tackle the crisis (Jha 2009). Money was directed to fixing roads and bridges in a number of provinces, though by late 2010, only $4 billion had been allocated by the federal government, and less than 30 percent of projects had been completed (Pinet and Weltman 2010). More than a quarter of the projects failed to report any progress. By spring 2011, the federal government removed another $1 billion in stimulus investment spending, and cumulative spending, including spending in all provinces, was reduced to $10 billion in total, or less than 0.4 percent of annual GDP.

In qualitative terms, the nature of the fiscal stimulus package was just as ineffective. The tax cuts had little stimulus effect, while costing the government roughly $32 billion a year (CCPA 2011). Personal tax cuts and tax credits reduced the federal government's fiscal balance by another $13 billion per annum. This not only worsened the federal deficit and placed provinces in even more difficult financial circumstances, it is estimated that by 2016, the

Harper government will have cut taxes by more than $218 billion during its time in government, effectively making it a priority for provincial governments across Canada to eliminate and restructure social programs.

Unemployment insurance reforms were equally unhelpful. In the early 1990s, Canada's unemployment insurance system provided income benefits for roughly 90 percent of the unemployed (Black and Shillington 2005). By 2005, after a series of "flexibility" improvements, only 40 percent of the unemployed qualified, and in cities like Toronto, with its high immigrant workforce and extensive non-standard employment, only 20 percent of the unemployed qualified.

In 2009, to overcome these problems and provide some income stabilization, the Conservative government introduced reforms to help the unemployed. But the impacts of the changes to EI were extremely limited. In December 2008, only 40 percent of unemployed Canadians qualified for benefits. In Ontario and Alberta, the numbers in early 2009 were even lower — 30 percent and 22 percent respectively (CLC 2009a). By the end of 2009, while the EI reforms meant that 50 percent of unemployed Canadians were now able to receive benefits (Jackson and Schetagne 2010), in Toronto, Vancouver and Montreal, fewer than 37 percent of the unemployed qualified for any kind of unemployment benefit (CLC 2009c: Table 4).

By the end of 2010, Canada had returned to "business as usual." In finance, after a strong rebound in the second half of 2009, stock market returns and Canadian bank profits soared in 2010. By fall 2010, Canadian financial markets had fully recovered from their March 2009 lows, bond issuance and corporate yields returned to pre-crisis levels, and bank credit continued to flow normally to businesses and households. The resource-heavy S&P/TSX index gained 13.4 percent in 2010, outperforming other advanced economies' indices and returning to the highs previously reached in the spring of 2008 (Pricewaterhousecoopers 2010b).

In the financial sector, even despite provisions for record credit losses in U.S. operations, all the major Canadian banks showed market returns in excess of 17 percent in 2009 and 14 percent in 2010. Many of Canada's major banks achieved record earnings on their domestic divisions, with the fastest expansion being in their mortgage and credit card operations (Pricewaterhousecoopers 2010b). Annual profits for CIBC, BMO, BNS, and TD soared over the course of 2010, as they each earned over $5 billion.

The resource sector also did extremely well in 2010. In oil, gas and mining, profits skyrocketed four-fold to $8.4 billion, as rising commodity prices and rapid growth in demand from China and India increased export prices (Statistics Canada 2011). Potash Corp in Saskatchewan saw similarly robust returns (Warnock 2011). In Canada's precious metal industry, double-digit growth is expected to continue for several years. Flush with surplus capital, multi-national resource corporations again rapidly acquired junior resource companies in the expectation of super-profits to come.

In October 2008, the *Economist* opined that government intervention and new and better forms of financial regulation and long-term policy planning were needed (at least in the short-term) if the world economies were to avoid seeing a recession slide into a full-fledged depression. The crisis, the magazine wrote, had the potential to undermine the "credibility of free-market capitalism" and "while the scale of the change is still unclear, a larger economic role for the state in general and a smaller and more constrained private sector can be expected, at least for the next few years." But, to date, little has changed.

Before the crisis, the financial and resource sectors were the most powerful economic, political and social forces in Canada. After the crisis, the financial and resource sectors are still the most powerful. During Canada's economic boom, manufacturing was in decline, there was a growing polarization between rich and poor, middle-income earners were dependent on debt, and public spending on physical infrastructure, education and social well-being was being slowly constricted. After the crisis, all these same trends continue.

CONCLUSION

Over the past decade, Canada's boom economy has provided unprecedented benefits for business and the affluent. Resource profits have exploded. Finance has reached new heights. Corporate CEOs have seen their bank accounts swell. But rather than better jobs and more secure futures for a majority of workers, most Canadians have seen their incomes stagnate and their work lives become more stressful. Unions are much weaker, with many having fewer members, others under severe attack in many provinces, and all seemingly more unpopular among the general public. Indeed, many union leaders and activists are more discouraged than ever, and private-sector unions, in particular, appear stuck in a downward spiral of workforce marginalization and political exclusion. But rather than governments using their power and influence to shape globalization in a way that is fair, to limit finance and redistribute our resource wealth in ways are sustainable, the second wave of neoliberalism in Canada has cast economic policy less on principles that would improve the well-being of the majority of workers than on making policies that serve the self-interest of a few — above all, the powerful economic interests in business, finance and resources.

To counter these worrying trends and develop policies that work for all citizens, Canadians will have to mobilize and press for coordinated responses to regulate, supervise and oversee financial institutions. Canadians also require policies that put the roles of market and government in balance and ensure that a strong state administers effective and progressive regulation. The power of special interests — especially those in natural resources — must be curbed. Job growth must be prioritized, in large part to generate higher wages and in turn shift the distribution of income in ways that will support more domestic consumption.

But making such changes in public policy, economic strategy, income distribution or work and industrial relations will be extraordinarily difficult. They not only require political will but more importantly political mobilization. They necessitate a politics that challenges the current economic thinking of powerful business interests and shows the clear need for alternatives. However, the problem today is that many unions are on the defensive after a decade of deindustrialization and the loss of jobs during the crisis of the past few years. Workers in atypical employment and poor jobs are often politically handcuffed, with many lacking the time, money and education needed to mobilize and organize for a better future. Moreover, between unions and the large numbers of women, immigrants and youth in non-unionized employment, there are often few ties and — even worse — growing resentment, further weakening the prospects of a new political coalition that will push for progressive policies that will benefit all Canadians.

If Canada's labour movement is to overcome these problems and move forward, then union leaders and activists need to engage with the current challenges of finance, deindustrialization and government deregulation. They must design policy responses to ensure robust growth that delivers a job-centred recovery and a sustainable "green" economy that benefits all workers. They have to press a more progressive political agenda that challenges market fundamentalism and the power of special interests in Canada's democracy. They also have to make labour law reform a key priority and implement new kinds of "open source" unionism that extends services, protection and education to non-unionized workers.

This is daunting. Neoliberal governments at both the federal and provincial levels have strong majorities. Finance and business are as strong and as profitable today as they were before the crisis. And unions — especially those in the public sector — appear caught in a downward spiral of defending their existing members yet condemned to becoming ever more unpopular to a wider public. Despite this, the argument for working-class organization in the wake of the economic crisis is more compelling than ever. To counter the power of business, workers and citizens need strong organizations that can mobilize, educate and protect basic rights and freedoms. To lead a social movement that helps people in all walks of life, unions need to connect with workers in more diverse ways. The task for the left, then, is to devise new forms of worker self-organization that are less dependent on the negotiation of collective bargaining contracts and far more focused on the struggle for justice and advancing the interests of working people in general. An essential first step is to identify and address the problems of Canada's "boom, bust and crisis" political economy.

2. THE SPOILS OF THE TAR SANDS
Profits, Work and Labour in Alberta

Diana Gibson and Regan Boychuk

After more than a dozen years of presiding over his "revolution" in Alberta politics, Premier Ralph Klein made his final appearance in the Alberta legislature on August 31, 2006, at the height of the oil boom. Finally freed from the political imperative to defend policy at the expense of honesty, Klein conceded that his critics had been right: his government had never had any plan for dealing with the boom. He claimed "no one could anticipate the phenomenal growth that was taking place"—it came "quite suddenly," catching him completely off guard (Fekete 2006: A1). But Klein should not have been surprised about the fevered pace of development because the oil rush was caused in great part by government policies. The tar sands boom in particular—multi-year, multi-billion dollar construction projects growing exponentially after 1997—was the direct and intended result of business mobilization and government reforms to tax and royalty structures.

What has since unfolded constitutes an enormous, business-driven social experiment in which vast amounts of public wealth have been transferred and concentrated into private (often foreign) hands at an astonishing pace. At the same time, public services and programs have been gutted through underinvestment. The result is that Alberta is now an increasingly polarized economy where, at the height of the boom, over 80 percent of the income went to the top half of households and the majority of Albertans felt they were not benefiting. Albertan workers have seen inflation price housing out of reach, incomes stagnate even as working hours increased, public services falter and job security erode alongside the increase in part-time and temporary work and poor working conditions. Albertans have paid a heavy price for this concerted experiment in governing for the few.

ECONOMIC BOOM

As the Klein era drew to a close, Cross and Bowlby (2006) noted that Alberta was "in the midst of the strongest period of economic growth ever recorded by any province in Canada's history": in 2005 Alberta's per capita GDP was 56 percent above the national average—the largest historical deviation in a century. GDP surged during the boom years, as evidenced in Figure 2.1. The *Financial Times* (May 8, 2007: 3), a leading global business newspaper, went a step further to call the tar sands boom "North America's biggest resources boom since the Klondike gold rush more than a century ago."

Figure 2.1 shows that in 2007 (the last year of available data), the oil and gas sector accounted for $87.5 billion of the total $255.8 billion provincial GDP. The sector accounted for as much as 37.5 percent of Alberta's total GDP over the 1997 to 2007 period (Carter 2011). This GDP growth was predominantly driven by the construction boom, fuelled by stunning levels of investment in the tar sands. In 1998, investment in tar sands capital and operating costs was less than $4 billion. By 2000, the figure had doubled to almost $8 billion and by 2005, it had more than doubled again to nearly

Figure 2.1 Oil and Gas Sector's Contribution to GDP in Alberta (Millions of Current Dollars)

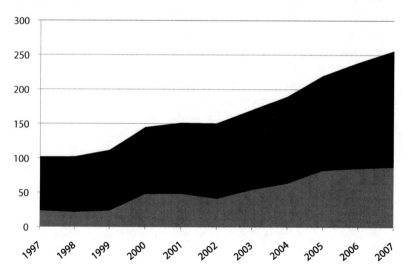

■ Total GDP (billions)

▓ Total Impact of Oil & Gas on GDP (billions)

Sources: Statistics Canada, CANSIM Tables 384-0002, 381-0015, 379-0025.

$18 billion. In 2008, annual investment in tar sands projects had climbed past $29 billion.

A residential and commercial construction boom paralleled this rapid development of tar sands production. With a rapidly expanding economy, Alberta experienced a population increase of approximately 46,500 persons annually in the 2000s—a rate that in relative terms was three times the national average. In turn, demand for housing rose and housing prices skyrocketed. Construction rose in tandem and by the mid-2000s, this sector accounted for 22.5 percent of Alberta's GDP. The bulk of this—64 percent—was in oil and gas.[1] But overall, construction employment accounted for over 10 percent of Alberta's workforce (compared to 7.4 percent nationally), the highest it has been since the 1970s.[2]

Who benefited from the economic boom? Most of the rewards from the unprecedented, globally notable growth in Alberta's white-hot economy went to corporations and the province's already hyper-affluent class. Over the last decade, Alberta's economy grew in lockstep with corporate profits. According to the Statistics Canada analysis, corporate profits were the biggest factors contributing to the surge in the province's GDP. Profits more than doubled, from $23.5 billion in 2002 to $53.1 billion in 2005, directly accounting for over half of all growth (Rowat 2006). In February 2007, Statistics Canada released a report that corporate operating profits had reached their second consecutive record high in 2005 (Statistics Canada 2007). The oil and gas sector accounted for much of this corporate profit, with the industry earning excessive pre-tax profits (defined as profits after royalties, land sales, exploration and operating costs and a normal rate of return). Over the last ten years, oil and natural gas companies operating in Alberta cleared more than $148 billion in pre-tax profit while contributing only $93 billion in royalties and less than $11 billion in land sales to the province for exploration rights (Boychuk 2010a). Average revenues in 2005 for the ten oil and gas companies considered in the Statistics Canada study were $5.2 billion each, an increase of 26.5 percent over average revenues in 2004. The average return on investment increased from 21.7 percent in the early 2000s to 23.1 percent in 2005. Of course, these extensive gains did not primarily go to Canadian corporations. Rather, mostly foreign corporations and foreign shareholders are benefiting; according to Statistics Canada, close to half of the assets and over half of the revenue in oil and gas extraction in Canada are foreign-owned.

Consistent with this trickle-up trend, executives have seen massive increases in their salaries and bonuses over the last few years, especially when stock options of up to $7.4 million are included. Likewise, only Alberta's richest 10 percent saw their incomes rise significantly while working fewer hours (Gibson 2007b: 12).

SOCIAL BUST

Corporations (mostly foreign) and the wealthiest classes in Alberta benefited enormously from the boom, as did those working in high-paid jobs in the tar sands. But the majority of Albertans saw their standard of living erode during this recent oil rush — due to rapidly rising inflation, particularly its impact on housing prices. The construction boom in response to the growth in tar sands operations led to shortages in materials and labour. Then the influx of workers into the province to fill the labour gap further heightened the demand for new construction, exacerbating the problem. Alberta's Consumer Price Index (CPI) increase was the highest in the nation at the height of the boom, hitting 5 percent in 2007. The construction price index was even higher and remained higher than inflation throughout the recession.

The combined forces of population growth and inflation also made for a housing crisis in Alberta. However, the tar sands construction boom dwarfed the boom in residential housing construction. The much better financed tar sands construction was able to bid scarce resources away from the housing sector, driving construction costs through the roof and house prices out of reach for many ordinary Albertans (Cross and Bowlby 2006: 3.6). For example, through 2006 and the first half of 2007, Calgary's new house price index increased 65 percent, while Edmonton's average single-family home/condo selling price jumped 52 percent (Gibson 2007b). In 2006, provincial housing prices increased by a record 31 percent and continued to rise as fast in 2007 and the first half of 2008.

As a result, housing affordability plummeted, and at least 20,000 Calgarians with a family income of less than $15,000 were paying more than 50 percent of their income for housing. Homelessness increased by a record 19 percent in Edmonton in 2006 alone. Consequently, more people were forced to use food banks, so much so that by 2009, the percentage of employed people utilizing food banks in Alberta was twice the national average (Food Banks Canada 2009: 22–3).

LABOUR BUST

Inflation has added a heavy financial burden on most Albertans as incomes have not increased to offset rising costs. On the contrary, evidence is mounting that incomes have actually stagnated while working conditions have deteriorated. The rising oil tide has not lifted the boats of Albertan workers; rather, the oil and gas boom has had profoundly negative impacts on the labour market.

The reality is that oil and gas extraction is capital rather than labour intensive: the sector has the lowest number of jobs per dollar invested of any industry in Canada. Of course, given the scale of the energy industry and taking a wider view to include indirect jobs associated with the sector (such as construction, supply, engineering and research and development), it has accounted for approximately 14 percent of total employment in Alberta (Alberta Government 2008). This is without a doubt a significant employment sector in Alberta, yet the jobs are often erratic and temporary. Over half of the workers associated with the tar sands boom are needed only for the construction phase and are out of work when that ends. While the jobs might be well paid, few are long-term or provide economic security for workers and their families. This makes Alberta very vulnerable to economic downturns, as was evident when the most recent recession hit, and construction came to an abrupt halt.

Alongside job insecurity, tar sands jobs often come at a high cost as living and working conditions are poor and hard on families. Over the past decade, between 16,000 and 25,000 mobile workers resided in remote clusters of modular trailers, while many living onsite in construction camps describe them as prisons (Dembicki 2010). The emotional toll of this is obvious. At the height of the boom, between 2006 and 2008, workers in the oil and gas industry were 35 percent more likely than the national norm to access employee assistant programs for addiction, and the rate had increased by 112 percent in just three years. Alcohol dependency rose steadily, with a 481 percent increase in employee assistance program usage between 2006 and 2008. Research indicates that the primary reason for these increases is "expansion of the oil sands projects and the ongoing recruitment of employees to support substantial growth" (Shepell•fgi Research Group 2009: 2, 4, 5). Yet even these alarming figures are likely underestimates. According to University of Alberta master of arts student Angela Angell (who interviewed tar sands workers, addictions counselors and labour experts over several years), the hospital emergency room is the public service most likely to be used in Fort McMurray; the least likely — social service agencies. According to one counsellor interviewed by Angell, 60 percent of workers with addiction issues do not seek help (Krogman et al. n.d.: 24).

Wages earned in the tar sands are hard won, and the general economic benefit of this industry does not extend far. Alberta's strong income growth was also not reflected in the wages and income of the average Alberta family. On average, hourly wages in Alberta did not keep pace with the high levels of inflation. In nominal terms, wages did increase between 2000 and 2005, but after accounting for inflation, real wages fell over this period. Most workers in Alberta sought to compensate for declining wages by working harder. And, as noted in a Statistics Canada (2007a) report, Albertans were already working harder than any other Canadians, averaging 1,880 work hours per year, the highest in the country. The Parkland Institute's analysis found that boom-time hourly wage increases did not account for the growth in incomes for the average Albertan. What income gains they had managed were the result of working more, not of getting paid more (Gibson 2007b).

As for those at the bottom of the wage scale, little changed. Statistics Canada numbers show that the percentage of all wage earners who were making less than $20,000 per year (2004 constant dollars) fell only slightly during the boom years and was actually still higher in 2007 than it was back in 1980 (Alberta Federation of Labour 2010). As shown in the results of a Parkland Institute study conducted at the height of the boom, most middle-income Albertans did not see their incomes rise along with the boom, and many lower income Albertans were actually worse off (Gibson 2007b).

During this stagnating wage boom-time, women, now a large low-wage workforce for employers, were particularly disadvantaged, and this trend has grown in the recent financial crisis. Between August 2008 and June 2009, there was an overwhelming net loss of jobs for 29,000 men over the age of twenty (Hamilton and Newman 2009). Yet by mid-2010, there was a 12,800 net increase in employment of women over the age of twenty. More families in Alberta are relying on women's lower wages to make ends meet. Yet women are increasingly working in low-paying jobs, resulting in more families living in a low-income situation. Wage disparity is illustrated well in the comparison of average median hourly earnings. During the first six-months of 2009, median hourly earnings were $25.43 for men over the age of twenty, versus $19.52 for women over that age. Furthermore, two-thirds of minimum wage earners are women. Half of women in the workforce earn less than $25,000 per year. Only 23 percent of women earn more than $45,000, in large part because they make up the vast majority of part-time workers (Phillips 2010). In 2009, women made up 70 percent of all part-timers in the province.

Another particularly vulnerable segment of the labour force comes from beyond Canada's borders. Construction in the tar sands has grown so rapidly that governments and employers turned to temporary foreign workers, as well as workers from elsewhere in Canada to supplement the workforce (Gibson 2007a). At the height of the boom, Alberta had 57,000 temporary foreign workers. These workers were employed everywhere from the tar sands, to Edmonton and Calgary staffing service-sector jobs, to Tim Hortons take-out windows across the province. The strategy turned out to be so successful for service-sector employers that the number continued to rise well after the re-cession hit. In 2009, there were 69,000 of these workers in Alberta, but they are not being brought in as potential new Canadian citizens; rather they are a temporary underclass of foreign workers, without the full rights of citizens and at the mercy of their employers and employment brokers.

Certainly there are few social security protections for temporary foreign workers. And the employment "safety net" that used to protect Canadian and

Albertan workers has been badly torn. Alberta's minimum wage was relatively low for most of the boom and only pegged to inflation at the end. Further, to ensure stagnant wages during the boom, welfare benefits were kept low. Between 1986 and 2008, welfare income fell by 23 percent for families of four and by 44 percent for individuals. Social assistance rates were also not pegged to inflation, and, even though it is the wealthiest province, Alberta has amongst the lowest rates (National Council of Welfare 2008a, 2008b). Even regulations on child labour were relaxed, with Alberta amending labour standards legislation to allow twelve-year-olds into the workplace.

For most Albertans, the oil boom has meant the rise of poor temporary jobs, increasing work hours, stagnating incomes, a new low-wage, temporary or part-time underclass of women and foreign workers and eroded social security programs. Hence, the results of the public opinion survey conducted by the Parkland Institute in March 2007 revealed more than half of Albertans felt they had not benefited from the boom, while 17 percent said they were worse off. Yet when asked if other Albertans were benefiting, the majority said yes (Gibson 2007b: 1). Albertans are under the illusion of the "Alberta Advantage" — just one that has somehow bypassed them as individuals.

GOVERNMENT FOR THE FEW

Did the Alberta Government have no control over the problem of intense social disparity amidst such enormous resource wealth, as Klein suggested upon his departure from office? Or were the social and labour issues discussed above a result of deliberate government policy?

The rapid investment in tar sands development that drove the boom was in response to concerted government policies, primarily low royalty rates. Investment rates are telling: from 1997, the beginning of the Klein administration's implementation of the new royalty regime, through to 2008, just prior to the financial crisis, $102 billion was spent on capital investment and another $59 billion on operations. But where did the policy of excessively low royalty rates originate? These low rates were implemented due to the demands of industry, with which the Alberta Government willingly complied. In relation to royalty rate restructuring, industry representatives assured Albertans that the royalty structure had been "thoughtfully developed with all stakeholders" through "collaboration among industry, government and other[s]" and only "adopted after extensive consultation" (Shell Canada Energy 2007: 9; ConocoPhillips 2007: 20; Imperial Oil 2007: 12). In reality, however, the tar sands royalty regime in place between 1997 and 2008 was "the result of a concerted effort on the part of representatives with expertise in business economic decision-making from six companies active in the Oil Sands" (National Task Force on Oil Sands Strategy 1995: i). The six companies whose executives drafted the regime were Syncrude, Gulf (now part of ConocoPhillips), Suncor, Amoco (now part of BP), Imperial Oil (controlled by ExxonMobil) and Canadian Natural Resources. Tar sands producers had written their own royalty rules, and they were adopted "in the main" (National Task Force on Oil Sands Strategy 1996: 6) by Alberta's government.

Public debates on royalties have intensified in the last few years. A blue-ribbon royalties panel was assembled to address the issue and it recommended raising rates from their current position near the bottom of all international oil producing countries. Albertans agreed with the move: 88 percent of Albertans did not think the province was getting its fair share from the industry, and 67 percent wanted the Stelmach government to implement the panel's recommendation to raise royalties (Alberta Royalty Review Panel 2007: 38). Instead, the Stelmach government began a series of backroom meetings with industry, then implemented a compromised and much watered down set of reforms. The global recession hit subsequently, along with the oil price crash, and even those moderate royalty reforms were revoked. Billions in incentives have been shelled out to the industry.

Due to low royalty rates, Alberta has gained relatively paltry revenues from the tar sands. Although this industry was responsible for much of the investment and construction booms, tar sands development was not responsible for the dramatic spike in Alberta's resource royalties in the middle of the boom. Once corporate capital expenditures, operating expenditures and royalty payments were written off, the effective percentage of the rent going to the government averaged out at a mere 8.9 percent over the 1992 to 2009 period. Therefore, while $205 billion worth of bitumen was produced from Alberta's tar sands since 1997, companies paid the province only $20 billion in royalties and land sales (Boychuk 2010b). The industry-friendly low royalty rates are effectively another subsidy to oil corporations, one that leaves the province with little benefit from the tar sands.

Under successive Progressive Conservative governments between 1999 and 2008, industry was granted more excess profit ($121 billion) than was collected in royalties and land sales ($104 billion). Though the industry cried foul after the new royalty framework was implemented, land sales, an indicator of investment interest, actually increased. The tar sands side of the industry barely experienced a blip during the recession and was back into strong growth, and again worrying about an overheated industry, by the end of 2010.

The story of oil and gas profits and royalty reforms in Alberta is a tale of wealth giveaways. In conventional oil and gas, the Alberta government set a very low target of capturing 20 to 25 percent of revenues, or 50 to 75 percent of rent. However, the Tory government has consistently failed to meet even these meagre targets. If the government had managed to collect even in the middle of this range it would have had an additional $37 billion in resource revenues between 1999 and 2008.

While handing over billions in tar sands rents to industry, consecutive Conservative governments have simultaneously weakened a far more stable revenue stream by cutting corporate and personal taxes. The province now has the lowest taxation rates and lowest rates of tax collection in the country. The combined federal/provincial general corporate income tax rate has fallen from 33.62 percent in 2005 to 28 percent today and is set to decline to 25 percent by 2012. The small business tax has also declined from 30 percent to 14 percent (Parkland Institute 2011). Alberta now has a revenue system far below that of the next-lowest taxing province, and Alberta's new taxation regime—a "flat tax" system—has further reduced the government's intake of tax revenue by as much as $5.5 billion (Parkland Institute 2009). This undermining of the tax base means that during recessions and economic downturns (such as Alberta experienced in 2008–10), the province faces deficit budgets and, therefore, cuts social programs (Gibson and Acuña 2011).

Social programs have long been at risk at the hands of the Alberta government; even before the pressures of the recession. Alberta entered the boom with a significant infrastructure deficit due to the lack of investment during the Klein years. During the recession of the early 1980s, general government spending peaked at 40 percent of GDP in Alberta, with the provincial government making up half of that. But by 2001, government expenditures had already fallen by a third, as tax cuts and austerity measures reduced general spending by more than 13 percent of GDP and cut provincial expenditures by more than 5 percent (Figure 2.2). Giving priority to eliminating deficits and implementing tax cuts, Alberta's Conservative governments reigned in public services and income transfer programs and sought to reshape their public sectors and wage bargaining systems by contracting out, privatization and job cuts (McMillan 2009).

Then came the tar sands boom, with runaway construction costs, dramatic increases in population and massive developments in oil and gas that required heavy public investments and new roads. All this eclipsed other spending on infrastructure. Figure 2.2 shows government spending compared to GDP, showing both total government spending and provincial government spending. It reveals that government spending on everything from infrastructure to hospitals and schools did not keep pace with the growth in the economy.

Budget-oriented management led to public officials laying off workers, introducing wage freezes and increasing job responsibilities. Privatization and marketization gave the provincial government and service employers new levers to enforce wage moderation. By 2008, government spending as a percentage of GDP had declined to forty-year lows, with overall spending bottoming out at 19 percent and provincial spending at 12 percent. Government investment in social services and infrastructure has not kept up with the new demands posed by the economic boom and resulting influx of workers. This has undermined program effectiveness and exacerbated rising inequality and poverty. The wealth of the boom was not redistributed to Albertans via stable public services.

An obvious example relates to services for women and families. Though it has had the strongest economy in the country, Alberta continues to allocate the fewest dollars for regulated childcare spaces among all the provinces. Now only 17 percent of children up to age five have access to a regulated care space—a figure among the worst in Canada. Nor do Alberta women have a provincial child benefit to help meet costs, or extended maternity/parental leave benefits, which would allow them to better balance their work and family lives. Single parents also feel the pinch of government neglect. Without adequate social supports, female lone parents have seen their market incomes drop and their ability to make ends meet decline. Today, families headed by single women who work are more likely to live in low income in Alberta than anywhere else in Canada (Phillips 2010).

The environment is another obvious example of the government's failure

Figure 2.2 Government Expenditure in Alberta (Percentage of GDP)

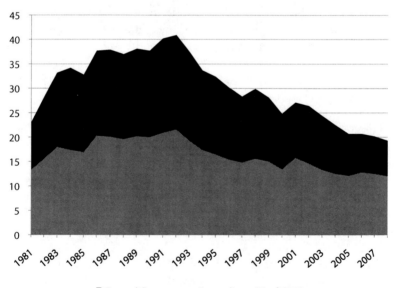

■ General Government Expenditure (% of GDP)

▩ Provincial Government Expenditure (% of GDP)

Sources: Statistics Canada Cansim tables 384004, 3840002

to invest and regulate in the public interest. Albertans can expect to be picking up the tab for pollution from the tar sands gold rush for years to come (Carter 2011). Many are already facing daily problems with water shortages, water contamination, air quality concerns and climate change inaction. The most direct impacts are being borne by the First Nations in the tar sands region. But the health and water impacts have been the heart of high-profile provincial and national controversy. Reports show that contaminants are being released into rivers throughout the north from the tar sands operations (Kelly et al. 2010). Communities and community medical personnel have raised concerns about cancer rates. But all Albertans, including future generations, are on the hook for the financial liabilities of the mining and tailings damage (Lemphers, Dyer and Grant 2010).

The Alberta government, favouring industry over the public, chose to capture very low revenues from its natural resources. At the same time, it cut taxes and neglected to invest in social programs and infrastructure that were stretched to the maximum by the boom. These were concerted policy options; they represent a choice made to govern for the affluent few while marginalizing the majority of Albertans.

CONCLUSION: MANAGING THE BOOM FOR ALBERTANS

Albertans have long called for a different kind of public management of their province. Rather than giving the resource over to industry with relatively limited benefit, the government could act in the public's interest. Clearly, as noted above, far more rent could be captured from the oil and gas sector for Albertans. Too much money from these publicly owned resources is currently being left on the table for the industry.

Tar sands development could also be paced to minimize the impacts of the rapid oil and gas boom on other sectors and to spread out jobs and economic growth for Albertans over the long term. Many different voices from across the political spectrum in Alberta have called for the government to apply the brakes. Notably, former Tory premier Peter Lougheed has frequently called on the government to pace development: "Do one plant, finish it and build another plant, finish it, do another plant—instead of having four of them go on at the same time," he recommended (Dyer 2006). Albertans agreed. A poll conducted by the Pembina Institute found that 74 percent of Albertans thought that the rate of development should be managed by the provincial government. The same poll found that 71 percent felt that new approvals should be suspended until the infrastructure and environmental problems could be addressed (Dyer 2006).

But the response from Ralph Klein to calls for a slowdown was unequivocal: in 2006 he told reporters, "I'm a firm believer in letting the market prevail and not putting in [...] government rules and regulations to control growth because they are so difficult to remove once they are brought in" (Jones 2006). In another newspaper article, he stressed: "To have a long-range plan would be an interventionist kind of policy which says you either allow them or you don't allow them to proceed. The last thing we want to be is an interventionist government" (*Fort McMurray Today* 2006). The grand irony, of course, is that the government *has* intervened—it has set royalty and tax structures too low in the tar sands sector, creating an uneven playing field and perverse incentives for uncontrolled development. The Stelmach government continued apace.

Where does this leave Alberta today, after a global financial crisis? In late 2008, national economists were predicting Alberta would be immune to the recession. But by early 2009 the province was leading the nation in recession indicators such as personal bankruptcies, foreclosures and job losses. Unemployment rates in Alberta's oil and gas sector peaked at 9.7 percent and at 12.9 percent in construction. Overall, 25,600 fewer Albertans were employed in January 2010 than in July 2008 (seasonally adjusted). In oil and gas, 19,000 jobs were lost (Emter 2010: 2, 9–15). The October 2009 caseload for people receiving income support had increased 37 percent in one year, though Alberta's social assistance funding has not kept pace with the greater need (Edmonton Social Planning Council and Public Interest Alberta 2009: 9–10). Over the course of 2009, 53,976 Albertans were assisted by a food bank, a 61 percent increase from 2008; 43 percent were children; 27 percent were working; 32 percent received social assistance.

Two years into the recession, its effects were continuing to take a toll. In July 2010, Alberta shed 13,000 full-time jobs, leaving the province with 53,000 fewer full-time positions after two years of recession. Most (50,600) were replaced with part-time positions. Oilfield service and forestry were still down 10,000 jobs. Alberta's EI beneficiaries jumped 40 percent, the biggest increase in Canada. Alberta also posted the smallest increase in Canada in wages and salaries (1.5 percent). Caseloads for social assistance increased further in 2009, to over 30,000 cases. In 2010, caseloads were 25 percent higher than 2009. Nonetheless, the provincial government's 2010 budget allocated $40 million less than they spent in 2009. Training programs, mostly for youth and First Nations people, were cut by $23 million; housing programs were cut by $94 million; Children's Services lost a third of its budget (Alberta Federation of Labour 2010).

Tools such as competitive royalty regimes, development pacing and planning, and the maintenance, at the very least, of public services and social protections could have been used to redistribute the enormous wealth being generated in the province and to weather the recent recession. But they were not. Instead, resource wealth in Alberta has consistently trickled up. Only Alberta's richest 10 percent of families have seen their incomes rise—in many cases significantly. Corporate executives have received record salary increases and bonuses, and foreign shareholders have seen unprecedented returns.

For the majority of Alberta's boom workers, inflation has eroded incomes even as they work more hours than ever. High levels of population growth have put unprecedented pressures on housing, pricing houses and rental accommodation out of reach. Social services and infrastructure have eroded. For those in low-wage and precarious employment, conditions are even worse, with growing numbers of poor, temporary jobs. Despite the clear evidence of rampant inequality, uncontrolled growth and a loss of control over much natural resource development in Alberta, the government refuses to act as a steward of the economy for the public good. Absent any mobilized interest by organized labour and the development of a strong and effective progressive political party, the economic boom in Alberta looks to bring few and often bitter rewards for many years to come.

Notes

1. Source: Statistics Canada CANSIM, Alberta, Series: Current prices: v687647 Gross domestic product (GDP), v687655 Gov. Structures, Private: v687659 Residential structures, v687660 Non-residential structures)
2. Statistics Canada CANSIM Table 282-0008, Labour force survey estimates (LFS), by North American Industry Classification System (NAICS), Alberta, 2008.

3. BOOM, BUST AND BLUSTER

Newfoundland and Labrador's "Oil Boom" and Its Impacts on Labour

Sean T. Cadigan

Fuelled by a decade of expanding offshore oil production, Newfoundland and Labrador cast off its have-not status in 2008 when it became a "have" province that no longer qualified for federal transfer payments.[1] At the time, Premier Danny Williams declared that Newfoundlanders and Labradorians' new-found wealth had made us "Proud. Strong. Determined. The Future is Ours" (Marland 2007: 79). But this future appears to depend on the continuation of an oil-fired economic boom, and at a closer look, the past decade has been more of a bust for much of the provincial economy, particularly the fisheries and forestry, sectors upon which many of the province's rural communities depended.

The oil sector has created some industrial spinoffs and jobs in manufacturing, construction and highly skilled professions. However, much of the wider economic spinoff has been limited. Growth in employment has occurred mainly in the provincial capital, St. John's, on the northeast Avalon Peninsula, and consists of unskilled, low-paying jobs. Women continue to work in such jobs, entering the workforce as cheap labour for the St. John's service sector. Skilled working people still regularly leave Newfoundland and Labrador to work elsewhere — most notably in the oil sands of Northern Alberta. So instead of a boom, the reality for many Newfoundland workers over the past decade has been a continuing struggle with low-wage work, growing job insecurity and the simple lack of permanent jobs in the province.

The bluster about the positive impact of the oil boom overlooks many of these problems. Indeed, rather than benefiting the entire province, the emergence of oil and gas in Newfoundland and Labrador has fostered a sharp divide between its rural and urban economies and has widened inequality in men's and women's participation in the labour market. Skilled workers, professionals and many of the construction trades have seen benefits out of recent economic growth. But unemployment, out-migration, seasonal migration of workers to other provinces and low-paid work at home continue to be a problem for many, especially for rural people and women generally.

BOOM

Broad indicators support the contention that expanded offshore oil production in Newfoundland and Labrador has triggered a tremendous economic boom. Since 2000, average personal incomes in the province have increased steadily. The size of the provincial labour force and participation in employment have remained fairly steady, and the province's unemployment rate has dropped. The boom has also led to impressive growth in provincial government revenues, consumer spending and gross domestic product (GDP). However, it is also clear that this boom has been much less impressive in generating more employment, especially in the rural areas beyond the region around St. John's.

In 2008, Statistics Canada proclaimed that Newfoundland and Labrador had entered a new era of prosperity on the strength of its oil exports. The province had "registered the largest single-decade turnaround in GDP per capita in Canadian history" (quoted in *Report on Business* 2008). Population decline had halted, and consumers were spending freely on cars, houses and retail products. Much of this good economic fortune has been attributed to the cyclical but steady rise in total oil production since the Hibernia platform first began to produce oil in 1997 (Table 3.1) (Gordon 2003; *Western Star* 2001; *Telegram* 2008; *Canada News Wire* 2002, 2001). Table 3.1 shows that oil projects accounted for more than $5 billion in royalties between 1997 and 2008, and by 2009 such funds accounted for roughly 28 percent of the province's revenue. The era of the oil boom has an important iron-ore and nickel mining component; together, mining and offshore oil developments have contributed significantly to provincial revenue and economic growth (Brautigam 2007; NL Department of Finance 2009). The benefits of the oil boom, however, have been concentrated in the St. John's area, which has approximately 37 percent of the provincial population. St. John's and its suburbs are home to much of the administrative, engineering, training, research, supply and air support services for the offshore industry and its spinoffs (Community Resource Services Ltd. 2003: 14, 20). Even before actual production began in 1997, the construction phase of the Hibernia project was boosting the St. John's region's housing markets (Beauchesne 2004). A decade later, press observers noted that St. John's hotels and retail shops were the big beneficiaries of the boom.

Table 3.1 Selected Economic Indicators, Newfoundland and Labrador (2000–2009)

	2000	2005	2008	2009*
Oil Production (in barrels)	52,798,311	111,269,370	125,245,251	97,679,170
Offshore Royalties NL ($ thousands)**	39,824	532,533	2,238,563	1,885,218
Mining Taxes and Royalties NL ($ thousands)**	20,611	22,218	216,945	75,572
Offshore Royalties,Mining Taxes and Royalties** as % NL Revenue	1.50%	9.99%	28.45%	27.87%
Per Capita GDP $	26,369	42,694	61,758	45,020
Personal Income $m	11122	13249	15641	16257
Wages & Salaries $m	5,421.3	6,608.7	7,986.0	8,375.8
Retail Trade $m	4760	5824	7009	7120
Labour Force (000s)	237.8	252.5	253.8	254.2
Employment (000s)	198	214.1	220.3	214.9
Unemploy. Rate %	16.7	15.2	13.2	15.5
Housing Starts	1,459	2,498	3,261	3,057
* estimates for all rows except "Wages and Salaries." ** all revenue figures are on an accrual basis for the fiscal year beginning 1 April				

Sources: Revenue figures are from Public Accounts of Newfoundland and Labrador 1997–2008 Volume I and Department of Finance 2010.

The oil boom has insulated some parts of the province — the St. John's area, the iron-ore mining communities of western Labrador and Happy Valley-Goose Bay and the communities near nickel mining at Voisey's Bay in central Labrador — from the economic difficulties of the rest of the province. The geographical units of observation used by government statistical agencies make analysis of regional variation difficult, but the most useful aggregate units are Newfoundland and Labrador's twenty economic zones, each with a regional economic development board.[2] A comparison of these zones shows that while the province's population has decreased steadily since its all-time high of approximately 580,109 in 1992 to 508,925 in 2009 (a decline of 0.77 percent), the population of the northeast Avalon Peninsula, which includes the St. John's area, grew slightly, by 0.88 percent, between 2001 and 2006, while decreases persisted in every other provincial economic zone.[3] Although the provincial unemployment rate for workers aged fifteen and older had dropped to 18.6 percent between 1996 and 2006, the rates are much lower in the mining areas of western and central Labrador zones (8.6 percent and 14.4 percent respectively). In 2006, the unemployment rate of 10.4 percent on the northeast Avalon Peninsula was much lower than the fifteen percent in 1996, while in Corner Brook, the site of the province's last active pulp and paper mill, the rate had dropped from 24 percent to 17.9 percent in the same period.

Although the unemployment rate had dropped from 35 percent in 1996 to 28.5 percent in 2006 for the other areas of the province, this remained much higher than the provincial average, especially areas dominated by oil or mining development, or the zones centred on the province's two major cities. On a per capita basis, personal disposable incomes have been much higher in the mining and oil centres of western and central Labrador and the northeast Avalon Peninsula than in other parts of the province. In 2006, for example, per capita personal disposable income in the province as a whole was $14,900, but was much higher in western Labrador ($22,000), in central Labrador ($17,200) and the northeast Avalon Peninsula ($17,000).[4] Consequently, while oil and mining development have contributed to overall economic growth and to more revenue for the province, the boom has largely benefited the St. John's region and the mining towns of Labrador.

BUST

But if the mining towns and St. John's have enjoyed the benefits of the boom, the economy has continued to be a bust for rural areas, which have seen declining employment in the fisheries and forestry sectors, population loss and lower incomes. Long before the oil boom, rural decline and urban growth were two trends that had defined the lives of many workers and families in Newfoundland. But the boom has reinforced these trends, and the oil, gas and mining sectors have yet to offset the steady decline of employment in the fisheries and forestry sectors since the late 1990s.

In 1992, for example, about 1,600 people worked in forestry and logging, and 9,300 people worked as fishers. By 2009, there were only 500 people working in forestry and logging, and 5,600 people remained as fishers. Over the same period, the total number of people employed in oil and gas extraction rose from 500 to 2,800. While rural Newfoundland and Labrador lost 4,800 jobs in fishing and forestry, the oil sector had generated only 2,300 extra jobs. Pulp and paper employment has been almost annihilated; 2,800 people worked in paper mills in 1992, but only 500 were left in 2009. About 7,800 people worked in seafood processing in 1992, while only 4,700 remained in such employment in 2009. Five hundred people worked in the support activities for oil and gas extraction in 1992, but employment in this area increased to 2,400 in 2009. Altogether, 5,400 jobs had been lost in paper and seafood manufacture, while 1,900 jobs had been gained in the support work for the oil and gas sector.

Construction work has been an important direct and indirect spinoff

from mining and oil development. However, even making the overly generous assumption that all construction may be related to the expanding oil
industry, it is clear that such employment has not fully compensated for the
loss of work in the fishing and forestry sectors (Figure 3.1). Jobs in the oil
industry pay extremely well, but the sector has not been "a significant direct
creator of jobs," as some have claimed (quote from a report on provincial
economic performance and living standards by Global Insight, cited in the
Beauchesne 2004: D1). While the oil, gas and mining sectors have generated
substantial new revenues for government, there is little evidence to show that
such resources have funded significant efforts to put other core industries —

Figure 3.1 Employment in Select Goods and Service Industries, NL

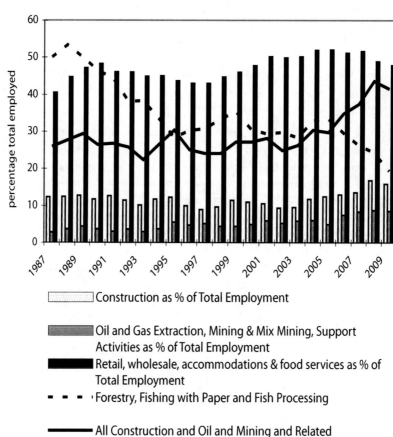

Construction as % of Total Employment

Oil and Gas Extraction, Mining & Mix Mining, Support
Activities as % of Total Employment
Retail, wholesale, accommodations & food services as % of
Total Employment
▪ ▪ ▪ ▪ Forestry, Fishing with Paper and Fish Processing

——— All Construction and Oil and Mining and Related

*Sources: Data compiled from Newfoundland and Labrador Statistics Agency (NLSA), "Employment
in Fishing Industry (NAICS1), Newfoundland and Labrador, Annual Averages, 1987 to 2009" and
"Employment by Detailed Industry (NAICS), Newfoundland and Labrador 1987 — 2009, Annual
Averages," January 2010.*

particularly fishing — on a more secure footing (Schrank 2005).

The fishing industry's troubles have been long-standing. In the 1950s, the provincial and federal governments viewed the salt fishery (with its largely small-boat inshore fleet and household organization of production) as backward. Hoping that landward industrialization and resettlement would encourage many people to leave the fishing industry, governments promoted a more capital-intensive fresh/frozen fish industry. Large offshore vessels would supply a small number of fish-processing factories. Although modernization of the fisheries proceeded, significant landward diversification never materialized, and many rural people have continued to work in fish harvesting and processing. Throughout the 1960s and 1970s, the provincial government permitted more fish plants to open as a means of economic development. The provincial and federal governments developed a variety of programs to encourage small-boat fishers to invest in larger boats and more efficient fishing gear (Cadigan 2002).

Although in 1977 the Canadian government took responsibility for exclusive regulation of all fishing efforts, domestic and foreign, within a 200-mile exclusive economic zone, to protect its industry from international over-fishing, fishing in the North Atlantic continued largely unchecked. While fishers diversified the species they caught, overall increases in the number and size of boats contributed to the collapse of many fish stocks and consequent moratoria on ground fisheries in 1992. The federal government's response to the moratoria was to use various compensation programs and, eventually, quota systems to encourage people to withdraw from the fishing industry. The winding down of moratoria-related programs throughout the late 1990s saw more migration from rural areas and also a boom in regional fisheries for invertebrate species such as shrimp and snow crab.

This growth in new fisheries prompted limited recovery in employment levels through 2005. But by diverting more effort down the food chain to species that depleted fish such as cod used to eat, the newer fisheries have proven more capital-intensive and have led to the over-exploitation of some new species. The fewer fishers who survived the catastrophic events of the 1990s have become the new, if still small-scale, capitalists of the fishing industry, despite their representation by the Fishers, Food, and Allied Workers, an affiliate of the Canadian Auto Workers (Neis and Kean 2003; Murray, Neis and Johnsen 2006; Ommer and Coasts under Stress Research Project Team 2007).

The forestry industry, too, has been in sharp decline, and the expansion of the oil sector in the province has done little to slow the decline of communities that depended on it. The demand for newsprint, the main paper product of the province, has been falling since 1980 as the industry becomes increasingly internationally competitive. Local forestry and sawmilling had long been adjuncts of the fishing industry in coastal Newfoundland, but industrial exploitation began in earnest with the opening of a massive pulp and paper complex in Grand Falls, in central Newfoundland, in 1909 and one in Corner Brook in the 1920s. Beginning in the 1950s, the paper companies focused on increasing productivity by reducing the labour force, especially in logging, the greatest source of employment in forestry. In 1951, for example, there were 10,333 loggers in Newfoundland, but twenty years later only 3,085 remained.

In logging and in the paper mills, the forty years since have seen a constant shuffling of corporate ownership, reductions in employment levels and benefits, more contracting out and a shift to unorganized workers in logging. Mechanized harvesting has eliminated jobs while stressing wood supplies. The ownership of the Corner Brook mill was transfered from Bowater to Kruger in 1984, and the new management implemented a form of lean production that characterized the paper industry as a whole. In addition to investing in labour-saving technology, Kruger reduced staffing levels in the mill, cut wages, discarded the seniority system, labour organization, family-based recruitment and apprenticeship training of the previous Bowater era, made layoffs and bumping a routine part of work at the mill and increasingly relied on casual labour (Norcliffe 2005; Ommer and Coasts under Stress Research Project Team 2007; Sinclair, MacDonald and Neis 2006). Although lean production has allowed the pulp and paper mill at Corner Brook to continue to limp along, the mills at Stephenville, in 2005, and Grand Falls-Winsor, in 2009, closed completely (NL Department of Finance 2006: 2–3; Morrissey 2007: A1; Roberts A1). As in the case of the fisheries, the forestry sector continues to experience severe economic decline, leaving rural areas largely untouched by boom conditions in other parts of Newfoundland and Labrador.

BLUSTER

A closer look at the nature of the boom suggests that there is a lot of bluster about how positive its impact has been on people's incomes and the employment opportunities it has generated in the province. Even in the St. John's region, which has been disproportionately enjoying the benefits of the boom, incomes for the majority of wage earners are lower than those in the mining areas of Labrador. This discrepancy is a reflection of the fact that employment growth during the oil boom has been mainly in the low-paid services sector (Figure 3.2).

The offshore sector's indirect impact in industries such as retail, wholesale, construction and hospitality must be considered alongside its direct impacts. While these indirect impacts are significant in terms of the sheer number of jobs created, most of this employment has not been in public-sector areas such as health care and education, where pay and working conditions are relatively good. Except the mining centres of Labrador, employment in the retail and wholesale trades, food services and accommodations sectors have been the most important source of employment in every part of the province during the boom (Figure 3.1) (Newfoundland and Labrador Statistics Agency 1996, 2001, 2006).[5]

Although it pales in comparison to the amount of work generated in the retail, wholesale, food services and accommodations sectors, construction has employed far more people than all goods production sectors or public service sectors, such as education and health care. But as important as construction work is to overall employment numbers, its positive impact on the provincial economy is still limited. Oil-related construction work tends to be cyclical, limited to initial project development rather than ongoing oil production. The production phase of oil and mining has not been enough to insulate the provincial economy from problems in the fishery or forestry, or to significantly diversify the province's employment base in primary production.

Figure 3.2 Employment by Sector and Gender, NL

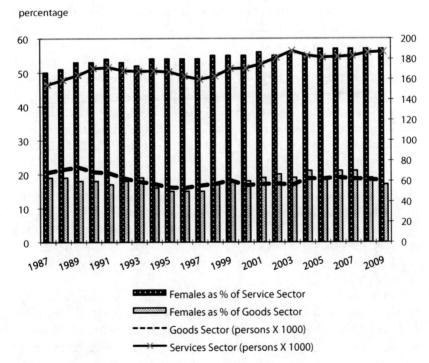

Females as % of Service Sector
Females as % of Goods Sector
Goods Sector (persons X 1000)
Services Sector (persons X 1000)

Source: Statistics Canada, Table 282-0008 — Labour force survey estimates (LFS), by North American Industry Classification System (NAICS), sex and age group, computed annual average (persons x 1,000)

The Royal Bank of Canada's Craig Wright put it plainly in 2007: "While the oil and gas industry accounts for roughly 15 percent of the economy, it has limited trickle-down effects, as we still see with weak employment growth and retreating construction activity" (Canada NewsWire 2007).

The limited nature of this trickle-down effect may be seen in the manner in which the oil boom has created a demand for far more low-paid service-sector workers than for better-paid, highly skilled workers, while reinforcing the gendered dimension of work. Women have constituted between 50 and 57 percent of all service-sector employees since 1987, but they have never held more than 21 percent of jobs in goods production (Figure 3.2). This demand for labour in the service sector reinforces a persistent disparity between the incomes of men and women. Since 1997, the average income derived by women from wages, salaries and commissions has ranged from 53 to 60 percent of men's. Areas such as retail trade and the accommodations and food services industries are disproportionately staffed by women and offer much lower wages. In 2008, for example, "over 70% of employees in the accommodation and food services industry earn[ed] less than $10 per hour" (NL Department of Finance 2008).[6]

While rates of unionization are relatively high in industries that employ mostly men, those that have been growing in the private sector since the oil boom, and which employ far more women, remain largely unorganized. Newfoundland and Labrador has historically had much higher rates of unionization than most provinces in Canada, but government retrench-ment policies in the 1980s and 1990s limited the collective bargaining rights and compensation for workers in public-sector areas, such as health care, which have been dominated by women. The labour relations climate of the province has been difficult for organized labour, but working men have fared better than women in securing collective bargaining rights and bet-ter pay. The rate of union coverage in the construction industry has risen steadily, from almost 22 percent in 2003 to 29 percent in 2008, and the rate in the mining and oil sector has ranged between 44 percent and 55 percent. Meanwhile, no more than 14 percent of workers in the accommodation and food services industries and just over 13 percent in the wholesale and retail trades are covered by collective agreements (NL Labour Relations Agency Online n.d.).[7]

Women also tend to earn much less than men because the preconcep-tions of male workers and employers have made it very difficult for them to enter highly skilled and better-paid areas of employment such as the oil sector. In Labrador City's iron mining industry, for example, male workers and employers expected women to stay in traditional service-sector work and/or unpaid domestic work rather than mine work. In 2001, women composed less than 5 percent of all workers in the offshore oil industry in

Canada, largely because its male-dominated work culture and employers' sexist suppositions limited women's recruitment. In Newfoundland and Labrador, the percentage of women working in the offshore sector reached no higher than just under 17 percent, in 2007 (Shrimpton and Storey 2001: 6–7; Statistics Canada 2010).

A SUPERFICIAL BOOM: CORPORATE PROFIT, RURAL MALAISE AND MIGRANT LABOUR

The economic boom from oil development and mining has had a limited impact on the fundamentally resource-driven nature of the provincial economy. While the mining and oil sectors have contributed to growth in the goods-producing sector, the service sector has remained the greatest contributor to provincial GDP growth in the financial and real estate sector (Figure 3.3). Oil development likely contributes indirectly to growth in the financial and real estate sector and to the wholesale, retail, accommodations and foods services sectors, while consumer confidence, driven largely by oil-related job creation, has encouraged retail sales and new residential construction. Non-residential developments, however, were responsible for almost three times the investment — $1.73 billion in contrast to $600 million (Community Resource Services Ltd. 2003), with oil- and mining-related construction being the most important components (Canada NewsWire 2000; NL Department of Finance 2002). Public-sector services, fuelled by oil- and mineral-related revenue at the provincial level, have also steadily expanded.

However, while much of the oil boom-driven real estate and retail activity looks impressive, it hardly constitutes an economic transformation of the province or a sound basis for long-term prosperity. Construction and retail trade remain relatively small contributors to the provincial GDP, generating a lot of low-paid and cyclical employment. The fishing and forestry sectors, so important to rural areas, have also languished during the so-called boom. The fisheries long served as a base industry for all of Newfoundland and Labrador and contributed disproportionately to GDP because of their strong links to other economic sectors (Roy, Arnason and Schrank 2009). But recently, along with forestry, the fisheries have become the least important direct contributor to the GDP. Retail and construction are the febrile companions of ailing fishing, fish processing and forestry industries in most of rural Newfoundland and Labrador; the oil boom has not provided the service or construction sectors with the strength to stand on their own. Although people in the St. John's area who work in retail, food services and accommodations may be getting more work and, perhaps, better pay, they are still poorly paid, especially if they are women.

The uneven impact of the oil boom on employment has thus created labour market problems for the province. The cyclical nature of oil-related construction work has not stemmed the overall tendency for skilled workers to look for more regular employment outside of the province. Consequently, local shortages of workers have continued to be a problem for the large scale projects like Hebron and for mining-related projects such as the nickel processing facility at Long Harbour, Placentia Bay, as well as for the aquaculture industry (*Chronicle Herald* 2008; *Telegram* 2008). Indeed, the out-migration of workers, particularly from rural areas, has been so significant that it may have contributed to lower unemployment rates in the province nearly as much as has employment associated with the oil boom (Gulf News 2006; NL Department of Finance 2005, 2007; Morrissey 2006).

While policy-makers fear shortages of skilled labour, the evidence of

Figure 3.3 Gross Domestic Product by Sector and Subsector NL

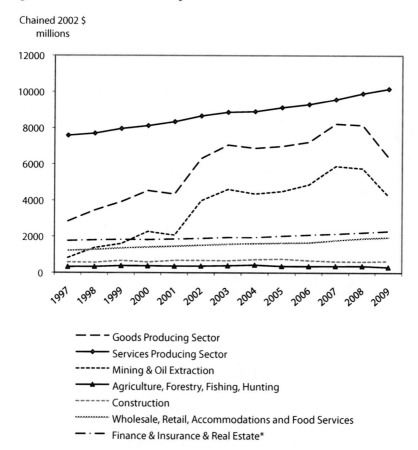

Source: Economics and Statistics Branch (NLSA), Department of Finance, Govt. NL, "Gross Domestic Product by Industry, Newfoundland and Labrador, 1997–2009 (St. John's 2010), http:/www.stats. gov.nl.ca/Statistics/GDP/PDF/GDP_Industry.pdf.

actual shortages appears to be mostly in the service sector, where demand for workers continues to grow. Amidst a troubled forestry sector in 2007–08, the Grand Falls-Windsor area Chamber of Commerce reported that the real labour shortages were in retail and food services work (Baird 2001; *Telegram* 2002; *Western Star* 2003; Hickey 2008). In 2009, the Newfoundland and Labrador Employers' Council (NLEC) encouraged its members to think about how they might recruit temporary foreign workers and other workers from abroad (McLean 2009a). The council's executive director, Richard Alexander, focused on the demand for poorly paid service-sector workers rather than better paid, skilled workers when he cited the example of "a Tim Hortons up in Labrador City, I believe, that has a number of temporary foreign workers from the Philippines" (Bartlett 2009).

Despite concerns about skilled-labour shortages, the demand for labour still seems to be in various less-skilled parts of the service sector. For example, tourism and hospitality industry operators in the region of Gros Morne National Park continued to find it difficult to recruit and retain employees because of out-migration and an aging workforce. The RED Ochre Regional Board, the body that manages Economic Zone 7 on the west coast of Newfoundland and includes Gros Morne National Park in its boundaries, sponsored workshops in the summer of 2009 that encouraged these operators to think about hiring "the retired and semi-retired" and college students who might be interested in an adventurous summer. The workshops recommended that employers consider that they could retain workers more cheaply through "non-cash rewards" such as nice thank-you letters rather than giving them better pay (*Northern Pen* 2009a). Such incentives were unlikely to meet the needs of the many people who had been going to Alberta for better pay, to the detriment of Newfoundland and Labrador employers.

The provincial government's response to the perceived labour shortage, meanwhile, has been to use federal-provincial labour market development agreements and a provincial poverty reduction strategy to "support" low-wage workers, reduce debts for education and provide various forms of assistance to immigrants and disadvantaged people so that they may enter the workforce (*Northern Pen* 2008, 2009b; Kelly 2009). Some commentators have suggested that the only way to retain workers — skilled or unskilled — is to ensure that they have decent pay and work security (Brake 2007).

In spite of all the talk of labour shortages, especially in the context of the oil boom, it is important to remember that Newfoundland and Labrador continues to have some of the highest unemployment rates in Canada. In July 2009, Statistics Canada revealed that the province's unemployment rate of 17.1 percent was by far the highest of any province and was nearly double the Canadian average of 8.6 percent. Although the unemployment rate in St. John's was much lower, at 8.1 percent, it was still higher than the rates in cities such as Halifax (6.0), Saint John (5.0), Quebec City (4.8), Ottawa (6.0), Winnipeg (5.3) and Regina (3.2) (*Telegram* 2008).

Since the oil boom, the demand for labour has increased, but it is of a type that many people do not want to meet. Even in areas closer to St. John's and the northeast Avalon Peninsula, local businesses have found it difficult to find workers. On the north side of Conception Bay and the south side of Trinity Bay, for example, research by the Mariner Resource Opportunities Network (M-RON, Economic Zone 17's regional economic development board) revealed that, in 2009, there were not enough people filling the employment opportunities available in the area. M-RON found that people continued to leave the area to seek work elsewhere, usually for better wages. George Parsons, the CEO of M-RON, suggested that economic development related to oil and gas and mining was not addressing the reasons why young people were leaving, which he gave as "the effects of declining industries, lack of year round employment, substandard wages, outdated services and infrastructure" (Bowman 2009a).

Many employers blame working people rather than the pay and working conditions on offer for the contradiction between persistently high unemployment and job vacancies during the oil boom. In the fall of 2009,

Figure 3.4 Percentage of Select Contributions to NL GDP (Income Based)

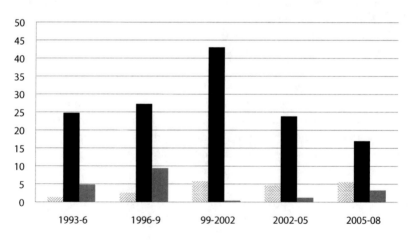

◌ wages, salaries & supplementary Income

■ Corporate profits before taxes

■ Net income of non-farm unincorporated business, including rent

Source: Growth rates calculated from "Table 1: Gross Domestic Product, Income-based, Newfoundland and Labrador," StatsCan, Provincial and Territorial Accounts: Data tables, catalogue number 13-018-X.

the NLEC's annual conference chose as a theme whether or not the work ethic of Newfoundlanders and Labradorians was in decline. The council had sponsored surveys of employers on a number of issues, including employment insurance and workers' compensation. Forty-one percent of the respondents indicated that they had an employee refuse work because she or he was eligible for social programs such as Employment Insurance. Forty-three percent of non-union firms and 62 percent of unionized workplaces indicated their unhappiness with the workers' compensation system, with almost 50 percent saying "it was ineffective in getting workers back to work in a timely manner" (Breen 2009). The Newfoundland and Labrador Federation of Labour responded by suggesting that the NLEC was trying to undermine social supports for working people. It might have also asked why such limited benefits as Employment Insurance were more attractive than the jobs available to many unemployed people in the province.

Job vacancies, work ethics and worker assistance programs have received a lot of public attention. But little notice has been taken of one area in which there has been a clear boom since 1997: corporate profits, which have escalated dramatically. Small businesses, on the other hand, have experienced very little growth in their net incomes, and wages and other income for working people have grown at a snail's pace by comparison (Figure 3.4). While the revenue that Newfoundland and Labrador derives from the oil sector has grown substantially, this must be set against the fact that the rate of corporate taxation has fallen by as much as two-thirds during the oil boom, in large measure because of the deals governments have agreed to with the private sector in order to secure resource development (Jim Stanford made a similar point in Stanford 2003).

CONCLUSION

The offshore oil and mining sectors have not yet fundamentally transformed the Newfoundland and Labrador economy. Many local economists feel that "all of the economic indicators point to an economy that is improving, indeed prospering" (Locke 2008). The province's record growth in GDP, recent budget surpluses largely founded on oil revenue, increased employment and growth in consumer spending in areas such as auto sales all suggest that Newfoundland and Labrador is in a boom. Conditions in much of rural Newfoundland and Labrador, however, have been more bust than boom, especially areas dependent on fisheries and forestry.

Despite all of the hype about the province's economic transformation, the greatest demand for labour has been in poorly paid and unorganized service-sector work and cyclically available construction work. Working women, on average, are enjoying fewer of the benefits of the boom than are working men. While the wages of working people have grown slightly, corporate profits, by comparison, have soared. Economic activity has grown in retail and related services, construction, real estate and the provision of government services, but these boosts increasingly rest on the revenue and labour generated by the oil industry while other goods production stagnates (McLean 2009b).

Studies suggest that oil production and related government revenue may start to decline rapidly after 2014, as the current pace of discovery will not ensure enough availability of oil to sustain the offshore industry at the levels upon which the economic well-being of the province has come to depend (Locke 2008). One of the problems the industry has always posed for Newfoundland and Labrador is that it requires a consistent and focused regulation to ensure maximum economic benefits for local people. "Non-renewable resources are not necessarily synonymous with non-sustainable benefits," argues one economist, but "they will be without the right choices" (Locke 2009; 1999: 36). Using royalties from offshore oil and mining to pay down provincial debt may help establish the environment in which to make such choices, but the province must decide what it wishes to invest in (Sinclair 2008). It remains to be seen how the economic boom will play out, but the evidence of the past ten to fifteen years suggests that talk of an oil boom is still mostly bluster, as many of the essential problems of the provincial economy remain unaltered.

Notes

1. This chapter is part of the project "Oil, Power and Dependency: Global and Local Realities of the Offshore Oil Industry in Newfoundland and Labrador," with co-investigator Peter R. Sinclair and funded by the Social Sciences and Humanities Council of Canada.
2. Established by federal-provincial agreements, the boards' goals are to develop integrated strategic economic plans in coordination with relevant public and private institutions in their regions. The Newfoundland and Labrador government's Community Accounts has created data tables for zones based on Statistics Canada and other sources.
3. Growth rates calculated from data derived from Newfoundland and Labrador Statistics Agency (NLSA), Government of Newfoundland and Labrador, compiled by the Community Accounts Unit based on information provided from the Census of Population 1996, 2001 and 2006 Statistics Canada (StatsCan).
4. Data on per capita incomes come from NLSA, Govt. NL, Compiled by the Community Accounts Unit, based on Canada Customs and Revenue Agency summary information as provided by Small Area and Administrative Data Division, StatsCan. Unemployment rates compiled by the Newfoundland and Labrador Statistics Agency Community Accounts Unit based on custom tabulations from the Census of Population 1996, 2001, and 2006.
5. Evidence on employment in specific economic sectors as a percentage of total employment throughout the province for the 1996, 2001 and 2006 census years

may be found in tables available from the NLSA, Compiled by the Community Accounts Unit based on custom tabulations from the Census of Population 1996, 2001, 2006, Statistics Canada.

6.   The provincial minimum wage in 2008 was $8 per hour, but has since risen to $10 per hour, one of the highest in Canada.

7.   The data on men's and women's incomes is from Statistics Canada, Table 282-0073 — Labour force survey estimates (LFS), wages of employees by job permanence, union coverage, sex and age group, unadjusted for seasonality, computed annual average (current dollars unless otherwise noted), CANSIM (database), Using E-STAT (distributor). The percentages of union coverage are from Labour Relations Agency.

4. STEEL CITY MELTDOWN
Hamilton and the Changing Canadian Steel Industry

Stephen R. Arnold

On November 7, 2010, United States Steel Corporation locked the gates of its former Stelco plant in Hamilton, Ontario, putting nine hundred workers on the street until they agreed to the company's demands for radical changes in their pension plans. The company's action followed a similar eight-month lockout of workers at its Lake Erie plant in Nanticoke, south of Hamilton.

The Stelco strike of 1991 had nearly paralyzed the city and dominated news coverage for its duration. In those days, however, a Stelco strike involved 10,000 workers, and its effects rippled through the entire local economy. The current confrontation, involving fewer than a thousand employees, was felt far less. That lack of major impact has caused some people to pose the question once considered unthinkable: What would life in Hamilton be like without the steel company?

How did a once vital industry come to such a sorry condition? What has this decline meant for Canada as a whole, and more specifically, for the workers and communities that once depended on steel as the basis for their local economy and the well-being of thousands of families and dozens of social institutions? What does the future look like for nine hundred locked-out workers?

In an effort to understand how this state of affairs developed, this chapter examines the history and current state of the Canadian steel industry through the stories of the Hamilton-based giants Stelco and Dofasco, now U.S. Steel Canada and ArcelorMittal Dofasco. Aspects explored include developments in the world steel industry that led to the rapid decline of employment, both Canadian companies coming under foreign control, the sharp difference between the trajectories of employment at the firms and their current state and future outlook.

HISTORICAL BACKGROUND

In the opening decade of the twentieth century, Canada's steel industry consisted largely of small metal-working shops clustered around the transportation hub of Hamilton, Ontario. In 1910, financier Max Aitken, the future Lord Beaverbrook, arranged a series of transactions that brought five small firms making steel and a few related products together into an integrated operation called the Steel Company of Canada, later shortened to Stelco. Two years later, in 1912, American foundry man Clifton W. Sherman founded the Dominion Steel Casting Company, which came to be known as Dofasco. The companies established their plants side by side on Hamilton's bay front, a location that gave them ready access to water and rail transportation of crucial supplies such as scrap, limestone, iron ore and coal. Coupled with cheap hydro-electric power, a protective wall of national tariffs, local government land, capital grants and generous tax incentives, both companies thrived.

Initially, Stelco became the larger of the two, using external financing to create a wide range of products. It also became known as the company that stressed the use of established technologies rather than new ideas. Over the decades Stelco poured its money into refining proven methods, for example stretching the life of the open-hearth furnace into the 1960s. Dofasco, by comparison, remained a small, locally owned and highly specialized manufacturer relying on purchased iron and scrap to produce castings for the railway and mining industries of northern Ontario and Quebec. During World War I the company was so focused on the production of munitions that it almost collapsed with the coming of peace. The firm was saved in 1921 by two events: the opening of a new universal plate mill and the granting of a patent for the casting of railway undercarriages. Other innovations quickly followed: in 1928, Dofasco built Canada's first hot-rolling mill, and in 1935 the company discovered a way to produce hot strip steel, an essential ingredient for tinplate.

This remained the basic structure of the industry in 1945, at the end of World War II. Hamilton was the undisputed centre of the Canadian industry, its mills producing about half of the country's steel. By the 1970s, this would rise to 70 percent (Corman, Luxton and Livingstone 1993: 25–26). In the years that followed, Dofasco continued its innovative ways: in 1954 it became the first steel company in North America to begin using a basic oxygen furnace, a more efficient way of making steel than the traditional open hearth method. Dofasco also introduced the country's first continuous galvanizing line in 1955.

By 2003, Canada boasted the seventh largest steel industry in the advanced capitalist countries (behind Japan, the United States, Germany, Italy, France, Spain and the United Kingdom). Canada's leading companies, Stelco, Dofasco and Algoma, accounted for 70 percent of domestic production, and until 1990 all three companies ranked among the top fifty firms in the world in terms of tonnage produced. In the few years since 2003, however, Canada has fallen to the status of "a relatively minor producer in global terms," with annual production around 16 million tonnes, less than 2 percent of the world total (Livingstone, Smith and Smith 2011: 15–16). What brought about that decline?

STEEL INDUSTRY DECLINE

In the 1980s, the industry fundamentally changed, going into a long period of decline that led ultimately to Canada losing control of a basic strategic industry. Starting with the recession of 1981, the story of Canadian steel has been one of struggle, job loss, plant closures and rapid and intense consolidation. Many forces have been identified as contributing to the decline of Canadian steel. A partial list includes changes in the auto industry that severely reduced the amount of the metal used in vehicles; the decline and disappearance of industries such as appliance making in Canada; the four-fold increase in oil prices imposed by OPEC in 1975; and an unprecedented build-up of inventories in the hands of steel users, which gave steel makers an exaggerated sense of demand for their product. That led to an unwarranted and ultimately unsupportable expansion of production capacity.

Many in organized labour argue that a major portion of blame must also be attributed to trade pacts such as the Canada-U.S. and North American free trade agreements, which removed national protections from the Canadian industry. Global trade conditions, especially the impact of the massive Chinese steel industry, unhampered by the burden of legacy, environmental and health and safety costs borne by North America's domestic producers, must also be considered. Other developing countries such as India have also entered the global steel business under similar conditions (Corman, Luxton and Livingstone 1993: 1; Hogan 1994: 16–17).

In Canada, those factors resulted in the share of the domestic market taken by foreign steel increasing from about 15 percent in the 1980s to 30 percent by the mid-1990s. Restructured American companies, aided by the Canada-U.S. Free Trade Agreement, more than doubled their share of the domestic market, to roughly 16 percent, while the share of the American market commanded by Canadian firms fell by half, to about 2 percent. The situation was exacerbated when free trade was extended to all of North America, granting low-cost Mexican producers unrestricted access to Canada and the United States. All Canadian producers suffered major market losses despite continued cost reductions (Livingstone, Smith and Smith 2011: 17).

The impact of those changes was severe. Simply stated: "The world now has more steel plants than it knows what to do with, a persistent overcapacity of around 20 percent" (Livingstone, Smith and Smith 2011: 5–6). The countries with the greatest overcapacity are also the ones making the greatest efforts to sell their excess production overseas at low prices, forcing producers, chiefly in North America, to cut costs any way they can. That has clearly been the pattern in Canada. Although Canadian producers were relatively efficient at the start of the crisis, when its effects began to be felt here in the 1980s, labour cost reductions were the first tool taken up by management. The result, discussed in more detail below, was that the companies entered the twenty-first century with no new hires for almost a generation and a large portion of their workforce nearing retirement age.

But a unique feature of the Canadian industry in terms of this general description of the world situation is the general delay in global impacts. The Canadian steel industry outperformed most of its competitors for over a decade, as measured by profitability, capacity utilization and employment stability. Part of this can be attributed to the Canadian industry's generally conservative approach to adding production capacity, a low exchange rate that allowed Canadian firms to hide the impact of generally lower productivity, natural advantages of easy access to cheap raw materials and secure domestic markets shielded from offshore competition by high transportation costs, at least until the arrival of free trade.

This period of sustained profits enabled the Canadian companies to make capital investments in new technology to catch up with Japan and Western Europe and to replace a declining domestic market with exports to the United States. That happy situation could not continue forever. Capacity utilization peaked at 95 percent in 1979. In the recession of 1981, however, it plunged to 55 percent (Livingstone, Smith and Smith 2011: 16; Corman, Luxton and Livingstone 1993: 20–21).

Faced with the challenges of competition from low-cost producers granted free access to this market, the North American steel industry responded with a cost-cutting drive that included corporate re-organizations, plant renovations and closures and a massive reduction of industrial jobs. Wherever possible, payroll costs were slashed by the adoption of technology. Overall, the human consequence of this cost-cutting logic in steel was "the most massive single-industry job losses in the history of capitalist manufacturing, with widespread disruption of the communities that had grown up around these large integrated steel plants" (Livingstone, Smith and Smith 2011). Between 1974 and 2000 more than 1.5 million jobs disappeared, about two-thirds of the North American steel workforce. In the period between 1980 and 1995 alone, employment in the industry fell from 460,000 to less than 225,000 (Corman, Luxton and Livingstone 1993: 10; Livingstone, Smith and Smith 2011: 5).

An expansion in North American production capacity left the industry with the ability to produce more steel than it could sell. The result was a campaign of competitive price-cutting by domestic producers, who hoped to preserve their market share. As price wars spread and steel firms continued to experience a general fall in the level and rate of profit, the drive to re-organize and become more "efficient" intensified, although few firms showed a real willingness to reduce their overall production capacity, fearing they would be left short when demand returned (Corman, Luxton and Livingstone 1993: 16–17).

THE HAMILTON STORY

In Hamilton, this trend had a much more severe impact on Stelco, where more than two-thirds of the labour force at Hilton Works (the company's main plant) were either laid off or retired between 1980 and 1993. In 1970, for example, the company employed 21,497 workers. The number rose steadily until it peaked in 1981 at 26,263. In that year, in the face of a severe recession and after a lengthy strike, the company slashed slightly more than 4,000 jobs to cut total employment to 22,104. That reliance on employment reduction has continued unabated. The company entered the 1990s with 14,348 workers. By 2005 Stelco, then under bankruptcy protection, employed 8,500 in total. In 2011, employment stood at around 900.

Dofasco, both as an independent company and as part of the ArcelorMittal chain, has followed the same employment trajectory. But for Dofasco, the changes have been accomplished largely through attrition and thus far less wrenching. Dofasco went from 8,600 workers in 1975 to 5,200 in 2010 (Corman, Luxton and Livingstone 1993: 25). The main impact of these changes in employment has been in the ranks of production workers, where jobs requiring heavy physical labour have been slashed in favour of technical, maintenance and service employees generally, and trades workers in particular (Corman, Luxton and Livingstone 1993: 36–37).

Battered by these global forces and a lengthy strike in 1981, Stelco sank into desperate financial straits. The company reported its first ever losses during the 1982–83 recession and only returned to modest profit levels by 1990. During that same period it saw its debt load rise to nearly 50 percent of capital assets. When another recession hit during the early 1990s, followed by another lengthy strike, Stelco was highly vulnerable. In both the 1981 and 1990 strikes United Steel Workers of America bargained from its traditional position of improving wages and benefits, assuming the recession would eventually pass and union and company would return to "business as usual." Management seemed to share this view — the 1981 settlement contained an increase of 50 percent over three years.

It is tempting to blame the United Steel Workers for the problems Stelco faced following those bitter strikes. By this view, the union should have realized the recessions of the 1980s and 1990s were different from previous dislocations, that the employer was in much changed condition from previous negotiations and that wage and benefit demands would have to be moderated accordingly. This view, however, requires attributing to union leaders a level of self-sacrifice for the company that is simply not part of their make-up.

As the leaders of Stelco's locals were fond of saying during the company's 2004 to 2006 journey through bankruptcy protection, workers do not join unions to move backward. They join in order to achieve continuous improvement in their situation. To the union leaders of that day there was never any doubt that the company would eventually return to profitability. The element that wasn't factored into the union's equation, however, was the way the world market would be flooded by cheap subsidized steel from Europe and the Third World. That, coupled with the drop in demand triggered by the recession, was a blow for which the company was not prepared (Corman, Luxton and Livingstone 1993: 21–24, 27–28).

Stelco was also hampered by other problems during this period. One was its long tradition of clinging to established technologies; where Dofasco had moved to the new basic oxygen furnace in the 1950s, Stelco had clung to open heart production methods until the late 1960s. The same held for the adoption of continuous casting technology. When Stelco finally took a major technological leap and built its Lake Erie plant, a result was to send the company into the 1980s with a vastly enlarged debt load. A modernization of the Hamilton plant in the 1990s left the company with a cost-disadvantage of about $30 a tonne in a glutted market where import penetration rose from 16 to 25 percent. In 2000, steel prices plunged by $100 a tonne for some grades, dropping the company into another major loss (Clancy 2004: 158–161). Early in 2004, the company finally buckled under these strains and sought bankruptcy protection in an effort to restructure its finances.

As noted above, the first response of Stelco managers to these problems was sharp and deep labour force cuts. Between 1981 and 1983 the company's workforce was reduced by 30 percent, from 29,000 to 21,000. This set a pattern that continued through the next generation as the strategic planning of Stelco managers no longer assumed the eventual resumption of expanded steel production. Instead, cutting costs became an overriding survival imperative — layoffs of over 1,500 followed a 106-day strike at the end of 1990. Aside from adding called-back employees in market upturns in 1984 and 1994, gradual employment reductions occurred in every year since 1981. While Stelco and Dofasco continued to be the largest employers in Hamilton, both steel companies only employed a total of about 14,000 people by 1995, or about 7 percent of the regional workforce (Livingstone, Smith and Smith 2011: 20, 23).

One impact of that shift has been a steady aging of the Stelco workforce. In 1981, for example, the average seniority in the plant was over thirteen years and the average age was thirty-seven. Over 40 percent of workers were under thirty-five years of age and less than 40 percent were over forty-five. The mass layoffs of younger workers starting in 1981 were followed by early retirement incentives that combined to quickly create a middle-aged workforce; by 1989, the average age was forty-four and the average seniority was twenty-one years. By 2003 the average age was fifty with seniority of twenty-eight years. At that point, only around 10 percent of the remaining workforce was under forty-five, and most of the rest were at or near eligibility for retirement.

The situation was aggravated by uncertainty during Stelco's tortured journey through bankruptcy protection. At the start of the process in 2004, still less than 10 percent of the decreasing workforce at Hamilton Works was under forty-five. By late 2009, half of the 2007 workforce had retired and the proportion under forty-five remaining was up to about a third and nearly 20 percent were under thirty-five. At that point, the dwindling Hamilton Works unionized labour force had an average age of forty-five and average seniority of nineteen years (Livingstone, Smith and Smith 2011: 25, 29, 163).

By comparison, Dofasco remained relatively profitable and steadily increased its capital assets through the 1980s, surpassing Stelco in net worth by 1985. This achievement was partially due to a decision to concentrate on flat-rolled products for the large and relatively stable consumer durables market. Dofasco was certainly not without its problems during this period; for instance, 1988 marked the start of its ill-fated Algoma investment. While buying Algoma seemed sound — it would give Dofasco a new source of ingots for its expanded rolling mills — the purchase was doomed by plunging prices in a glutted world steel market, a four-month strike at Algoma and increases in interest rates and the Canadian dollar (Corman, Luxton and Livingstone 1993: 23).

Another factor widely held to have given Dofasco a major advantage is the fact that its workforce is not unionized. Initially the labour policies of both companies were basically paternalistic, although Dofasco's founders managed to maintain a "family image" with open-door communication, a recreation centre, a huge annual Christmas party and profit sharing. Stelco's policies were clearly harsher, leading in 1946 to the formation of Local 1005 of the United Steelworkers of America, often cited as one of the most militant union locals in Canada. While Stelco suffered periodic strikes that interrupted supplies to its customers, Dofasco workers were kept happy by being given whatever raises the unionized workers won at Stelco. In effect, they had all the benefits of being unionized without having to assume any of the risks. As a result of the 1981 Stelco strike and the layoffs that followed, for the first time Dofasco employed more workers than Stelco — 11,400 to 9,700. U.S. Steel's website says total employment is 3,550. That number includes production employment of about 800 at the Lake Erie Works and about 900 production workers at the former Hilton Works plant in Hamilton. But with the shutdown of the Hamilton plant, employment at the Lake Erie works in the wake of the lockout has remained at 800.

Dofasco also reduced employment through this period, but the vast majority of this was accomplished through attrition. Moreover, as Dofasco served a different market than Stelco, concentrating more on the value-added steel grades demanded by the auto industry, the company was able to sell more of its product into the contract market, thereby maintaining higher employment levels. Stelco, by contrast, had more of its production dedicated to the commodity steel grades that sold in the spot market, where price fluctuations were much greater, cyclical conditions harsher and layoffs more likely.

Since 2007, both companies have been foreign-owned — Stelco after being purchased by U.S. Steel from the hedge funds that financed its 2006 emergence from bankruptcy protection, and Dofasco by ArcelorMittal after a bidding war for what was considered a jewel of the Canadian industry. Since their changes in ownership the companies have followed remarkably different trajectories. Stelco's story has been one of assets sales and closures and a seemingly endless cycle of worker layoffs in a desperate search for renewed profits, while Dofasco's employment has remained relatively stable, and its new owners announced investments of $250 million in the Hamilton facilities in January 2011, which were only partially scaled back ten months later (Arnold 2011c, 2011d).

STEEL AND THE GLOBAL RESTRUCTURING OF LABOUR

The dawn of the twenty-first century found the Canadian and North American steel industries still facing a massive set of challenges despite years of difficult restructuring. Open hearth furnaces had been phased out across North America, and the mini-mills had risen to virtual parity with the integrated producers and were invading the high-end, flat-rolled market with their products. The Canada–U.S. and North American free trade agreements had created continent-wide markets with the promise of a level playing field for cross-border trade. Producers had even begun to join bigger corporate blocs through a series of mergers that started in the late 1990s.

These large-scale developments were not enough to save jobs or keep the industry running. Competition in the steel industry was intense. The vast expansion of steel production in Asia, in China in particular, but also in South Korea and Japan, put all other national steel industries under pressure to lower costs and boost capital spending (Fairbrother, Stroud and Coffey 2004). In 1991, Asian producers had 33 percent of total world production. By 2001, Asia had captured more than 40 percent of the world steel market, feeding its own as well as other national markets and often selling steel at below world prices to capture an even greater market share.

In order to compete, European Union countries and Russia expanded their steel output. But all steel producers began to feel the pinch of declining prices because of two major events in the 1990s: the collapse of the Soviet Union and the financial Asian crisis of 1997, both of which led to a rapid decline of global steel consumption and consequent overcapacity of production. The reduction in steel consumption totalled more than 30 million tonnes, leaving producers with over 50 metric tonnes of unsold crude and unfinished steel products. In such conditions, prices plunged. Steel companies shut down production and laid off workers.

In North America, steel prices became disconnected from general business cycles. Volatility was the watchword. The cost structures of many of the North American integrated mills were higher than the most efficient world plants, "so even when demand was strong, profitability was problematic." The problem was so bad that in 2001 the number-two U.S. producer, Bethlehem Steel, had a negative net worth of $170 million. In 2003, it followed NTV and National Steel into court-supervised bankruptcy protection (Clancy 2004: 37).

Over the course of the 1990s, average output at Canadian mills had risen an average of 8 percent, while apparent consumption (output plus imports minus exports) had risen to 20 million tonnes. Stelco and Dofasco both invested heavily in capital upgrades, increased their shares of coated steel for the auto market and promoted new products in the construction field. Despite these gains, the import problem was growing; from an average of 25 percent of sales in the first five years of the 1990s to 39 percent in the last five years, foreign steel companies captured an ever-larger share of the North American market. The Canadian industry pushed for anti-dumping cases against foreign producers and criticized the Canadian International Trade Tribunal for what it called a "timid" response (Clancy 2004: 140).

In the absence of national solutions that focused on the protection and growth of domestic jobs, the steel industry underwent a further major transformation that saw the emergence of international corporate giants and competition shift from the national to the international level, with companies undertaking global restructuring efforts to lower costs, reduce workforces and overhaul collective agreements and union pension plans (Bacon and Blyton 2000.). Faced with declining industries, many governments across Western Europe sold off their national steel enterprises, often at bargain-basement rates to the largest corporations. With new sources of international finance, companies like Mittal Steel, Arcelor and ThyssenKrupp went on international buying sprees, acquiring companies in all international markets in order to give themselves a competitive edge. Other international giants, like POSCO

(South Korea), Nippon Steel and NKK (Japan), grew by signing joint venture agreements that gave them the opportunity to grow beyond their national borders and make profits from consolidated operations. In less than fifteen years, more than 70 percent of the world's large integrated steel companies changed ownership and came under the authority of larger corporate conglomerates (Bacon and Blyton 2000: 12–15).

The result was a drastic reduction in domestic steel businesses and the rise of international steel companies that have done everything possible to lower costs, cut wages and reduce employment, especially of its unionized workforces. With the capacity to operate facilities around the world, global multi-nationals have gained new opportunities to transfer production (or at least threaten to) from less to more profitable or potentially profitable sites. These global companies closed plants. They outsourced work. They reworked collective agreements. Companies also expanded non-union plants, instituted inhumane line speeds, cut benefits and discarded injured workers wherever possible.

Throughout the steel industry, this has forced many workers to accept much greater workloads, far fewer job guarantees and many more temporary employees and contractors. In a stronger position to impose uniform conditions across plants, international companies have told unions that plant survival and new investment are wholly dependent upon unions acceding to certain conditions, such as restricting wage claims and accepting inferior pension payouts and defined contribution plans.

The concentration of ownership among fewer MNCs has also led to the rapid spread of new technologies and the rise of "mini-mills," which have demanded greater workforce "flexibility" (i.e., more shift work at lower rates) and lower pay rates, while providing greater opportunity for employers to establish a non-unionized workforce. Throughout the United States, the common trend for new steel companies is to either establish non-union factories or negotiate local contracts with pay systems linked to performance and employee share option schemes that pay little back to workers (Livingstone, Smith and Smith 2011).

In Hamilton, these trends have seen the end of both Stelco and Dofasco as stand-alone operations and their absorption into global companies. Stelco was purchased by U.S. Steel in a deal announced in August and closed in October 2007. The purchase price of the company was $1.9 billion, consisting of $1.1 billion in cash, to a trio of hedge funds — Tricap Management of Canada (formerly Brascan and part of the Bronfman family empire), Appaloosa Management of New Jersey and Westface Capital of New York. Together these firms controlled 76 percent of Stelco's shares: stock they had been given at $5.50 a share for a value of around $140 million. After seventeen months, that $140 million ballooned to a $1.1 billion payoff. The balance of the purchase price was the assumption of debt. That was all separate from Stelco's pension and health-care liabilities of between US$1.3 billion and US$1.5 billion. The purchase price amounted to $38.50 per share, a premium of almost 43 percent over the closing price on the previous trading day. In a statement that today causes many to shake their heads, U.S. Steel president John Surma said in an interview: "Stelco is a much improved company than it was before, " adding he had no plans to reduce Stelco's workforce of about 3,600 or to close operations. He told a reporter at the time: "We wouldn't be putting this kind of money into a company to shut it down" (Powell 2007: A1).

Before the U.S. Steel purchase, Stelco was something of a wallflower at a party where global companies were looking for any chance to break into the lucrative North American steel business. The Russian company Severstal considered an offer, India's Essar Global and Ukraine's Metinvest toured the plant, picked through the books and asked questions, but none made an offer. ArcelorMittal, which had been quietly eyeing the plant, stepped up its research and then disappeared. At the end of the process, only one made a formal offer. At that time, U.S. Steel was in a strong growth-by-acquisition process that had seen it triple in size since 2000. The Stelco acquisition made it the world's fifth largest steel producer. In addition to agreeing to pay a significant premium for the shares, U.S. Steel also guaranteed the company's $1.4 billion in pension and healthcare liabilities, chipped in an extra US$31 million to the pension shortfall, retired $760 million in debt and endowed a research chair at McMaster University. Finally, it gave undertakings to the federal government to maintain employment at 3,100 workers, to make capital investments of $200 million over five years and to increase exports from Stelco by 10 percent (Powell 2007).

The only serious opposition to the deal was raised by the United Steel Workers, who argued not against the purchase itself but against clauses that permitted U.S. Steel to cancel earlier Stelco commitments to contribute excess cash to the pension shortfall and not to pay dividends until the unfunded pension liabilities had been eliminated. Lawyers for Stelco, U.S. Steel and the Ontario government argued that the union's goals were accomplished by U.S. Steel's excess contribution and its unconditional guarantee to meet pension-funding obligations (*Hamilton Spectator* October 31, 2007: A15).

Despite its promise to maintain production and employment in Canada, in the wake of the economic recession starting in late 2008, U.S Steel shut down its Hamilton and Lake Erie blast furnaces indefinitely and began a series of large layoffs that by March 2009 led to the dismissal of all hourly employees — about 1,700 workers at Hamilton Works and 1,100 at Lake Erie Works. When recovery started in 2009, U.S. Steel's American plants dramatically increased the amount of steel they produced for Canadian customers while the former Stelco plants sat idle. As steel markets continued to recover, U.S. Steel called back 800 workers in June 2009 to produce coke at Hamilton Works for U.S. Steel mills and to avoid costly severance payouts (Livingstone, Smith and Smith 2011: 154).

In an op-ed piece written for the *Hamilton Spectator* at the time of the sale, union leader Rolf Gerstenberger sounded an eerily prescient warning about the potential outcome of the deal: "We are under no illusions that USX will guarantee jobs, pensions or anything of value in the community that comes in conflict with its primary mission to make profit for its U.S. owners.... Whatever USX says now, one year from now it could be a completely different story with fine reasons stemming from `global competition' or a business downturn" (Gerstenberger 2007).

In 2009, there were less than 1,000 workers left in the Hamilton plant, running the trimmed-down operation of coke ovens, blast furnace and caster, doing maintenance and operating the Z-Line finishing mill. At that point, the unionized labour force was about 7 percent of its 1981 size. With the shutdown of the entire plant for much of 2009, many workers were forced to retire in the wake of indefinite layoff because their pensions were greater than their unemployment benefits. Between the March 2009 shutdown and mid-2010, there were over seven hundred retirements; in late 2009, about two hundred of the 942 workers in the plant were eligible to retire, many in their late forties and early fifties. By mid-2010, plant numbers were down to about 850 as many of those eligible for retirement at a fairly early age continued to take it. The issues of renewing this aging workforce and coping with the loss of the knowledge of these experienced workers were becoming painfully obvious to all (Livingstone, Smith and Smith 2011: 160). By 2012, the Hamilton plant was shut and there were no plans to re-open it.

Dofasco's absorption into the new global steel industry was only a partly different story; it and its 6,400 employees were the much sought-after prize in an international bidding war among European giants looking for a way into the North American market. The Hamilton steel maker was seen as a desirable target because it had been consistently profitable, produced more iron ore than it needed through its Quebec Cartier Mining asset and is located in close proximity to several major automakers.

The bidding started in November 2005 when Arcelor SA made a C$4.3 billion hostile takeover bid for Dofasco. A few days later ThyssenKrupp emerged as a white knight, making a friendly bid of $4.8 billion. Arcelor ended the bidding in January 2006 with a final offer of $5.6 billion. Days later, Mittal Steel shocked the world by offering US$22.8 billion for Arcelor. Mittal made Dofasco a pawn in its global power play by hatching a side deal to flip the Hamilton firm to ThyssenKrupp if it was successful in getting Arcelor. In

April Arcelor attempted to thwart Mittal's advances by shifting ownership of Dofasco into a non-profit Dutch foundation. The move built a virtual fence around Dofasco, making it difficult for Mittal to sell and creating regulatory problems for Mittal in the North American tin-plated steel market.

In May, Mittal completed its takeover of Arcelor with an enhanced offer of US$33 billion. The American Justice Department raised antitrust questions about the size of the new company because it owned numerous steel operations in North America, including Cleveland-based International Steel Group, Inland Steel in Illinois, Weirton Steel in West Virginia and Georgetown Steel in South Carolina. Mittal also owns three former subsidiaries of Stelco. The Americans demanded that ArcelorMittal's footprint be reduced by offloading either Dofasco or the Sparrows Point plant in Maryland. Sparrows Point was eventually sold to U.S. Steel (Powell 2006).

From the beginning, ArcelorMittal executives made it clear they had big plans for the Hamilton icon. In an interview with the *Hamilton Spectator* in June 2007, newly appointed ArcelorMittal Dofasco president Juergen Schachler said Dofasco would be "one of the flagships" of its new owners and was expected to play an important role in its North American strategy. That role would be bolstered by a number of capital investments, including a $60 million pulverized coal injection system (Arnold 2007a).

Dofasco's change in ownership involved some reductions in employment, but they were not as severe as the wholesale slashing of staff at Stelco. From the workforce of 6,400, the company cut seventy-five summer student positions and a number of casual jobs and offered permanent staff not eligible to retire a special severance package of three weeks' pay per year of service plus $2,000 toward an approved education program. Those job cuts were blamed on the effects of Canada's soaring exchange rate — the company noted that a one penny rise in the exchange rate of the dollar cost it $20 million off its bottom line (Arnold 2007b).

THE U.S. STEEL PENSION DISPUTE

U.S. Steel has brought a new component to the long-running steel industry obsession with cost cutting: a relentless campaign to reduce the cost of worker pensions. To that end, in August 2009 it locked out its workers at its Lake Erie plant for eight months until they agreed to a two-tiered pension plan that offered a defined benefit pension to current staff and a defined contribution scheme to new hires. The difference between the two types of pension plan is important. A defined benefit system pays a pension usually based on some negotiated percentage of average earnings multiplied by years of service. As the name implies, it is a defined monthly retirement income. Under Ontario law the pension fund pool created by employee and employer contributions must hold enough money to meet all current and estimated future pensions if the company were to go out of business. Any shortfall, called an unfunded liability, must be made up by the company over a legally mandated period of ten years. A defined contribution system, on the other hand, works in basically the same way as a registered retirement savings plan. Workers and employers make contributions to the plan over the years of employment. At retirement, the monthly pension paid by the plan is dependent on the amount saved and its investment performance over the years. In addition, U.S. Steel has demanded an end to pension indexing for retirees in Hamilton. Under a system negotiated in the 1991 contract retirees are entitled to have their monthly payments increased according to a formula balancing increases in the cost of living with the performance of pension plan assets. In 2009 that formula produced a raise of just under 1 percent, or $10 per $1,000 of monthly pension.

At the time of its bankruptcy protection filing, Stelco's main pension plans were $1.2 billion short. Today the shortfall is basically unchanged because of years of disastrous stock market returns. U.S. Steel has claimed repeatedly that being forced to make up defined benefit pension shortfalls places it at a crippling competitive disadvantage against other American and global firms. It also notes that under American law many companies were able to simply walk away from pension obligations.

Union officials hold that it would be a betrayal of both retirees and future workers to give in to the demands of the company. Union leaders argue that even if the company agrees to maintain the defined benefit system for the current staff that pensions could eventually be taken away as workers retire and surrender their power to shape union negotiations in the future. Union leaders point out that retirees are the are ones who fought the strikes of the past to win the benefits enjoyed today. Negotiating those benefits away would be an action of base betrayal. Workers on the picket lines in January 2011 shared these views (Arnold 2011e, 2011f):

> Eventually people have to know we create the wealth, the world was created on the backs of labour and we have to get back to those roots. Governments have to look after the people and if they won't then we're going to put somebody in power who will and that's eventually what's going to happen.

> These public unions see it too. If we give up our fight they're going to lose their pensions as well.

> When people are seventy-five years of age they shouldn't have to come down here and fight for their pensions. They've kept their end of the bargain. For U.S. Steel to come in and say we're going to take that away when the CEO makes $14 million a year there's

something not right in society. We're not greedy, we just want a fair piece of things.

The conflict became the longest labour dispute in Stelco's hundred-year history in March 2011 and was not resolved until October 2011, when the union finally admitted defeat and accepted the company's pension demands. In exchange retirees were given a one-time payment roughly equal to the indexing they would have received for three years. Through the confrontation union members were bolstered in their determination by a decision to award them Employment Insurance benefits, which, combined with strike pay of $200 a week, gave most a lock-out income of about $600 a week, roughly two-thirds of what they made when they were working (Arnold 2011g).

At the same time, a lawsuit against the company launched by the federal government seeking financial penalties now totaling more than $15 million for failing to live up to its production and other promises remains mired in procedural appeals by the company. Action on the substantive issue of the suit isn't expected before the summer. In addition, the United Steel Workers have been granted intervener status and are asking for $44 million in lost wages during the company's Canadian shutdowns. Welland-based Lakeside Steel, a former Stelco division, is asking for a court-ordered sale of the Stelco assets.

Aside from their intervention in the federal lawsuit, workers focused their anger through a series of demonstrations, denouncing the company and governments at all levels for their failure to take firm action. Union leader Rolf Gerstenberger said at one such demonstration on January 29, 2011, "Part of our message is that the government should play their role in looking after public right, after the interests of the people rather than the monopolies. We're hoping somebody there gets the message it just isn't acceptable to buy us, shut us down twice in two years. It's not good for Canada, it's not good for us. That's what we'd like to have some action on" (Arnold 2011).

Workers remain concerned about their future under the pension scheme demanded by the company, but they also want to get back to the jobs that support their families. As one said in an interview after the January 2011, rally:

> I've been retired eight years and I can see my surplus money going down and I hate to think what it's going to be like in another eight years without the indexing. I raised a family of three at Stelco, it was good to me, but I'd like to see other people get into Stelco at the same age I did and be able to raise their families as I did mine and we can't when we're not there working.
>
> Most of us left parts of our bodies in Stelco when we left. I don't have any use of my left hand, I have two artificial hips. I was

a millwright, I did a hard job but it served me well. I just want our people of Hamilton and area to give their families what I was able to give mine and we're not going to be able to do that unless we get back working.

I'm seventy now and I hate to think what it's going to be like if I live to be eighty, I'm just not going to have the dollars. I want to be able to hold my head up, have a respectable retirement and not live in poverty and go for social assistance. I just want a payback for the work I did and for the body parts I've left. (Arnold 2011)

CONCLUSION

Given the developments over the past decade or more, it is worth pondering the impact of China's steel industry on global steel making and on the likely further significant contraction of the Canadian steel industry. China accounts for about 40 percent of total global steel capacity and perhaps as much as 50 percent of operating capacity. In the last ten years, it has increased its crude steel production by over 400 million tons, and increased its share of world production from 15 percent to almost 50 percent. On average, since 2001, China has added twice the size of the Canadian steel industry every year. China is already the world's largest steel producer, accounting for 45 per cent of global output, and is home to six of the world's ten largest steel makers. The mainland's total capacity, which is set to hit 940 million tons this year, already outstrips demand by 220 million tons, according to Shanghai-based research and consulting firm Mysteel (Roberts 2012).

That huge capacity will weigh heavily on the future of the industry. Steel making is capital intensive and involves relatively high fixed costs, an equation that provides a real incentive for producers with significant excess capacity to increase production. Given China's phenomenal growth, its producers are inclined to boost their exports even more. Export subsides only exacerbate this situation and contribute to the widespread dumping of steel at below-cost prices (Warrian 2010: 91). For Canada's steel workers the results are likely to be dire — further contraction, further restructuring, further retirements and further job losses.

The Canadian Steel Producers Association concludes that such a dooms-day scenario "would be devastating in their dimensions and implications" (*Algoma News* June 1, 2010). The Canadian Steel Producers Association es-timates its industry has a multiplier effect of approximately 3.3:1 — that is one additional manufacturing job and 2.3 additional service-sector jobs for every direct job within the industry. If Canada were to lose its steel industry, it would not only hurt the steel industry and the steel workers, but many of its communities as well. Already there is much evidence of this. The extended shutdown of U.S. Steel's facilities in Nanticoke and Hamilton has created crises for local businesses, a collapse of local public finances and erosion of the tax base for critical social and health services (Warrian 2010: 23–24)

Leo Gerard, the international president of the United Steel Workers, argues that if Canada wants to avoid this bleak future, the first step will be to develop a national industrial strategy aimed at preserving some level of production in Canada. In January 2011 he told a *Hamilton Spectator* reporter:

> Steel is a basic material for the equipment and infrastructure that make up modern life. Without control of this fundamental industry Canada cedes a great deal of control over its future to the boards of directors of foreign companies whose only duty is the production of "shareholder value."
>
> Today, Canada does not have any meaningful domestic steel manufacturing. It has some large steel service companies like Samuel Manu-Tech, but they have no large company that makes steel. In fact the Canadian steel industry is now primarily American, Russian, Brazilian and Indian, which is a shame.
>
> One thing I've learned in my work as president of the Steelworkers is, when you talk to people in other countries they understand that in order to have an industrial economy you've got to have a steel industry. You can't make anything, not a thing, you can't make a computer, a car, you can't make a railroad, you can't make a building or a school or anything without steel.
>
> America is down to three domestic steel companies, Canada is down to none and there's no industrial strategy or manufacturing strategy. We're getting our lunch eaten by those who have a strategy.
>
> The only ones who don't have a strategy are Canada, the United States and Great Britain. Each of them have bought that free market baloney. There's no free market, markets are regulated. (Arnold 2011a)

Professor David Livingstone and former Local 1005 president Warren Smith suggest four possible national strategies for Canada to deal with the U.S. Steel — and Canada's — situation: another foreign takeover, repurchase of the company by Canadian private capital, turning the former Stelco into a crown corporation or supporting some form of worker ownership. In their analysis, only worker ownership provides a viable and long-term model. Continuing with foreign takeovers, they claim, will only give Canadian workers more of the same: companies that buy operations around the world, close less efficient plants and lay off workers. Nor would the repurchase of the former Stelco be any better. The likely scenario, as was seen when Stelco emerged from bankruptcy protection, would be a quick turnover and layoffs in hopes of a fat profit. As to the idea of turning the former Stelco into a crown corporation, they note there is no legal reason this couldn't happen — but it is largely a question of political will, a will that deficit-obsessed governments lack today.

Livingstone and Smith are more impressed with the possibility of some form of worker ownership, perhaps along the cooperative model developed by Mondragon in the Basque region of Spain, rather than the business "partnership" models trumpeted by corporations today. In the cooperative model, all workers have a vote in the direction of the company, decisions are made in regular assemblies, the highest-paid manager does not receive more than six times the compensation of the lowest-paid worker, and profits are retained within the firm. Livingstone and Smith argue that there is a long tradition of cooperative ownership in Canada and suggest that, with the right kind of government and financial support, such a model could work for both the Hamilton and Lake Erie plants of the former Stelco. Again, however, the hurdle to be overcome is that of political will (Livingstone and Smith 2011).

The last three decades have essentially stripped Canada of control of its domestic steel industry, and as Livingstone and Smith conclude, companies and industries that don't control decisions about their own development become branch plants whose existence depends on the fortunes of a larger company. The final question is simple: Does manufacturing and steel making matter to Canada? Canada's steel industry was born because of the confluence of advantages of access to raw materials, transportation infrastructure and available markets. Those still exist. What is lacking is the political will to capitalize on those advantages to the general benefit of Canada.

Part II

DEREGULATION AND CHANGES IN PROVINCIAL LABOUR MARKET POLICY, POLITICS AND INSTITUTIONS

5. THE BIGGEST ROLL-BACK OF WORKER RIGHTS IN CANADIAN HISTORY

The Campbell Government and Labour Market Deregulation in British Columbia

David Fairey, Tom Sandborn and John Peters

Over the course of a decade, British Columbia's government was transformed, and this has fundamentally changed British Columbians' perceptions of what government does and for whom it acts. From his election in 2001 until he stepped down in 2011, Gordon Campbell and the Liberal government implemented policy that is generous towards those at the top. Income inequality has skyrocketed, and instead of offsetting this rise, government taxes and benefits have actually worsened it. In a range of areas, from labour law to financial market regulation, Liberal public policy has reshaped the economy to favour the wealthiest segment of society. Most notably, the Liberal government has introduced policies that have seriously weakened organized labour and have made the labour market precarious for men and women, immigrants and youth alike.

Analyses of government and labour market deregulation often miss the fact that the this exercise of political authority is an extraordinarily powerful means for influencing the structure of "private" markets, which in turn that determines the economy's winners and losers and what kinds of jobs — good or bad — that workers have. Those in positions of power have an enormous influence over organized labour, the distribution of income, and the life chances of citizens. Too little analytical effort is devoted to assessing the real-world impact of changes in government regulations.

During Campbell's time in office, his Liberal government drastically altered the labour market, the balance of power between trade unions and employers, and the distribution of market income. The Liberals have not only passed laws that spurred the housing boom, they have rewritten labour legislation and redesigned labour regulatory agencies to influence how business and organized labour operate. The government has done everything possible to change legislation and overhaul administrative procedures to give employers the upper hand and to lower labour costs. In these and other ways, the new rules for the labour market have made a big difference in peoples' lives. What we now see developing is a declining labour movement, the rise of a small number of rich professionals and a growing majority of part-time, temporary, foreign and underpaid workers.

THE CAMPBELL GOVERNMENT AND THE BOOM

Over the past forty years in British Columbia, the provincial economy and the political parties in power have gone through distinct cycles of progress followed by long periods of business-friendly Social Credit or Liberal governments. But over the past decade, the province has taken a sharp turn to the "right" and there has been no effective counter by labour or the left.

Funded by generous Business Council contributions and using innovative organizational strategies, the B.C. Liberal Party under Gordon Campbell translated its mastery of an increasingly money-driven campaign world into durable election victories that consolidated tax cuts, deregulation and labour market flexibility policies. First elected in 2001, the Campbell government cut personal and corporate taxes by more than 25 percent in its first term. Then it imposed tight constraints on public spending and reconfigured social programs to exclude many of B.C.'s most vulnerable residents, including women, the disabled and the homeless (Mcbride and Mcnutt 2007).

It followed this up by cutting corporate tax and royalty rates for natural resource companies and by enacting new investment allowances that allowed companies to write off 100 percent of exploration and pre-production costs, as well as a further 33 percent for new capital costs annually (Natural Resources Canada 2010; McMahon and Cervantes 2009). Tax credits for oil and gas, mining and forestry were implemented to spur further rapid resource exploitation (Marshall and Newnham 2004: 17–19). This was then supplemented by the federal government allowing all mining companies to deduct 100 percent of provincial mining taxes and royalties from federal taxes. Further subsidies for road development, transport, storage and distribution were enacted to take advantage of the strong global demand for resources.

Housing, commercial real estate and urban investment were spurred by changes in tax codes, low interest rates and an estimated $6 billion in Olympic spending. Housing starts boomed along with prices. In the course of eight years, housing starts tripled, from 12,000 to more than 39,000 by 2007. Housing prices doubled, and by 2008, the average house price was nearly $500,000, the highest in Canada. Double-digit increases in housing prices from year to year and a massive expansion of construction and housing supply industries were also fuelled by speculation and overly enthusiastic realtor associations.

At the same time, the 2010 Olympics, led by the provincial and federal governments building new venues, expanding the Sea to Sky highway, providing $1 billion for the Convention Centre and the $2 billion Canada Line extension of the Sky Train, further spurred urban development and the construction industry (*Economist* 2009). Add to that the bailout of developers of the Olympic Village, a security budget and other costs, and government expenditures into British Columbia over 2003–2010 totalled in the billions, resulting in the most rapid economic expansion of British Columbia in decades.

With average annual growth rates approaching 6 percent annually, market price GDP increased from $129 billion to $210 billion from 2000 to 2009. Mining, oil and gas, finance and construction grew at record rates, more than doubling employment in these sectors. Jobs in construction nearly doubled, from 111,000 in 2000 to more than 220,000 by 2008. In finance, insurance, business and real estate, employment rose by more than 150,000 (BC Stats 2010). The growth in jobs spurred more debt-led consumption, as many took out home equity loans or new mortgages that were larger than existing mortgages in order to buy cars and boats, take vacations or pay bills. And with rising house prices, home equity fuelled ever greater levels of consumption. And as home ownership equity plunged, so too did savings out of disposable income fall to record lows.

However, most of the gains of this widespread boom went to the top 10 percent, and especially to the top 1 percent and the highest reaches of the top 1 percent. This followed the wider trends in Canada, where by 2007 the richest 10 percent had more 40 percent of all income, and Canada's wealthiest citizens took home almost a third of all income growth during the decade from 1997 to 2007. Similarly in B.C., the richer you were, the richer you became.

In 2001, B.C. already had one of the wealthiest elites, with the richest 10 percent of family units holding 54.6 percent of the province's personal wealth (compared to 53 percent nationally) (Kerstetter 2001). But over the course of the first decade of the twenty-first century, with tax cuts targeted to the wealthy and supporting financial returns, government policy ensured that economic gains went almost entirely to the richest 10 percent (Ivanova 2009). By 2005, B.C. had the largest income gap of all the provinces.

Unsurprisingly, this boom in wealth for the well-to-do was of limited benefit to the vast majority of workers in the province. Beginning in the early 2000s, the Campbell government turned back the clock in every area of labour legislation: employment standards, industrial relations regulation, the sanctity of freely negotiated collective agreements, industrial apprentice-ship regulation, workers' compensation and special legislation to undermine the free collective bargaining process in most of the province's major labour disputes. And by the end of the decade, the economy had turned into a night-mare for many workers. In 2007 provincial economic growth fell below its long-term average of 3 percent, and with the onset of the global economic crisis, growth fell to zero in 2008, before shrinking 2 percent in 2009. The Winter Olympics in early 2010 is credited with helping return the province to positive economic growth in 2010. However, the unemployment rate had jumped from 4.2 percent in 2008 to 7.6 percent in 2009, and remained stuck at 7.5 percent in 2010. In northern and interior regions the unemployment rate went even higher, averaging more than 10 percent in 2009 and 2010.

Table 5.1 B.C. Average Weekly and Hourly Wages

Year	B.C. Consumer Price Index (2002=100)	Average Weekly Wage	Real Ave. Weekly Wage	Percent Change	Average Hourly Wage	Real Ave. Hourly Wage	Percent Change
1997	93.1	610.31	655.54		16.83	18.08	
1998	93.4	618.90	662.63	1.1%	17.08	18.29	1.2%
1999	94.4	626.78	663.96	0.2%	17.28	18.31	0.1%
2000	96.1	639.37	665.32	0.2%	17.64	18.36	0.3%
2001	97.7	648.19	663.45	-0.3%	17.98	18.40	0.3%
2002	100.0	668.04	668.04	0.7%	18.59	18.59	1.0%
2003	102.2	683.68	668.96	0.1%	19.02	18.61	0.1%
2004	104.2	686.74	659.06	-1.5%	18.99	18.22	-2.1%
2005	106.3	704.49	662.74	0.6%	19.36	18.21	-0.1%
2006	108.1	726.02	671.62	1.3%	19.91	18.42	1.1%
2007	110.0	747.84	679.85	1.2%	20.49	18.63	1.1%
2008	112.3	780.85	695.33	2.3%	21.46	19.11	2.6%
2009	112.3	800.5	712.82	2.5%	22.21	19.78	3.5%

Sources: BC Stats and Statistics Canada, Labour Force Survey

The boom also did little to improve wages for the majority of workers. In the first five years of the Campbell Liberal government (2001 to 2005) average real weekly wages declined from $665.32 in 2000 to $659.06 in 2004, and remained below the 2000 level until 2006 (Table 5.1). At the same time the real average hourly wage declined from the $18.61 peak in 2003 until a marginal recovery to $18.63 in 2007. In the nine years from 2000 to 2009 the average weekly wage in B.C. went from 3.8 percent above the national average to 0.5 percent below and from second place to third place, behind Alberta and Ontario.

In the weakened and declining unionized sector of the labour market, in the period 2002 to 2010, major wage settlements provided for annual average wage increases in B.C. of 1.5 percent compared to 2.5 percent for all of Canada. And throughout the decade the average wage increase in all B.C. collective agreements barely kept pace with the rate of inflation. Rather than a boom for all workers, what the last decade meant for many of B.C.'s workers was a growing gap in income and wealth between the super-rich and everyone else.

THE DEREGULATION OF EMPLOYMENT STANDARDS

The Campbell government policy not only affected what people earned and how but also influenced many other fundamental economic decisions that businesses and workers made. Under the influence of multi-national and local employers, wealthy business owners and rich families, who poured vast new resources into efforts to shape the broader political climate, the B.C. Liberal government enacted a host of legislative and administrative changes affecting labour. Some of the most important reforms have been to employment standards and public-sector collective agreements.

So dramatic were the changes that University of British Columbia Sauder School of Business professor emeritus Mark Thompson, a former independent employment standards review commissioner, characterized changes to the *Employment Standards Act* and legislation governing public-sector collective agreements in the period 2001 to 2004 (including Bills 48, 37 and 56, and numerous Regulation changes, and Bill 29 in 2002, the *Health and Social Services Delivery Improvement Act*) as constituting "the biggest roll-back of worker rights in Canadian history" (Sandborn 2010b).

With business putting together all the pieces — the coordination of many companies toward shared goals, the creation of umbrella business groups to advocate for reduced taxes and labour market "flexibility" and the proactive shaping of political discourse through conservative think-tanks like the Fraser Institute — they created a political agenda that forced the Liberal government to enact a variety of deregulatory initiatives. Wherever possible, regulations were rolled back; where not, they were rendered ineffective.

In its spring 2001 provincial election campaign, the Liberal Party of B.C. targeted employment standards and industrial relations legislation for change in its "New Era" platform. The B.C. Liberals promised twelve employment policy actions based on the following: "To compete and prosper in the new economy, workers and employers alike need more flexibility and a modern work environment that encourages innovation and rewards creative thinking and increased productivity." After referring to a plan to cut income taxes, the election platform went on to state:

> We also have to restore workers' rights and modernize employment standards to ensure all workers are treated fairly and equitably. Our New Era is about liberating our economy and minimizing undue government intervention in people's lives. It's about giving employees and employers the tools they need to foster better working relationships and safe, healthy, dynamic workplaces. It's about giving working women and men the safeguards and incentives they need to participate fully and equally in the competitive global economy in which we all work and live. (Gordon Campbell and the BC Liberals 2001: 11)

The 2001 BC Liberal Party campaign platform on employment standards borrowed heavily from the 1999 election campaign platform of the Progressive Conservative Party of Ontario, in which it promised to "modernize" the Ontario *Employment Standards Act* to make it "flexible" and adaptable to the contemporary labour market. In November 2001, following their election in May, the new Liberal B.C. provincial government embarked upon a series of substantive changes to the *Employment Standards Act*, regulations under the Act and the system of administration and enforcement of the Act.

In announcing changes to the Act in May 2002, following a quick twenty-eight-day consultation process and senior staff review in November and December 2001, the minister explained: "These changes are designed to provide flexibility and encourage self-reliance so employees and employers can build mutually beneficial workplace relationships." The stated goals of the new legislation were the following:

- Protect vulnerable employees, particularly those in certain sectors.
- Encourage flexible workplace partnerships.
- Help revitalize the economy, specifically small business, by recognizing the needs and the realities of the workplace.
- Simplify the rules. (B.C. Ministry of Skills Development and Labour 2002b).

Changes in employment standards and industrial relations legislation and regulation were motivated by the Campbell government's belief that "the labour relations climate in British Columbia is often perceived as hindering investment in the province" (B.C. Ministry of Skills Development and Labour 2002a). As such, changes to the *Employment Standards Act* were explicitly designed to simplify the rules and advance a model premised on greater flexibility. To this end the Ministry has aggressively sought to introduce legislation that initiates "changes to employment standards that give employees and employers greater flexibility, reduce unnecessary regulation and bring mandatory penalties into force."

The provincial labour strategy and workforce development plan adopted by the Liberals was intended to address the "increasingly globalized marketplace where competition is tighter and competitive advantages more crucial" and, according to a provincial government statement, the "provincial and regional economies must be defined by a culture of increasing knowledge and innovation" (B.C. Ministry of Skills Development and Labour 2004: 1). Then Labour Minister Graham Bruce asserted that these "changes send an important message to the labour relations community and to investors. They say that B.C. is open for business and that we are prepared to make sure labour relations in British Columbia are balanced, fair-minded, and support growth and prosperity" (B.C. Ministry of Skills Development and Labour 2002b). The remedy to this increasingly competitive environment, according to the provincial Liberals, was the wholesale adoption of a flexibility model of labour regulation in which job security is undermined through the relaxation of employment standards.

Bills 48 and 37 in 2002 and 2003 made a total of forty-two substantive changes to the *Employment Standards Act*, thirty-five of which have had a negative impact on workers' conditions of employment (Fairey 2005). The first regulation change, in 2001, was the introduction of the $6 per hour minimum first job entry level wage for the first five hundred hours of employment, $2 per hour below the general minimum wage of $8 per hour. Intended to reduce the youth unemployment rate, the first job entry level wage demonstrably did not have that effect. The unemployment rate for fifteen- to twenty-four-year-olds increased from 13.9 percent in 2001 to 15.1 percent in 2002 and remained above 10 percent until 2005. During the brief economic mini boom and general above-average employment growth of 2006 and 2007, the youth unemployment rate fell to 7.6 percent, but then in 2009 jumped dramatically to 13.2 percent — double the overall unemployment rate for twenty-five- to sixty-four-year-olds.

Neither the $8 general minimum wage (established in 2001 before election of the Liberal government) or the $6 first job minimum wage increased during the first nine years of Liberal government (although minimum wages have increased since then and the first job minimum wage has been discontinued), while the cost of living increased by 15 percent and the average B.C. industrial wage increased by 23.5 percent. The injustice of such low minimum wages in B.C. was demonstrated by the results of research conducted by the Living Wage for Families Campaign (Richards, Cohen and Klein 2010). They calculated that the living wage in Metro Vancouver at which a household of two parents and two children can meet its basic needs was $18.17 per hour for each parent working full-time. It was not until May 2011 that the Liberal government, under a new premier, acknowledged the injustice of not increasing the minimum wage for nearly a decade and the inequity of the $6 first job minimum wage by instituting three staged increases in the general minimum wage and elimination of the the first job rate. However, in November 2011 and May 2012 the Liberal government once again froze indefinitely the minimum piece rate wages for farm workers who hand harvest fruits, berries and certain vegetables.

The following list describes other significant changes to employment standards and related enforcement practices made in the early years of the Campbell Liberal government that facilitated a continuing decline in workers' conditions of employment:

- exclusion of employees covered by a collective agreement from the core provisions of the Act;
- elimination of government supervision of the employment of children between the ages of twelve and fifteen — now the lowest standard in Canada;
- elimination of the requirement for employers to post workplace rules consistent with the Act and to post hours of work in places of employment, or to give twenty-four hours' notice of shift change;
- reduction of minimum call-in pay provisions where the minimum daily hours were reduced from four to two hours;
- new "hours averaging agreement" provisions allowing employers to enter into agreements with individual employees to forego their rights to overtime pay after eight hours per day and/or forty hours per week so that they may be required to work up to twelve hours per day without overtime pay provided their hours of work do not exceed an *average* of forty hours per week over a four-week period;
- reduction of statutory holiday provisions whereby in order to qualify for a statutory holiday with pay an employee must have worked for at least fifteen of the thirty calendar days before the holiday, effectively eliminating statutory holiday pay for many part-time employees. In addition, employers are no longer required to schedule another day off with pay for employees required to work on a statutory holiday,or to provide such employee with a paid day off in lieu of the holiday;
- reduced employer liability for wage payment violations whereby retroactivity was reduced from two years to six months, directors or officers of companies no longer bear personal liability if the

company is in bankruptcy or receivership, and farm producers are no longer liable for the unpaid wages of farm workers employed by farm labour contractors;

- introduction of employee "self-help/do it yourself" procedures as the first step in the filing of complaints, requiring employees to initially make their complaint to employer, and to then run the gauntlet of protracted complaint processing procedures involving the Employment Standards Branch;
- a 33 percent reduction in Employment Standards Branch staff, a 47 percent reduction in enforcement officer staff, and the closure of half of the Employment Standards Branch offices; and
- Employment Standards Branch termination of active random auditing of employers as an effective enforcement tool in sectors with a history or pattern of non-compliance.

Of particular significance were changes to employment standards with respect to the minimum standards and protections for farm workers, especially those employed through farm labour contractors. These changes involved the following:

- disbanding the inter-agency Agriculture Compliance Team (ACT), a highly successful multi-jurisdictional program that proactively enforced regulation in the agricultural sector and encouraged direct communication between staff members and the predominantly Indo-Canadian farm workers;
- a return to a complaint-dependent (rather than proactive) enforcement system, despite the vulnerability of immigrant and migrant farm workers, the power of farm labour contractors and a history of unscrupulous violations of regulations that led to establishing the ACT in the first place;
- elimination of the requirement that farmers retain records of wages paid to employees of farm labour contractors on their properties and creation of exemptions from farmers' liability for workers' unpaid wages, shifting liability to farm labour contractors;
- reducing the minimum piece rates payable to farm workers by approximately 4 percent, by deeming piece rates to include statutory holiday and annual vacation pay;
- excluding farm workers who are paid hourly from entitlements to statutory holiday pay and annual vacations;
- reducing from four to two hours the minimum hours to be paid to workers who are transported by farm labour contractors to farms; and

- initially reducing overtime pay for work in excess of 120 hours in a two-week period from double time to time and a half. Subsequently, by regulation, excluding farm workers from all overtime entitlements.

By the end of the decade, as Simon Fraser University professor Marjorie Griffin Cohen noted: "The removal of union members from Employment Standards protections, the exclusion of farm workers and other changes in Employment Standards mean that at least a third of the workforce has been removed from ESA protection."

THE ATTACK ON ORGANIZED LABOUR

The election victory of Gordon Campbell changed the playing field in favour of management and against organized labour. By stacking the Labour Relations Board with their own appointees and rewriting the established legal framework for recognizing unions, the Liberals provided new opportunities for companies to develop and implement long-term plans for conducting business in a union-free environment. Outgunned in terms of money, organization and focus, unions were unable to effectively organize or politically challenge the government. The consequence was that in the space of nine years, the Campbell government so successfully reformed labour legislation that there are now few real limits on employers that pursue vigorous anti-union activities.

The most significant *Labour Relations Code* amendments in 2001 (Bill 18) and 2002 (Bill 42) involved the following:

- reintroduction of mandatory union representation votes and elimination of the card-check system of automatic certification of a union when the union can demonstrate majority workplace support for certification;
- amendments to the unfair labour practices provisions, subsequent Labour Relations Board (LRB) interpretation of amendments and failure of the LRB to provide effective remedies in the face of increasing evidence of unfair employer practices to prevent unionization;
- elimination of special sectoral bargaining provisions of the Code applicable to collective bargaining in the construction industry;
- making all public education employment an essential service; and
- mandating that the LRB must exercise its powers and perform duties under the Code that, among other things, fosters the employment of workers in *economically viable businesses* and encourages

cooperative participation between employers and trade unions in resolving workplace issues.

The above changes combined with precedent-setting interpretation of the Code by a new business-friendly Labour Relations Board, contributed greatly to decline in union density. The ending of card certification and first-contract arbitration across the province proved enormously effective in weakening union attempts at organizing. It meant that the era of the moderate employer campaign against union organizing drives was now over. Henceforth, management could hire lawyers and consultants who ran campaigns that bordered on — and often crossed the line into — illegality with little opportunity for challenge or oversight.

Such reforms in labour legislation have set off a long-term and chronic pattern of union decline. Faced with a hard choice — devote their dwindling resources to organizing or spend their money and time on increasingly uncertain provincial actions to promote new rules and protect old one — many unions have retreated from organizing and instead sought to merge with other unions. Some unions, faced with the costs of organizing the rapidly expanding numbers of non-union workers, have made cuts to education

Figure 5.2 B.C. Union Density — Public and Private Sectors (Percentage of Total Employed)

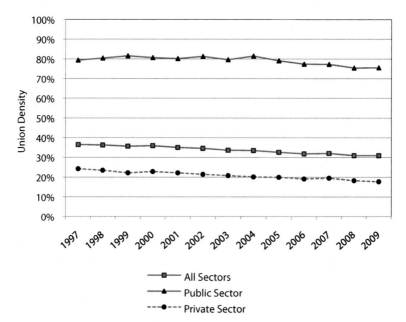

Source: Statistics Canada, Labour Force Survey Estimates.

programs and withdrawn from labour organizations in order to focus simply on collective bargaining issues. As a result, the number of employees granted union representation has declined significantly, from an average of 8,762 per year in the period 1994 to 2000 to an average of 4,000 per year in the period 2002 to 2009. Backing away from more forward-looking and aggressive organizing strategies, unions saw the number of new certifications granted to individual workplaces decline from an annual average of 353 in the period 1993 to 2001 to 112 in the period 2002 to 2009. During the latter period, the number was less than 100 in every year except 2005 and 2007.

In addition, the certification success rate went from an average of above 65 percent in the period 1993 to 2000 to an average of 50 percent in the period 2002 to 2009 (below 50 percent in five of the eight years). As a consequence, union density in B.C. has declined more dramatically than in the rest of Canada, and now hovers around 30 percent — a long drop from the 40 percent rate in 1991 and lower than the overall Canadian unionization rate for the first time ever. While union density in the B.C. public sector is now about 76 percent, in the private sector it is down to just 18 percent (Table 5.2).

Repeal of the sectoral bargaining provisions of the Code for the construction industry flew in the face of the long recognized and thoroughly researched uniqueness of labour relations in construction. In many provinces, provincial labour laws make special institutional arrangements to facilitate the orderly acquisition, operation and retention of collective bargaining rights for construction workers. This roll-back contributed to a steep decline of unionization in the B.C. construction industry, from 34 percent in 2001 to 20 percent in 2009. Likewise, the repeal of the *Skills Development and Fair Wage Act* in August 2001 — legislation that had required fair wages and occupational training programs on all public construction projects — also undermined employment conditions and labour relations in the construction industry. The elimination of Highway Constructors Limited, a government company that provided centralized hiring of all construction labour on highway projects through a single agency, led to fewer employees receiving adequate health and safety training and less priority given to equity hiring.

AD-HOC LABOUR LEGISLATION

Beyond the rewriting of legislation to shift the balance of power in management's favour, unions were also hurt by ad hoc labour legislation imposed on unionized workers in order to end strikes, impose collective agreements, enforce the arbitration of collective agreements and strip collective agreements of freely negotiated provisions. Between June 2001 and November 2009 no less than fourteen pieces of legislation were enacted to seriously restrict and undermine unions' collective bargaining power.

The most notorious and egregious piece of anti-union legislation was

Bill 29, the *Health and Social Services Delivery Improvement Act*, enacted in January 2002 (Camfield 2006). This unprecedented legislation was passed in the middle of the term of a negotiated three-year provincial agreement for the Hospital Employees Union and other unions who represented health-care, long-term care and community social service workers. The goal of Bill 29 was to lay off thousands of workers, contract out work and terminate the equity wage provisions of the community social services collective agreement, all in order to cut health-care labour costs. The legislation not only gutted hospital and community social service collective agreements, it terminated an earlier government commitment to pay equitable wages to workers in social services. On top of this, under Bill 29, health employers were given the opportunity to hire an entirely new workforce at half the wage rate and with far fewer benefits, i.e., no pension or long term disability plans and very limited vacation, sick and health and welfare benefits (Stinson, Pollak and Cohen 2005: 13). To limit the possibility that their only union representative — the Health Employees Unions (HEU) — would re-organize these mostly immigrant and visible minority women workers, the three multi-national service organizations (Aramark, Sodexho and Compass) took the unprecedented step of approaching a number of other unions to offer them "voluntary recognition agreements," in which the terms and conditions of employment were established by mutual agreement prior to hiring the workforce.

While almost all of the unions refused this offer, one local of the Industrial and Allied Workers of Canada (IWA) agreed to sign six-year voluntary recognition agreements with the three multi-nationals with wages ranging from $10 to $11 an hour. And although the HEU successfully challenged these agreements at the Labour Relations Board and managed to re-organize the vast majority of these new workers, the wages and benefits levels agreed to by the IWA were inherited by HEU. As a result, in less than a year, B.C. went from having the highest paid to the lowest paid health-support workers in the country (Cohen and Cohen 2004: 16).

The health-care unions affected by Bill 29 did appeal this legislation to the supreme courts of B.C. and Canada, and in June 2007 the Supreme Court of Canada issued one of the most important decisions in Canadian labour history by declaring, for the first time, that collective bargaining rights are protected by the Charter of Rights and Freedoms and that the B.C. Liberal government did not have the right to unilaterally strip provisions from the health-care unions' collective agreements (Centre for Constitutional Studies 2007). However, while the court decision was a precedent-setting victory for the entire union movement and provided some monetary compensation for the laid-off workers, it did not reverse the very significant setback experienced by the 8,000 workers who were laid off. Nor did it help the privatized health-support workers, who were not allowed to bargain with other health-care workers and were subject to essential service legislation, which prohibited them from striking. In addition, as a result of the changes set off by Bill 29 and other health-care restructuring, the major public-sector unions have continued to engage in increasingly destructive raiding drives, which have undermined solidarity in the B.C. labour movement and made it more difficult for unions to conduct comprehensive, public advocacy campaigns in the support of public health care and the end to privatization.

Other ad hoc legislative changes have been just as harmful to B.C. workers. For example, B.C. residents injured at work were less likely to qualify for compensation (and would receive less compensation if they did qualify) than they would have in the 1990s. In 2002 the B.C. government and Workers' Compensation Board made major changes in the laws and policies that govern the workers' compensation system. Those changes were enacted after an aggressive lobbying effort by employers claiming that the system had become economically unsustainable. The resulting reforms were based upon no discernable principle other than that of reducing costs for employers. However, these alternations have come at a profound cost to workers and to the treatment and benefits that injured workers receive under the compensation system. A combination of legislative amendments, ongoing policy revision and structural change has resulted in thirteen significant changes to the WCB and to compensation benefits for injured workers. The most significant of those changes are as follows:

- the effective elimination of pensions based on the actual long-term loss of earnings of injured workers;
- the effective elimination of vocational rehabilitation assistance, which helps injured workers return to the workforce;
- appeal processes that have become increasingly technical, difficult to understand and inaccessible to injured workers;
- functional pensions that are now only payable to age sixty-five rather than for life; and
- the reduction of benefit rates by 13 percent — from 75percent of gross income to 90 percent of net income.

Consequently, the number of so-called loss of earnings (LOE) pensions granted has fallen from an annual average of around a thousand before the changes to only sixty-eight during the sixteen-month period from February 2006 to June 2007. During that period, 96 percent of the injured workers who applied for an LOE pension were denied.

THE EXPANSION OF PRECARIOUS EMPLOYMENT

The changes detailed above, along with other legislative and regulatory initiatives, have created a province in which it is shamefully possible to work full-time and still not be able to house and feed yourself adequately. More and more, government has given up on any serious attempts to regulate labour and worker safety. In-work poverty and low-wage work have grown to a rate higher than anywhere else in Canada. More and more, government has facilitated employers bringing in temporary foreign workers by the thousands but has denied them the right to settle and make a life in Canada.

Employers in the private and public sectors alike have sought to take advantage of these reforms. In agriculture, the provincial government entered into an agreement with the federal government in 2004 to permit the employment of temporary agricultural workers by farm operators under the Seasonal Agricultural Workers Program (SAWP). British Columbia growers in the Fraser and Okanagan Valleys took full advantage of the SAWP and within a few short years had some 3,400 temporary foreign workers competing with immigrant farm workers to produce cheap food with highly exploited labour.

Fruit and vegetable farmers trying to compete with industrial growers in the United States either directly employed Mexican farm labour at just above the minimum wage or hired contractors to employ immigrant men to pick fruit at piece rates. In 2005, it was found that 80 percent of these hand harvesters were illegally forced to return some of their wages to contractors. In addition, many were paid less than the minimum piece rate and many who resided at their worksites were only being paid for about eight hours, five days a week, but were working ten hours per day, seven days a week. Workers brought in from Mexico under the SAWP found they were similarly exploited.

Agricultural workers sadly discovered that farm work was often a deadly business. Three men were killed and another two severely disabled working in an enclosed space on a Langley mushroom farm in 2007. Others paid the price of working for negligent and unethical employers by being crowded into unsafe vans for transport between fields. In one tragic case three East Indian women were killed and another thirteen injured when an overloaded and under-equipped van belonging to a farm labour contractor flipped over on a rainy highway outside Chilliwack in 2007. In 2010, workers from several African nations employed by a contractor to do silviculture work for the provincial government were housed in filthy conditions, subjected to death threats, worked fifteen-hour days and paid erratically and at a lower rate than promised.

The construction industry has been an equally negligent employer of cheap — often foreign — labour. In 2006, controversy swirled around a group of European ironworkers brought in to work on the Golden Ears Bridge project (Sandborn 2006a). That same year, thirty-five Central and South American tunnel workers hired on Vancouver's Canada Line rapid transit project joined the Construction and Specialized Workers Local 1611 after telling union organizers they were being paid substandard wages and provided with housing and other benefits inferior to those the company gave their European workmates (Sandborn 2006b).

This dispute, which dragged on through numerous Labour Relations Board hearings, led to an historic B.C. Human Rights Tribunal ruling that held the Latin American workers had experienced wage and benefit discrimination while working on the Vancouver project. The tribunal ordered the employer to pay roughly $50,000 to each of the thirty-five temporary foreign workers involved — the difference between what they had been paid and what other workers performing the same work had been paid. The employer has appealed the tribunal decision, and as of this writing the case has not been heard.

In the B.C. construction industry, union density declined from 34.1 percent in 2001 to 20.3 percent in 2009. In the infrastructure construction lead-up to the Winter Olympics and the housing construction boom years of 2006 to 2008, the number of non-union construction workers increased from 45,600 in 2001 to 85,900 in 2006, to 96,200 in 2007 and to 115,500 in 2008.

At the end of 2009 there were 69,038 temporary foreign workers in B.C., the second largest number in any province behind Ontario, with 94,762, and the B.C. number represented 24.5 percent of all temporary foreign workers in Canada. From the end of 2001 to the end of 2009 the number of temporary foreign workers in B.C. increased by a huge 317 percent. As in the rest of Canada, this dramatic growth in the employment of temporary foreign workers is concentrated in employment requiring low-level skills and education, paying very low wages and having no systematic inspection or enforcement of legislated minimum standards or employment contracts.

Women have been particularly impacted by the shift to low-wage, temporary and part-time employment. Statscan research from May 2009 showed that in the past thirty years, 45 percent of "core age" women (fifteen to twenty-four years old) worked part-time versus just over 20 percent of men the same age. In 2009, B.C. unemployment rates went up to 8.7 percent for men and 6.8 percent for women. In July 2009, 31.3 percent percent of employed women in B.C. held part-time jobs versus 13 percent for men. Women are working more of the casual and non-standard jobs that are increasingly the norm (B.C. Stats 2010).

The results of this growth in precarious employment — more people in low-wage "mcjobs" — are not surprising. Statistics Canada reports that

346,100 B.C. workers earned less than $12 an hour in 2008: almost one in five of all employed workers. Of this total, 182,400 earned less than $10 an hour. The $12 figure is significant partly because it's a very conservative estimate of what the Organisation for Economic Co-operation and Development defines as a low-wage job. According to the OECD, a low-wage job pays less than two thirds of the median wage, or the wage at the exact midpoint of the wage scale.

When low-wages are examined on an annual basis, the figures are even more disturbing. According to social policy analyst and former director of the National Council of Welfare Steve Kerstetter, some one million British Columbians earned less than the annual median wage of $25, 722 (Sandborn 2010a). People who worked part-time the entire year wound up with earnings 47 percent below median earnings. The age group twenty to twenty-four had median earnings of only $12,970. Statistics for August 2005 showed that only 34 percent of the age group with employment income were full-time students. That percentage dropped slightly during the school year, and the students who worked then normally worked part-time. Women too worked more low-wage and part-time jobs. These trends all appear to be getting worse.

The prevalence and persistence of low wages in B.C. over the first decade of the Liberal government is further demonstrated by the high provincial rates of poverty. From 2001 to 2008, according to the National Council of Welfare, B.C. had the highest provincial poverty rate, reaching a peak in 2002 and 2003, when the provincial rates were 38 percent and 33 percent respectively above the national rate. The B.C. poverty rate declined slowly from 2004 to 2008, but remained 21 percent above the national rate in 2008. High overall poverty rates have meant that child poverty rates in B.C. have also been the highest in the country in recent years (B.C. Campaign 2000 2010). Throughout B.C, there are thousands of people working two, three, sometimes more jobs in order to make ends meet, somehow piling those exhausting duties on top of caring for children and relatives while striving to gain the education needed to escape the low-wage treadmill.

THE FALTERING UNION RESPONSE

Confronted by such political and economic trends, B.C. unions have sought to establish new and effective means of bargaining and to build wider provincial strategies that will allow them to pressure employers and governments. Over the past ten or so years, many have tried out new organizing strategies; others have initiated lawsuits hoping these would force the government to back down. However, the results have often been much less than expected, and unions are finding themselves with their backs against a wall with few places to turn.

Several public-sector unions, backed by the Canadian Labour Congress, successfully filed complaints against the Liberal government with the International Labour Office (ILO) of the United Nations. In August 2001, on an appeal of the B.C. Teachers' Federation, the ILO ruled that parts of Bill 18 — the *Skills Development and Labour Statutes Amendment Act* — that made education an essential service under the *Labour Relations Code*, were in violation of international labour conventions.

In November 2001, unions representing teachers, school support workers, health-care workers and nurses filed a formal complaint with the ILO that Bills 15 and 18 were contrary to Canada's obligations under international labour standards. These complaints were later joined by complaints from the Canadian Labour Congress (CLC) and several provincial and national unions that the B.C. government's Bills 2, 15, 18, 27, 28 and 29 violated ILO conventions and freedom of association principles regarding free collective bargaining and the right to strike. In March 2003 the ILO ruled that the six pieces of labour legislation imposed by the Liberal government violated international agreements, but the provincial government took no action on the ILO's urging that it repeal or re-write the offending laws.

Overall, few unions have instituted more militant strategies or sought out allies to pressure firms and governments to protect jobs and implement more ecologically responsible business practices. Nor have unions yet developed better bargaining, advocacy or political strategies to provide strong counter measures or alternatives. The most notable labour victory (mentioned above) was that of the Hospital Employees Union in court against Bill 29 (Camfield 2006). The legal challenge brought by HEU and the B.C. Government and Service Employees Union and other health-care union groups led to the Supreme Court of Canada striking down sections of the legislation because they deny the freedom of association guarantee of the Charter's section 2(d) (Centre for Constitutional Studies 2007). The court ruled that these sections violated citizens' rights "either by disregarding past processes of collective bargaining, by pre-emptively undermining future processes of collective bargaining, or both."

But, despite the victory, as mentioned previously, many of the health workers in private care companies ended up with very little bargaining power. Indeed, some workers in long-term care were no longer considered to be in health care, but rather were simply "service employees," and therefore could not bargain with other health-care workers. In addition, these marginalized workers in private health care are effectively unable to go on strike, as a Labour Relations Board decision has designated the essential service levels in long-term care (i.e., staffing levels during a strike) at 100 percent.

Likewise, the response of organized labour in B.C. to temporary foreign worker issues has been one-step-forward and two-steps back. Remarkably free of the racism that has blemished union responses to offshore workers in times past, B.C.'s labour movement has organized new workers into existing unions, set up storefront service centres to meet their needs and called on the government to allow guest workers a pathway to citizenship. These efforts are led by the United Food and Commercial Workers through their Agricultural Workers Alliance, which operates ten storefront organizing centres across the country, including three in B.C.: in Surrey and Abbotsford in the Fraser Valley and in Kelowna in the Okanagan Valley, where several successful organizing drives have been conducted in recent years (Sandborn 2008). For the first time in B.C. history, foreign workers imported to pick crops were allowed to join a union. Migrant workers at Greenway Farms in Surrey voted to join the United Food and Commercial Workers (UFCW) of Canada. The historic certification was granted with the support of more than 75 percent of the roughly forty affected workers and came on the heels of a seasonal workers contract in Manitoba, the result of renewed UFCW efforts to organize farm labourers across Canada.

However, across the agricultural sector in B.C., hundreds of thousands of workers remain non-unionized. Even though the provincial government in 2002 effectively reduced the minimum piece rates payable to farm workers by approximately 4 percent, by deeming piece rates to include statutory holiday and annual vacation pay under the *Employment Standards Act*, many farm workers are not even paid the piece rates they have contracted for. And even if they are paid the statutory minimum piece rates, their hourly pay often comes to less than the minimum wage.

Predominantly immigrant farm workers employed by farm labour contractors often do not receive pay for the two hours or more of daily travel time while being transported from Vancouver to worksites as far afield as the ginseng farms in the Upper Fraser Valley. Others are compelled to return part of their wages to the labour contractors in return for falsified records of employment. Still others are not paid for several weeks at a time or until the end of harvesting contracts. In addition, harvesters are frequently not permitted to have lunch breaks.

Because of the many setbacks and defeats over the last few years, organized labour has fallen further and further behind. Unions have launched a number of significant strikes, but the results have often been meagre if not disastrous. In the province-wide strikes of the nurses and health science professionals, the CAW Metro Vancouver transit workers in 2001, the ferry workers and coastal forest industry workers in 2003, the Hospital Employees Union in 2004, teachers province-wide in 2005 and CUPE ambulance paramedics in 2009, defiant workers had significant public support. But in each case, the unions were forced into very consequential capitulations. Union members were left with the bleak reality of real-dollar wage and benefit losses, or found that at the end of the strike, their jobs had been downsized or contracted out.

CONCLUSION

Traditional explanations of union decline often highlight how unions and the labour market more generally have been hurt by the major changes in B.C.'s and Canada's economy. The decline in key resource and manufacturing industries — forestry, pulp and wood mills, capital-intensive mining, machinery and equipment parts, and fishing — cost hundreds of thousands of union jobs. The slump in the American housing market led to significant further layoffs in resource industries. The growth of construction, transportation and service industries also allowed for the vast expansion of a non-union workforce. Private-sector facilities are now predominately non-union, and throughout the province, new factories and workplaces have remained resolutely anti-union and managers have defeated — time and again — efforts by unions like the CAW and HEU to organize new workers.

However, such explanations miss much of the truly epochal transformations of the past decade or more and how the Liberal government turned its back on workers and much of the middle class. Regulatory changes and aggressive ad hoc legislation ended strikes, reshaped contracts and imposed wage cuts and job losses. The rules governing union representation campaigns have given employers a major advantage in resisting efforts to organize. The law dealing with secondary boycott and organizational picketing makes union activity especially subject to prosecution. At the same time, new employment standards legislation has given employers — both large and small — ample opportunity to hire workers at ever declining rates of pay. As a result, many employers have begun to see the collective bargaining process as an opportunity to rid themselves of unions. When agreements are about to expire, employers demand major concessions that unions are unable to accept. Forced to strike, unions are left at a major disadvantage when employers threaten to leave or downsize their operations. For non-unionized workers, the situation is equally problematic. With limited protection, more workers than ever are employed in part-time and temporary jobs, and more workers are taking on extra jobs in the attempt to make ends meet.

Why have many citizens failed to respond and the wealthy been so successful in setting the agenda? Certainly the fact that few citizens pay attention to politics has played to the advantage of the well-to-do. Because of media concentration in newspapers and television stations in B.C. and across Canada, citizens lack important resources to form grounded views and informed votes. In particular, citizens lack knowledge and information about what governments do or don't do to address problems. But so too has the clout of ordinary voters fallen — especially those who have been on the losing end of the "boom" economy. In the 2007 provincial election, voter turnout was 48 percent, with the wealthy twice as likely as middle-income voters to vote. Today, B.C. Liberal party positions and opinions are those of their highest income constituents. For constituents in the bottom third of the labour market, there is no congruence between their opinions and those of their representatives.

Unions were not only hurt by the Campbell government pushing them under a fast-moving train of economic changes. They were hurt politically as well. In an era when an organized voice was needed more than ever, the steady decline and fragmentation of unions means there is no longer an effective counterweight to the rising influence of those at the top. Added to this, many leaders of organized labour have lost sight of the need to organize and to maintain the spirit of the movement, and union's political power has dwindled to miniscule proportions in comparison to the economic power that corporations, developers and banks now wield.

To counter these trends, unions have to rediscover what it means to be a "worker's movement" — something more than a scattering of organizations concerned with money, member numbers and economic power, significant though all these factors are. Rather, unions need to find new ways of ac-tivating and using the energies of workers. This means fostering solidarity across unions and occupations, and it requires leaders who are willing to trust one another and who are committed to sharing power with the union's rank and file.

Over the past decade and longer, organized labour has spoken a great deal about approaching this goal, but it has, in practice, just as regularly retreated from it. To amend the laws that have done so much damage to workers across the province, unions again have to take up the challenge of organizing and create a movement that gives it a far more powerful voice. Resisting the "greatest roll-back in worker rights" will require nothing less.

6. WHITHER THE QUEBEC MODEL?

Boom, Bust and Quebec Labour

Peter Graefe

When we speak of boom and bust, we think of wild swings in economic fortunes, of the roaring twenties and the dirty thirties, or of a town like Murdochville, Quebec, which boomed when copper was found and then shuttered its doors when the ore ran out. It is tempting to think of the past fifteen years of Canadian economic development in this same frame: a long expansion followed by the shock of the 2008–09 global downturn. And when we consider Quebec, we can certainly observe the pendulum swing of boom and bust, and the deep social transformations that accompanied it: the consolidation of a neoliberal political economy in Quebec, the transformation of people's expectations about what was normal in terms of work and income, and the reduction of policy alternatives. In this picture, Quebec does not stand out as a distinct society offering possible alternative paths to other provinces, but rather is just one example among others of the neoliberal transformation of provincial economies.

Even with a relatively high rate of union density and with a more developed set of stakeholder institutions where unions sit with business and government, the general direction of labour through the boom and bust has been in line with the rest of the country, with workers and unions experiencing worsening wages and many more working in low-wage employment. However, if Quebec stands apart from other provinces at this conjuncture in any way, it has less to do with greater union power than the success of maintaining and expanding public policies that provide some real (if slight) material compensations for those exposed to neoliberal labour markets. Yet even these policies appear to be a rapidly disappearing, and the Quebec Model — which seeks to maintain economic competitiveness in order to foster social inclusion and cooperation among all segments of Quebec's society — looks to be in jeopardy.

The analysis in this chapter falls into four parts. The first looks at economic growth and the manner in which Quebec capital restructured itself over the boom years. The second considers the boom and bust cycle and its effects on labour markets, particularly their remarkable stability through the boom years. The third part looks at the state of Quebec's unions. It argues that even though unions have been successful in maintaining their size and coverage of the workforce, there are a number of worrying signs that they are only protecting a core labour force while leaving the vast majority to low-wage and insecure employment. Finally, I look at the limited capacity of the labour movement to influence public policy and the labour market, and I consider what the future may hold.

THE BOOM YEARS: GROWTH AND RESTRUCTURING

As with the Canadian economy as a whole, Quebec enjoyed a decade and a half of solid growth from the mid-1990s to the financial crisis of 2008–09. While not matching the explosive growth of the 1960s, these were nevertheless boom times of the sort not seen through the preceding fifteen years. The steady growth in real GDP from 1985 to 1989 (at 2.9 percent annually) was bracketed by the dismal periods of the early 1980s (0.8 percent average annual GDP growth, 1981–84) and early 1990s (1 percent, 1990–94). Growth in the 1980s spawned an exuberant surge in commercial construction in Montreal, leading to gross overcapacity into the early 2000s. By contrast, while the robust growth of the late 1990s (3.4 percent for 1995–99) cooled in the early 2000s (1.9 percent, 2000–04), this continued growth was enough to soak up significant unemployment, by 1999 bringing the unemployment rate below the 1989 trough and briefly dropping the rate below 7 percent in 2008, just prior to the economic crisis. Not only were unemployment numbers down in the early 2000s, but the relatively buoyant labour market shortened the average duration of unemployment from 37.5 weeks in 1997 to 15.2 weeks in July 2008.

In overall terms, the picture was fairly rosy. Nominal GDP rose continuously throughout the 1990s and 2000s, and by 2008, led by finance, real estate and construction, GDP in Quebec topped $300 billion (Figure 6.1). The reality was more mixed. Over the long term, Quebec's average annual GDP growth of 2.1 percent over the 1981–2007 period compares unfavourably to the OECD average (also the Canadian average) of 2.8 percent and to the Ontario and United States rates of 3 percent. However, on a per capita basis, growth in Quebec over that period (45.7 percent) was the same as in Ontario (46.8 percent), although well behind Canada (53 percent) and especially the OECD and the United States (66 percent). This reflects both the narrowing of the productivity gap with Ontario and the rest of Canada, and a widening of the gap in productivity growth rates with the OECD and the United States (Joanis and Godbout 2009).

But beneath this story of growth rates was the continued reinvention of Quebec capital. In the 1960s, the Quebec government created a series of public institutions and crown corporations in order to regroup small francophone businesses into larger concerns that might compete as "national champions" (Graefe 2000, 2003). While some analysts in the 1970s could see this "state capital" as a lever to strengthen a francophone Quebec capitalist class around a more autonomous and social democratic development strategy, at no point in the subsequent quarter century has there been any evidence of such nationalist aspirations.

Indeed, if anything, Quebec and Canadian capital rallied to American models of neoliberal restructuring. The Montreal Board of Trade merged with the Montreal Chamber of Commerce, bringing together the major representatives of English Canadian and francophone Quebec capital. Boards of major corporations integrated American and Canadian enterprises. Also merged were francophone business leaders into the networks of English Canadian capital. As William Carroll's (2004) study of the Canadian corporate elite suggests, the percentage of corporate directors of leading Quebec firms with French Canadian surnames jumped from 12 to 31 percent

Figure 6.1 Nominal GDP for Quebec, Selected Sectors (Millions of Current Dollars)

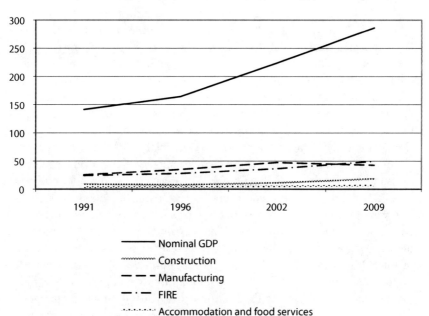

Source: Institut de la statistique du Québec.
Note: FIRE refers to finance, insurance, real estate

from 1976 to 1996. Similarly, firms like Videotron, Quebecor, Metro and Bombardier emerged as players tied into the Canadian corporate network.

And beginning in the 1980s and continuing over the past few decades, the globalization of Quebec government and economy has continued apace. Since the early 1980s, businesses — Quebec, Canadian and international alike — have been unanimous in their belief that successful development requires significant state spending and tax cuts, deregulation and privatization. The business community has also been strongly in favour of trade liberalization. Quebec's unique array of state financial institutions, particularly the Caisse de depot and the Société général de financement, have aggressively pursued "maximum financial returns" rather than strengthen aspects of the province's industrial "structure." Consequently, the Caisse has focused on short-term returns, and indeed only about 9 percent of its total investments are in the Quebec private sector (Tremblay 2009). The focus on returns resulted in the Caisse having an historic investment loss, of $39.8B (25 percent), in the financial crisis of 2008, as it held a large share of toxic "non-bank-sponsored asset-backed commercial paper."

In addition, over the past decade or so, Quebec capital has been further transformed. "Financialization" and the increasing importance of financial capital compared to non-financial capital in determining the rhythm and expected return on investment have come to mark Quebec's economy. From 2000 to 2007, financial products, activities and industries grew rapidly, to 17 percent of provincial GDP, versus 17.6 percent for manufacturing, with the increase in GDP of $12.1 billion over the 2001–07 period, mirroring the decline in manufacturing of $15 billion (Figure 7.1). As with the the Caisse, the new emphasis by large provincially based firms on maximizing returns in global financial markets over and above domestic economic development likely smoothed over some of the earlier divisions between Quebec and non-Quebec capital and led to a relatively peaceful subordination of Quebec capital under the wing of Toronto-based financial concerns (Beaulne 2009).

Financialization also reflected a change in perspective concerning foreign investment and control. While Quebec has always been "open for business" in terms of foreign investment, from the 1960s into the 1980s the state did intervene through various instruments to protect strategic firms and sectors. By the late 1990s, this protective reflex was much weakened. The purchase of grocery giant Provigo by Ontario-based Loblaws was the clearest signal of this. Other examples include Rio Tinto's purchase of Alcan, even if this implied the shuttering of the Bécancour aluminium complex, and the blessing given to the merging of the Montreal and Toronto Stock Exchanges.

The growth of finance and change in corporate operations was likewise responsible for greater labour market polarization and "dualization" between those workers with good jobs and those in precarious employment (Emmenger et al. 2011; Palier and Thelen 2008). As elsewhere, private service-sector job growth took a "good jobs/bad jobs" track. Certainly, young professionals did well by strong job growth in finance, insurance, real estate and professional services. But this was matched by growth in low-wage service-sector employment in restaurants, accommodations, cleaning and tourism. This dualization can be seen most clearly when we turn to labour market developments.

LABOUR MARKETS

Jobs and Job Quality

Despite the economic boom and Quebec's commitment to a more "inclusive" society, it is remarkable how many jobs have remained low-wage, part-time and precarious throughout Quebec. From the 1970s through to the mid-1990s, the churning of the labour market greatly increased part-time and other atypical work as well as self-employment. Of the 670,000 jobs added in that period, fully a third were in self-employment, nearly two-fifths were part-time, and only a quarter full-time (Table 7.1). Over the most recent boom years, this distribution of one-third atypical jobs has remained unchanged. From 1996 to 2009, part-time work increased slightly faster than full-time work (26 versus 18 percent). Similarly, atypical work (which includes temporary, part-year and self-employment as well as part-time) remained at 37.2 percent during this time. In other words, the rate of part-time and atypical work, which had been increasing rapidly over the previous two decades, stabilized during the boom. "Good times" meant that roughly two-thirds of new jobs were in standard employment.

The situation looks a bit rosier in terms of job quality, with the share of jobs classified as low-quality declining from 26 to 20 percent between 1997 and 2009, and that shortfall was recuperated almost entirely by high-quality jobs, which rose from 26 to 32 percent. However, this indicator is a bit of an overstatement, bringing together measures of wages, qualifications and hours of work into a very simplified three-category breakdown, while excluding the category of the self-employed. Note also that someone working thirty to forty hours a week for $15 an hour (in 2002 dollars) in a job with high qualifications would be considered to have high-quality work, even though that would provide an annual salary of $30,000 or less (Institut de la statistique du Québec 2010b).

Overall, it is hard to foresee much improvement in job quality, particularly given the polarization of service-sector employment and the decline in manufacturing. With the bust starting in 2008, the goods-producing sector was hard hit, losing 32,500 jobs in 2009. This sector was already bleeding jobs through the middle years of the decade, in part from the rising dollar and from mounting trade barriers to the export of wood products, which wiped out 58,000 jobs between 2004 and 2008 (essentially more than cancelling out the 50,000 jobs created in this sector since the 1991 recession). A study of cases where there were more than ten manufacturing layoffs in the 2003–08 period demonstrated that fully a third of the cases involved the definitive closure of the operations. Just under three-quarters of these closings were in the low technology manufacturing sectors of textiles, clothing, wood and paper (Jalette and Prudent 2010).

Table 6.1 Employment by Status and by Sector in Quebec

	2001	2009	% change
Total employment	3 402 800	3 844 200	13%
Full-time permanent	2 164 900	2 414 500	12%
Permanent part-time	334 200	442 300	32%
Temporary part-time	153 700	155 200	1%
Temporary full-time	251 900	267 600	6%
Self Employed	498 000	564 600	13%
Manufacturing	628 000	532 200	-15%
Construction	137 600	210 500	53%
Primary	93 100	87 400	-6%
Accommodation and food service	203 300	231 100	14%
Retail	542 400	626 300	15%
Finance, insurance, real estate	183 700	224 100	22%
Public and private services	2 552 100	2 979 600	17%

Source: Institut de la statistique du Québec 2010a.

This situation of declining employment in manufacturing in the 2000s provided a mirror image of the 1990s: while manufacturing bounced back after the 1991 recession and financial services struggled, the 20 percent drop-off in manufacturing employment since 2004 has been compensated by strong growth in finance (16 percent), insurance and real estate (30 percent) and professional services (28 percent) over the same period (Table 6.1; Koustas 2010). As such, the post-2008 slowdown only lowered Quebec's GDP by 0.3 percent in 2009 and pushed unemployment up to 8.5 percent, which is considerably below the rates of the recessions of the early 1980s and early 1990s. But the small size of the aggregate impact should not hide the differential impact on manufacturing workers nor the regional impacts of the decline in forestry.

Earnings

In terms of earnings the story of the boom is one of relative stagnation for the bottom half of income earners and a concentration of gains in the top earners, leading to increased income inequality. Incomes for families in the bottom half did rise a little through the boom years but not enough to recover from the drop in the early 1990s recession. The median incomes for each of the bottom deciles remained lower in 2003–06 than in 1976–79, having fallen from $53,900 in 1976 to $51,900 in 2007 (Couturier and Schepper 2010). So while per capita wealth grew by about half over this period, the bottom half of the income distribution did not shared in this increase. Indeed, in terms of their share of total before-tax income, the bottom seven deciles registered a 6 percent loss from 1976–79 to 2003–06, while the top decile increased its share by 5 percent. In terms of after-tax income, it is only the top decile that increased its income share — by at least 1 percent.

This result is particularly surprising given that women's labour force participation increased from 41 to 61 percent over this period, suggesting that the hours of paid work performed in these families increased substantially. The average family with children provided 14.2 more weeks of paid work in 2006 than in 1976. The poorest 30 percent of families increased their hours of work by 11 percent, and middle-income earners by 16.5 percent. Hours-of-work data for the 1997 to 2006 period, where incomes did tick up slightly, tell a similar story of greater work effort for thin returns. For instance, families with children in the second lowest decile worked on average eighty-six more hours per month in 2006 than in 1997, for a meagre increase in monthly income of $781.

Meanwhile, families in the top decile worked nineteen more hours a month, but pulled in an extra $4,043 for that effort. Similarly, families and income earners in the second highest decile increased their work hours and increased their monthly incomes by $1,277 over the same period. This pattern of earnings gains being concentrated among upper income earners was common in other provinces as well. Earnings inequality in Quebec, as measured by the Gini coefficient, was below the Canadian average after the 1980s recession, but has moved in lockstep with the Canadian trend, edging up from .33 in 1992 to .36 in the early 1990 and to just under .35 in 2006. Consequently, the boom years enabled the bottom half to make up most of the losses from the early 1990s recession but not to break the pattern of forty years of stagnant incomes. In contrast the top income earners and wealthiest — whose incomes did not move much from the 1970s to the early 1990s — have seen their incomes rise significantly and continuously since then (Couturier and Schepper 2010; Joanis and Godbout 2009).

Inequality and the Social Wage

These stories of increased work effort for diminishing returns and of growing inequality in labour market outcomes fits very well in the Canadian picture, although Quebec actually comes off better; there is less inequality and poverty in Quebec than in other provinces after the tax and transfer system has done its work.

Relative poverty in Quebec has been below the Canadian average for at least two decades, and between 1996 and 2006 poverty rates in Quebec continued to fall. The poor in Quebec were also on average closer to the poverty line and less poor than those elsewhere in Canada. In addition, while inequality has slowly increased in Quebec, for instance with the post-tax and transfer Gini coefficient for economic families creeping from about .28 in the boom years of the late 1980s to just over .30 through the 2000s, this increase is well below the Canadian trend line. Indeed, while Quebec's Gini was close to the Canadian and Ontario averages in the 1970s and 1980s, it came uncoupled during the 1990s recession and is now .02 to .03 below those elsewhere in Canada.

Lower inequality in Quebec appears to be based on three factors, two of them related to public policy choices. The first factor is that salaries among the top francophone earners did not rise as rapidly as elsewhere in Canada and North America. Thus, while the top 1 percent of wage earners grabbed 11.2 percent of all wage income in Canada and 18 percent in the United States, in francophone Quebec, they only took 6.5 percent (and 14 percent in anglophone Quebec). While an analysis for this outcome has yet to be produced, a plausible explanation is that francophone corporate leaders have a tougher time casting themselves as mobile within a continental labour market. As such, they are less able to assume the role of indispensable pharaohs deserving of jewel-encrusted salaries.

The two public policy factors that account for comparatively lower levels of poverty are that the Quebec tax system's top tax bracket is set at a slightly higher rate than in neighbouring jurisdictions (26 percent in Quebec versus 22–24 percent elsewhere) and that Quebec has done a great deal by way of pushing income into the lower deciles through "family friendly" policies, child benefits and tax credits to parents in low-wage work. For example, depending on family configuration and level of earned income, Quebec child policies provide income supplementation at two to three times the level of the Ontario Child Benefit. And the relative strength of these measures can be seen in the fact that the tax and transfer system reduces the Gini coefficient by 0.143 in Quebec versus 0.109 in Ontario, or in other words by roughly a third (Joanis and Godbout 2009).

Some of the negative impacts of wage stagnation and greater income inequality were cushioned by family and child-care programs in Quebec.

Here again the province has stood out from the rest of the country in crafting policies reflecting the reality of an "everybody works" labour market. The flagship initiatives are the universal low-cost early childhood education system and a parental leave insurance outside of the Employment Insurance system.

Quebec's "$7/day daycare" program dramatically increased the number of licensed spaces available in the province at the beginning of the 2000s, as well as made initial strides in increasing the quality of care and the wages of child-care providers (Jenson 2010). While, some of the more progressive potentials in this system (community control, non-profit structure and upward pressure on working conditions) were stalled or reversed under the post-2003 Liberal government, the policy continues to provide working parents with a very different set of financial and accessibility constraints around child care than found elsewhere in Canada. The parental leave plan likewise provides the possibility of wage replacement during a maternal or paternal leave to a much broader range of workers than in the rest of the country, as it is based on a relatively low threshold of earned income rather than the much more stringent Employment Insurance conditions, which disqualify many workers in other provinces.

THE STATE OF ORGANIZED LABOUR IN QUEBEC

When boom times bring little improvement in job quality and more inequality, is that a sign that the labour movement is missing in action? Into the 1990s, the Quebec labour movement presented a proud profile in Canadian labour circles. They could point to tangible gains: maintaining high rates of union density, ongoing participation in policy-making through representation in economic and social development boards and commissions, leadership in improving industrial relations legislation (e.g., an anti-scab law) and the social wage (e.g., child care, social housing, family benefits). This set of achievements has sometimes been packaged as part of the "Quebec Model," showcasing Quebec as an exemplar of a more egalitarian development path precisely because of the effectiveness of unions at the bargaining table and in politics. But the survival of this model for labour and for labour input into policy now hangs in the balance, dependent on how successfully organized labour rides out the boom and bust cycles in the global and national markets.

Representation
The recent boom and bust were not the best of times for organized labour in Quebec, but the swings in the economy had a relatively muted impact on the ability of the major union federations to reproduce themselves as organizations. From 1997 to 2009, the number of employees with union coverage increased from 1.1 million to 1.3 million. This increase in numbers was largely proportionate to the growth of the labour force, such that union

density hovered in the range of 39–41 percent over the period, starting at 41.5 percent in 1997 and ending at 39.8 percent in 2009. The decline was felt most in the private sector, where coverage fell from 28 to 26 percent.

This overall density thus remains roughly 8 percentage points higher than the Canadian average and 10–12 percentage points above the average for Ontario. Nearly half the gap with Ontario can be explained by much higher union densities in health and social assistance in Quebec (3.4 points of the overall 11.6 point gap between provinces in 2005) and manufacturing (2.2 points of the 11.6 gap) (Labrosse 2006). In the big picture, Quebec unions have been treading water for a decade, maybe sinking a centimetre deeper under the surface but not at a rate that would create enough of a sense of urgency to radically alter their tactics and strategies.

Table 6.2 Union Membership and Union Coverage in Selected Sectors, Quebec

	1997 Membership	1997 Coverage	2009 Membership	2009 Coverage
Primary	14 600	26.30%	10 800	21.40%
Construction	42 600	48.40%	88 600	57.90%
Manufacturing	225 400	41.20%	187 000	37.10%
Retail	80 600	19.60%	109 000	19.60%
Accommodation & food services	23 800	14.10%	24 100	11.60%
Health Care & social services	187 800	67.20%	268 900	64.40%
Finance, insurance, real estate	31 500	19.30%	37 800	20.30%

Source: Institut de la statistique du Québec.

This does provide a portrait of stability, but a breakdown of the areas of gains and losses reveals a more problematic picture (Table 6.2). On an industrial basis, we notice the loss of 38,000 unionized jobs in manufacturing and a decline in density from 41 to 37 percent between 1997 and 2009. The only sectors that experienced a comparable drop were primary industries (26 to 21 percent of the unionized workforce), information culture and leisure (0 to 31 percent unionization rate — based mostly on the sector growing by 25 percent while union numbers remained constant), restaurant and hospitality (14 to 12 percent, representing anaemic membership growth in an expanding sector) and health and social services (67 to 64 percent, an additional 80,000 new members not being enough to keep up with job growth in the sector).

One should not read too much into such broad categories and aggregate numbers, but they do indicate a weakening of bargaining strength as the manufacturing and primary sectors shrink and restructure their previously well-paid workforces, a loss of strength in the expanding consumer service sector and the difficulty of keeping up in organizing health and social service jobs, perhaps as these are increasingly located in smaller organizations outside the public service.

The unions did make gains elsewhere, particularly in construction, a booming sector where density increased from 48 to 58 percent between 1997 and 2009, more than doubling the number of members, from 42,600 to 88,600. There were also density gains in transportation and warehousing (48 to 51 percent), finance, insurance and real estate (19 to 20 percent) and "other services" (15 to 16 percent). In sum, at least at the level of organizing workers at a rate to maintain stable density, the story of the boom was of gains in construction masking losses elsewhere.

The boom in construction has itself turned out to be a bit of a poisoned chalice, as the close relations between high-ranking union leaders and "controversial personalities" (a journalistic euphemism for people with suspected linkages to organized crime) has caused the labour movement, especially the Fédération des travailleurs et travailleuses du Québec (FTQ), to have a serious image problem. The ex-director general of FTQ construction, Jocelyn Dupuis, had to resign in early 2010 after revelations of defrauding the union with restaurant receipts, and it was later revealed that the lawyer investigating the fraud for the union had had several sumptuous meals with Mr. Dupuis at the union's expense. While the $200 tip for their waiter might evince a touching solidarity with service workers, charging $1026.80 to the union for a dinner for two did little to generate public support for unions as vectors of positive social change (Lévesque 2010).

A couple of bright spots in the comparison of 1997 and 2009 would be the increased density in establishments of under twenty employees (16 to 19 percent), among temporary workers (34 to 40 percent) and among employees who had been in their job for less than a year (21 to 25 percent) or for between one and three years (26 to 32 percent). At such an aggregate level, it is hard to tell whether the growth in construction is bleeding into these categories to improve the results, but the optimistic interpretation would be that the unions have had minor success in organizing some of the more insecure sectors of the labour market.

Of course, unions are not fan clubs, so beyond the simple question of maintaining membership is one of how well unions have performed in collective representation. Perhaps the most visible transformation of the Quebec labour movement is the change in militancy, at least as measured in a willingness to strike. In the 1976–80 period, strike activity in Quebec peaked, with an average of 343 work stoppages a year and over 3.5 million days lost. Through the 1980s, these rates dropped, with about a hundred fewer work stoppages a year in the 1986–90 period and 1.6 million days lost.

Employers' associations praised the newfound maturity and responsibility of unions in the 1990s, as rates dropped further to an average of 122 strikes per year in the 1996–2000 rebound and just under 500,000 days lost. This is one-seventh of the peak in absolute numbers but an even smaller fraction when the fact that total employment increased by over 50 percent in this period is taken into account. The use of legislation to impose collective agreements on provincial public-sector employees over most of the past quarter century explains some of the drop-off, but the drop is also significant in the private sector. The number of strikes remained stable through the first half of the 2000s, but because of an increase in the length of labour conflicts, the number of days lost rose to 909,672. This reflected a change in the causes of work stoppages. Wage disputes, while still constituting the cause in 45 percent of strikes, fell by a quarter, while disputes tied to subcontracting tripled in the 1997–2006 period. Not surprisingly, when conflict pits workers looking to keep their jobs against employers seeking a free hand to subcontract as they see fit, the result can be long, bitter strikes. Conflicts over pensions and benefits also increased significantly in this period, with a similar tendency of increased willingness of workers to stay on strike.

Collective Bargaining

In terms of collective bargaining outcomes, the boom of the late 1990s and 2000s permitted private-sector employees to increase their real incomes by about 3 percent from the trough of the early 1990s bust, although the policy of continued public-sector austerity in order to fund tax cuts meant that the real incomes of public employees declined by 1 percent through to 2006, and by a further 4 percent following the five-year contract imposed by the province in 2005. These losses in the public sector reflected not only the aggressive strategies of government negotiators to contain labour costs but also union organizational difficulties. Union bargaining power has been hamstrung by the resource intensity of bargaining across such a diverse sector, particularly where all the major union federations are present and involved in raiding each other in the open period before negotiations. Unions have a history cooperation but they also compete, especially when engaged in collective bargaining with the province during periods of cutbacks and government austerity measures, which has further hampered a unified and coordinated response. So even the most recent public-sector agreement, signed in June 2010, failed to make up the ground lost in past agreements, despite the unions abstaining from raiding each other.

The portrayal of recent concessionary contracts as "victories" has raised questions about the strategic capacity of the Quebec union movement to represent public-service workers, since it did not seem to take the obvious steps of mobilizing its membership and developing public recognition about the importance of public services in order to improve its bargaining position. Similar criticisms were made in 2005 about the weakness of the labour movement's response to the draconian imposition of a public-sector contract by a government that was at its nadir of popular support (Mandel 2010; Charest 2009).

One significant loss over this period was the end of the collective bargaining decree system in a number of sectors. The decree system, which was unique to Quebec in North America, allowed for the extension of a collective agreement to an entire sector (such as women's garments or corrugated board and cardboard box). It provided a form of protection that stood somewhere between minimum wage laws and real collective bargaining rights. Through the late 1990s and early 2000s, about a third of these decrees were abolished, leaving about 50,000 employees without their previous protection. The union failure here was not in collective bargaining *per se*, since it was the government that abolished the decrees in response to employers arguing that the decrees made firms uncompetitive in international markets. But the fact that the unions were unable to mount a challenge in defence of the lowest-paid parts of the manufacturing workforce did have the effect of further moving wage setting in this sector away from union influence.

So too the introduction in collective agreements of more managerial flexibility to weaken seniority rights and of contracting-out clauses also suggests a weakening of union power. These concessions to managerial rights were partially compensated by an increasing share of collective agreements that provide the benefits of the core workforce to more atypical employees. But most agreements still allow management to employ a reserve of less well-paid and less protected employees to deal with seasonal or unforeseen surges in production (Jalette, Bourque and Laroche 2008).

It is risky to draw conclusions from specific cases, but these developments strongly suggest a situation where unions are securing the position of a core labour force while agreeing to flexibility and subcontracting provisions that in the long run are likely to erode that core. After all, with the growth of a less secure labour market, employers now have a credible threat to flexibilize even core employment in order to remain competitive, and this diminishes working-class solidarity by enabling an insider/outsider division where the core labour force is seen as living unjustly "high on the hog" while the outsiders work harder and struggle to get by.

Further evidence of this divide between "insiders" with good jobs and often union collective bargaining protection and "outsiders" with poorly paid and insecure employment can be seen in changes in job quality, discussed earlier. Between 1997 and 2007, union work was characterized by a stable distribution of 16 percent low-quality, 49 percent middle-quality and 35 percent high-quality jobs. This essentially means that the observed overall distributional shift of 3 percent of jobs from low quality to high quality took place entirely in the non-union sector, which in turn suggests that, to the limited extent that the mix of job quality improved through the boom, this improvement had more to do with the mix of jobs created and destroyed than with union efforts to improve the quality of existing jobs (Institut de la statistique du Québec2010b) .

In sum, in riding through the boom and bust, Quebec's labour unions showed remarkable stability in expanding their membership and maintaining something close to historic levels of union density. Given the drop in unemployment and the persistence of wage inequality, one might have expected to see more success in recruiting new members. On the other hand, given unions' expansion into sectors with historically low unionization and the downward trend in union densities across the West in the current period, one might have expected the unions to be less successful than they ultimately were.

Similarly, in terms of collective bargaining, the unions managed to make some headway, but the question remains about whether this is simply shoring up the position of a core labour force rather than pulling up working conditions across the labour market. Indeed, if we think back to the data on income distribution, it appears that tax and transfer policies have been more decisive than collective bargaining in lifting standards of living in the bottom half of the population.

THE QUEBEC LABOUR MOVEMENT: HALF FULL OR HALF EMPTY?

What do these trends of inequality, growing low-wage work and the faltering of the Quebec Model mean for the future ? Does the success of unions in maintaining their membership point to the continued capacity to shape labour markets and economic outcomes? Or instead does it reflect success in protecting a dying breed of "labour market insiders," with the loss of capacity to push up work and wages in the growing service sector? Does the relative levelling off of labour market flexibilization signal a "new normal" where a third of jobs are atypical, or do the unions have an opening to re-regulate labour markets? Or will the projected labour market tightening related to population ageing open new opportunities, not only for better wages and working conditions but also for better training and retraining?

As this chapter shows, even if the Quebec Model continues to outperform the Canadian one in terms of holding poverty and income inequality in check, it is hardly a gold standard. Despite significant economic growth and reduced unemployment, a third of the labour force is stuck in non-standard employment, wages are stagnant, and a retreat in union strength has been masked by the boom in unionized construction jobs. As elsewhere, the boom years have been years of feast for the richest and stagnation and continued insecurity for the rest. As talk turns to austerity as the way to pay back the debts incurred during the latest crisis, the measures that tempered inequality are on the chopping block. The Quebec Model, indeed, is a shadow of what it once was and risks becoming a yet paler imitation of its old self.

If we look back at the boom years, there are reasons to be sceptical that the labour movement will take a leading role in re-regulating labour markets or improving living standards. Certainly, Quebec's unions have supported the sorts of income supplementation and collective services that succeeded in marginally transforming the wealth of the boom into improved living standards for the many. But unions were not in the forefront of the push for them: to take the case of the family policy package (child care, parental leaves, enhanced income supplements to families), the women's movement, the family movement and early childhood development experts were far more involved both in the "insider" crafting of policy and the "outsider" push for its adoption. Similarly, when the Parti Québécois (PQ) government opened the door to improved labour standards in the dying days of its 1998–2003 mandate, it was the advocacy organization for poorly protected workers, Au bas de l'échelle, that most successfully organized to win improvements to minimum labour standards and their extension to more categories of workers in December 2002.

Moreover, even when issues central to the long-term health of the labour movement have been on the table, such as the reform of the Labour Code in 2000, the labour movement was not successful in pushing changes that would have made it easier to organize the sorts of private service-sector jobs that are a key source of new employment creation. Similarly, when the post-2003 Liberal government rolled back union rights around subcontracting and representation in the health and social services sector, the unions managed to mobilize public shows of force in terms of days of action but were unable to translate these campaigns into a reversal of the roll-backs, let alone limit concessions on jobs and contracting out.

If this assessment of the labour movement's short-term prospects is accurate, then what other constituencies might push working conditions one way or another? Those making up the bottom 50–60 percent of the income distribution have on occasion successfully pressured the government to redistribute a modicum of income with taxes and transfers, and lower income earners have also seen the expansion of collective provision in areas such as child care. Social movements such as the women's movement have also done much to politicize the deficiency of minimum wages and labour standards.

But the right in Quebec has invested just as heavily in recent years in developing think-tanks and political vehicles to rally the disaffected. Led by upper- and middle-income earners and supported by a large section of blue collar workers, this coalition of "haves" and think-tanks has definitely slowed the pace of positive social change under Charest's Liberal government — so much so that today the elite consensus that the public should pay for the global economic crisis through budgetary austerity is now the common operating assumption of all political parties in Quebec, which suggests that further cuts to social services and income transfer programs are in the offing.

At the workplace level, if unions retreat into the protection of a core workforce, it is hard to believe that public policies can succeed in preventing employer strategies of expanding the use of a flexible and less well-protected workforce or in pushing up wages and working conditions above a fairly low floor. Indeed, if the Quebec labour movement were to remain silent and unable to mobilize wider public support, it is likely this retreat would imperil the survival of any version of a "Quebec Model" that pushes up the social wage. After all, to the extent unions look like they are protecting insiders, they lose moral credibility in speaking for — let alone mobilizing — a broader working class. For example, when pushed in tough bargaining during the late 1990s into signing "two tier" contracts, which provided new hires with worse terms of pay and employment, it was the unions (and not the employers) who met with public outcry. It is perhaps here, then, where the changes below the surface appearance of continuity in union strength most strongly presage unhappy tomorrows.

To avoid that outcome, the Quebec labour movement will have to show much more originality in its organizational, workplace and political strategies. In this respect, the challenge is not much different from that facing the labour movement elsewhere in Canada. Although it starts from a higher base in terms of union density and has developed better insider policy leverage through the tradition of the Quebec Model, it faces the same challenges. In terms of organizing, the issue is one of trying to organize the private service sector within a legislative framework more conducive to unionizing large manufacturing workplaces. In terms of bargaining, the union focus on decentralized workplace bargaining is no longer pulling up wages as trade pressures depress wages in open sectors and as the fragmentation of private services prevent meaningful pattern bargaining that improves wages and job security for all. In terms of politics, three terms in power by a neoliberal Quebec Liberal Party (2003–present) may not have rolled back the Quebec Model, but they certainly have made it seem increasingly out of date. The opposition PQ does not show much enthusiasm for reviving it either. While the PQ favours certain improvements to the social wage so as to foster social cohesion, they tend to see this as a *quid pro quo* for maintaining a *laissez-faire* attitude to liberalized labour markets and decentralized industrial relations.

There are no quick and easy alternatives for organized labour in Quebec: it is easy to say "organize more, employ new strategies, improve outreach to the unorganized, link up with social movement struggles, re-engage the realm of partisan politics and state policy" and so forth. But as with the Canadian labour movement, there have only been halting and partial steps taken on all of these fronts, and few more sustained and better-resourced efforts. The similarity of the challenges facing Quebec labour and labour in the rest of the country should hopefully lead to a more productive and grounded dialogue between Quebec labour and Canadian labour, specifically about organizational, bargaining and political strategies. However, the Quebec Model appears increasingly outdated, and given the increased fragility of both the unions and the Quebec Model coming out of the boom and bust, far more problems than solutions lay on the horizon ahead.

Part III

NEW CHALLENGES FACING LABOUR

Organizing, Health and Safety

7. INDIGENOUS WORKERS, CASINO DEVELOPMENT AND UNION ORGANIZING

Yale D. Belanger

We don't need you people to find solutions for us. That's been our problem all along. Where were you in the '60s, '70s and '80s when we needed union support? We will find our own solutions because all your solutions are half-baked.
—David Ahenakew, former chief, Federation of Saskatchewan Indian Nations

After thirty years with the federal civil service, Arnold Ahenakew decided that working for the Northern Lights Casino in St. Albert would be a welcome break from the monotony of retirement. So in 1999 he accepted an entry-level position during the casino's early days of operations. Disturbed with management's poor treatment of employees and its refusal to respond to grievances, as well as the comparably low wages contrasted with employees working at the provincial non-Native casinos, Ahenakew invited the Canadian Auto Workers (CAW), the nation's largest private-sector union, to organize a union (Burton 2002: E7). In the close-knit world of provincial First Nations[1] politics, Arnold soon discovered that his cousin, former Assembly of First Nations grand chief and Federation of Saskatchewan Indian Nation (FSIN) official David Ahenakew, opposed his actions.

A long-time critic of non-Native agents insinuating themselves into the exclusive domain of sovereign First Nations economic development issues, David claimed that the employee grievances originated with "people who shouldn't be there — lazy, marginal workers." Expressing concern that casino unionization would lead to unionization of First Nations, inevitably driving Aboriginal employees to seek out union counsel in lieu of working with community leaders, he clearly intimated that provincial First Nations leaders would go to great lengths to resist union organizing (Parker 2001: A6).

Little did the two cousins realize that their ideological differences would be played out when casino management and First Nations political leadership confronted casino employees working as union organizers. A three-year battle ensued involving all levels of the Canadian courts, which was followed by the prompt certification and equally swift dissolution of the CAW as labour advocate. This opening salvo by Northern Lights employees and later attempts in 2002 by Painted Hand organizers to certify Yorkton's Public Service Alliance of Canada foreshadowed what has since developed into a significant issue: First Nations leadership's resistance to Aboriginal attempts at labour organizing. It is problematic that First Nations leaders are wilfully ignoring what the Supreme Court of Canada in 2007 acknowledged to be a constitutional right: to bargain collectively (*Health Services and Support — Facilities Subsector Bargaining Association v. British Columbia*).

Perhaps more troubling is the politicizing of the labour-business relationship by First Nations leaders, which thus obscures workers' rights. In this milieu the FSIN, which in turn oversees the Saskatchewan Indian Gaming Authority (SIGA), informs casino management's responses to labour advocacy. The FSIN has developed far reaching strategies to counter attempts at labour organizing; these include petitioning the Canadian courts, refusing to negotiate with union representatives and increasing wages at First Nations casinos. The conflation of politics and economics is complicating what are already multi-faceted worker-owner relationships.

The FSIN is not alone in this recent world of labour advocacy occurring within First Nations casinos, which are often the newest economic engines of development. The Rama-Mnjikaning First Nation, Casino Rama's home community, and the Mississaugas of Scugog Island First Nation, which operates the Great Blue Heron Charity Casino, have both contested similar efforts. They also insist that the Aboriginal right to self-government and existing treaty rights shield First Nations casinos from provincial legislation and thus union dictates. The FSIN argues that labour unions are not traditionally "Native" and that their "un-Indigenous" nature is and should remain foreign to First Nations culture (Pitawanakwat 2006: 32–33). Most resistance strategies have succeeded. Casino Rama resisted the Teamsters and five other unions, while SIGA on two separate occasions broke organizing resolve (Belanger 2006a: 159–162). Only the Great Blue Heron Charity Casino failed as a union buster.

A number of troubling trends characterize the varied attempts at containing unionism, but perhaps most disturbing is that this new generation of First Nations leaders fail to acknowledge that their own employees — Aboriginal and non-Native alike — actively court the unions. Equally problematic is the discovery by labour advocates working with gaming employees that most of their contacts demonstrated a general lack of union and labour consciousness, which undermined organizing efforts (Belanger 2011). Several independent and intersecting forces have led to this situation.

Significant Aboriginal union participation in the early 1900s diminished noticeably after the 1920s. Limited work opportunities led to minimal labour union participation, and when union membership was possible, Aboriginal workers often felt unwanted in organizations that perpetuated the racism that contributed to their marginalization. It should come as no surprise that Aboriginal people attached limited value to seeking skilled, permanent employment and refused to aggressively agitate for re-inclusion in unions that historically failed to provide them sanctuary. Yet it is notable that internal requests and aggressive lobbying for unions at First Nations casinos has occurred repeatedly in recent years. In addition to demonstrating casino employees' dissatisfaction with working conditions, this trend also hints at the evolution of a labour consciousness that undoubtedly threatens First Nations leaders. This movement demands investigation, in particular the conflicts that have arisen in response to Aboriginal and non-Native employees challenging First Nations business owners and how the protagonists counter one another in the contemporary world of Aboriginal economic development and labour advocacy.

FIRST NATIONS CASINO DEVELOPMENT, 1996–2010

In the decade and a half that they've been operating, First Nations casinos have become a ubiquitous feature of the Canadian gaming industry and emerged as economic powerhouses in their own rights. Casino Rama in Ontario and the River Cree Casino and Resort in Alberta are recognized as two of the nation's largest destination resorts. Seventeen First Nations casinos across the country employ more than 8,700 workers. Capitalist-oriented Aboriginal leaders trumpet these facilities as much needed instruments of economic revitalization but have proven extremely resistant to efforts by the workers in these casinos to unionize.

For many, the birth of the Canadian First Nations gaming industry dates to 1996, the year Casino Rama opened in Ontario and four casinos opened in Saskatchewan. The use of gambling revenues by First Nations, however, dates to the 1984 launch of a government-sanctioned, community-based lottery operated by the Opaskwayak Cree Nation in Manitoba. Captivated by the nearly one hundred American Indian bingo operations grossing an estimated $200 million (combined) annually, First Nations leaders in Saskatchewan and Ontario initiated research during the 1980s to evaluate the potential of situating casinos on reserves (Belanger 2006a), and by 1987 they were aggressively lobbying officials in several provinces to permit reserve casino operations (Cordeiro 1989: 1). These efforts corresponded with the American Indian gaming industry's rapid expansion following two key U.S.

Supreme Court decisions: *Seminole* (1981) and *Cabazon* (1987). The former halted the State of Florida's interference with the economic activities of the Seminole and was interpreted as restricting all states from interfering with tribal economic activities, including bingos and other gambling operations. The latter led many tribal leaders to conclude that the individual tribes controlled Indian gaming (Reid 1990: 17).

First Nations leaders in Canada adopted the popular U.S. tribal sovereignty model in the early 1990s, and soon several First Nation communities proclaimed an inherent right to establish casinos and other economic development projects outside of provincial oversight (Belanger 2006a). The Canadian courts determined, however, that First Nations did not possess a sovereign right to control reserve commerce or economic development. As a result, all reserve casino facilities were subject to provincial legislation. In due time this would have implications for casino workers seeking legal protection from interference with their rights by First Nations operators.

By all accounts, casinos appeared an economic development mechanism capable of effectively countering endemic reserve impoverishment. According to the Harvard Project on American Indian Economic Development, established in 1987 (Cornell and Kalt 2006), First Nations were engaged in nation building, or a policy of legitimate self-rule. The Harvard Project's research determined that legitimate self-governance required First Nations leaders to take control of their communities and guide the economic development decision-making process. Under the historical Indian Affairs bureaucratic model, outside administrators directed reserve economic development, leading to an inevitable conflict of interest between government desires and community-based political and economic agendas. Harvard researchers encouraged First Nations leaders to acquire control over local development as one aspect of a larger overarching process they coined "practical sovereignty" (14). The Harvard Project's research findings suggest that practical sovereignty if properly implemented will lead to greater local control over decision-making, permitting First Nations to benefit from good policy decisions and suffer the consequences of bad policy decisions.

With the spirit of practical sovereignty guiding their actions, First Nations leaders from Ontario and Saskatchewan willingly negotiated gaming agreements with provincial officials in an effort to jump-start their economic development strategies. Considered an economic panacea whereby revenues would be utilized in much the same way provinces used these monies — to improve local services and infrastructure — First Nations by the 1990s were openly rationalizing legalized gambling similarly to provincial officials as a "legislative blessing ... based on the premise that the social good of the activity outweighs any negative consequences" (Smith and Wynne 2000: 32). Reserve casinos also had two unique features entrepreneurial First Nations leaders prized: (1) they were local businesses generating operating revenue and onsite employment; and (2) the business model attracted start-up capital from partners willing to absorb a portion of the financial risk.

The First Nations gaming industry's rapid expansion followed. As of 2010, there were seventeen First Nations casinos operating in the provinces of British Columbia (one), Alberta (five), Saskatchewan (six), Manitoba (two, with a third planned) and Ontario (three). Of these, two in Ontario (the Golden Eagle Casino in Kenora and Blue Heron Charity Casino on Scugog Island) are charity casinos. The remaining fifteen are for-profit casinos operated in association with American and Canadian casino operators. Nova Scotia First Nations, meanwhile, operate several video lottery terminal (VLT) sites.

The First Nations casinos range from destination-type resorts, such as the Enoch Cree's $178 million River Cree Resort just west of Edmonton, which boasts six hundred slot machines, forty table games and a poker room, to more modest operations, such as the $11 million Casino Dene at Cold Lake, Alberta, which houses 150 slots and ten table games. Success is measured variably. Casino Rama, near Orillia, Ontario, netted $1.2 billion from $5.2 billion gross revenue between 1996 and 2007, whereas the Aseneskak Casino on the Opskwayak Cree Nation, adjacent The Pas, Manitoba, lost money its first year and continues as a lower-revenue operation. The provincial revenue distribution formula in Ontario ensures that all First Nations in the province benefit, but having to allocate the revenues among 132 First Nations radically curtails per capita disbursements.

In other provinces, similar trends are evident. In its first four years of operations the First Nations Development Fund (FNDF) of Alberta produced nearly $278 million for First Nations' use, and five casino charities made roughly $140 million during the same time period. In Saskatchewan the First Nations Trust accumulated $374 million from 2002 to 2010 for use by the seventy-five provincial First Nations. The South Beach Casino Limited Partnership in Manitoba produced net earnings of $7,139,404 in 2007 and $5,585,321 in 2006 from combined $48,232,924 gross gaming revenue. Despite a rough start, the Asensekak Casino near The Pas, Manitoba, turned a $1.6 million profit in 2007, an increase of $839,000 from 2006. In B.C., the St. Eugene's Mission Resort in Cranbrook netted approximately $7.4 million between 2002 and 2009. Between 1997 and 2010, the thirteen gaming First Nations in Nova Scotia pocketed nearly $419 million (including a combined contribution from the Sydney Casino) from the 403 VLTs they control.[2]

The Canadian First Nations gaming industry is still modest in comparison to the U.S. Indian gaming industry, where 233 tribes (including two Alaska Native villages) in twenty-eight states with gaming compacts operate 411 gaming facilities, including casinos, bingo halls and pull-tab operations. In 2008, the U.S. Indian gaming industry generated $25.9 billion in gross gaming revenues (National Indian Gaming Association [NIGA] 2008). The seventeen First Nations casinos in Canada, meanwhile, net approximately $750 million annually.

Unlike American Indian tribes, which manage gaming revenues generated by reservation casinos, First Nations have limited say over how gaming revenues are distributed. The province of Ontario took 20 percent of Casino Rama's gross revenues for provincial operations until 2008, when the provincial First Nations successfully sued the Ontario government to recover these revenues (see Belanger 2006a; Manitowabi 2007). Similarly, the Saskatchewan government assigns 25 percent and Alberta 30 percent of annual First Nations gambling revenues to their respective provincial treasuries. At the community level, forty-four of Alberta's forty-five First Nations may apply to the FNDF for project funding; however, the revenue distribution formula allocates the five First Nations hosting casino operations 45 percent of all revenues. An additional 10 percent assigned to the FNDF is divided accordingly: 5 percent of the revenues are distributed equally among the thirty-nine non-host First Nations, and 5 percent is available for proscribed project funding, which is circulated according to a formula that considers population size and geographic location. In the last three years, this 10 percent annual allocation has been in the neighbourhood of $25 million. In Manitoba in 2007, $378,571 was distributed to each of the South Beach Casino Limited Partnership's seven member First Nation communities (Grant Thornton 2007: 2–3), while each of the seven Aseneskak Casino partner First Nations received $72,000 (Aseneskak Casino: The Pas/Opaskwayak Cree Nation 2007: 1–2). Provincial First Nations in B.C. do not benefit from Casino of the Rockies operations; the profits produced to date are limited and have a minimal provincial impact.

These data reveal the First Nations gaming industry's variable impact nationally, even if First Nations leaders guiding struggling economies remain loyal to the enterprise (Table 7.1). In June 2010, for example, the First Nations Summit of B.C. announced the creation of a gaming commission. Angered at the premier's refusal to distribute a portion of provincial gambling revenues to all First Nations, years of unsuccessful lobbying efforts compelled the gaming commission's creation, which could lead the way to a casino operating on First Nations land or legal action seeking to secure a percentage of provincial gambling revenues (CBC News 2010a).

Table 7.1 First Nations Casino Revenues, 1997–2010

Nova Scotia (1997–2010)	Ontario (1996–2007)	Manitoba (2002–2010)	Saskatchewan (2002–2010)	Alberta (2006–2010)	B.C. (2002–2009)
$418,988,842	$1,200,000,000	n/a	$373,896,612	$418,470,711	$7,387,212

Shortly thereafter, First Nations leaders in Saskatchewan announced their intention to establish a national Aboriginal gaming commission, ostensibly to gain more control of what they described as the huge revenues generated by First Nations casinos (*CBC News* 2010b). As chief of Saskatchewan's Little Black Bear First Nation and the former FSIN grand chief who oversaw the potentially debilitating SIGA revenue mismanagement scandal in the early 2000s Perry Bellegarde proclaimed, the national gaming authority "all about sovereignty and jurisdiction and exerting that and occupying the field so that we can in turn have our own First Nations gaming act."

In spite of modest returns all First Nations casinos at the time of this writing are profitable, permanent fixtures of First Nations politics that increasingly come to guide long-range economic and community development strategies. They have also met original expectations by providing Aboriginal employment, which is benefiting local economies. Interestingly, as discussed below, First Nations leaders do not foresee an improved job market facilitating the entry of unions into their gaming industry.

ABORIGINAL CASINO EMPLOYMENT

Setting aside the politically fractious and costly First Nations sovereignty debate for a moment, the First Nations gaming industry has fulfilled one of its primary objectives: to employ First Nations individuals. From the beginning First Nations leaders argued that gaming was more than a means of generating quick money to satiate local needs; if properly managed it would create local employment opportunities, thus improving local well-being.

In 2006, gambling produced 135,000 full-time gaming-related jobs nationally, resulting in $11.6 billion in labour income. Factoring in jobs created through gaming spinoff, the industry supports 267,000 full-time jobs nationally, more than 8700 for First Nations workers (Canadian Gaming Association 2008: v, vi, 17). The majority of First Nations casinos have exceeded employment expectations (Table 7.2). None have to this date failed or closed doors, and all in recent years have produced a profit. The more impressive stories emanate from Ontario, Saskatchewan and Alberta.

In Ontario, Casino Rama, the largest single-site employer of First Nations workers in Canada, boasts an annual payroll of $140 million and close to 3,700 employees (McKim 2008). The Gold Eagle and Northern

Lights Casinos in Saskatchewan originally expected to employ 170, with a combined payroll of $4.5 million. In 2008, they employed more than 700, with a combined payroll of $24 million (Saskatchewan Indian Gaming Authority 2008: 23, 25). SIGA's 2,100 employees in 2008–09 achieved a payroll exceeding $69 million, up $31 million from 2006–07. The five Alberta First Nations casinos' payroll for the 1,200 employees at the casinos and the First Nations charities (206 are of Aboriginal descent) is estimated at more than $34 million.

Table 7.2 First Nation Casino Employees 2008–2009

	Total Casino Employees	Employees of Aboriginal Heritage	Percentage of Aboriginal Employees
Ontario	4850	585	12
Saskatchewan	2200	1365	62
Alberta	1200	206	17
Manitoba	268	149	56
British Columbia	250	50	20
Nova Scotia	n/a	n/a	n/a
Totals	8768	2355	27

Source: Author's own calculations based on interviews

The positive impact of reserve casinos is usually immediate, and Casino Rama is an excellent example. Within a few years of its 1996 opening, unemployment at Mnjikaning dropped from 70 to 8 percent, and band staff jumped from 50 to 230. By 2000, there were close to twenty-five private and band-owned businesses operating. The Mnjikaning Kendaaswin Elementary School opened in 1998 to both First Nations children and those from neighbouring non-Native communities, followed by the community building its own fire department, establishing a first-response emergency unit and creating a tribal police unit that works in conjunction with the Ontario Provincial Police. Water and sewage treatment facilities were also constructed to service the local community and the needs of nearby businesses (Belanger 2006a). A 2000 study reported that Casino Rama generated $862 million annually in economic spinoff, of which 68 percent benefited the Orillia area (McKim 2008). This study is unique, as only one other study exists nationally to provide insight into First Nation casinos' spinoff effects (Williams, Belanger, and Arthur 2011). We are limited concerning our knowledge of working conditions or how wages at First Nations casinos compare to their non-Native counterparts.

Available data detailing worker wages at individual casinos make it difficult to compare First Nation casino employee wages with those of their non-Native counterparts. The Saskatchewan example is instructive, however. Despite a court decision compelling SIGA to negotiate a collective agreement, it refused to do so until grievance procedures and the collection of union dues were worked out. The CAW petitioned the Saskatchewan Labour Relations Board to resolve the issue, followed by a government-appointed mediator rendering the following decision in January 2002: dealers wages would rise from $9.19/hour to $13.05; pit bosses would go from $13.52/hour to $14.85; and slot technicians would go from $10.92/hour to $13.65 (*Saskatoon Star-Phoenix* 2002: A6). Six months later workers received a 28 cents-an-hour pay raise, and workers employed between June 1, 2000, and June 1, 2001, received an additional $650 in retroactive pay (Parker 2001: A6). Despite these gains, workers decertified the CAW in December after SIGA honoured the pay raises while providing full dental and medical coverage and pensions. The pay raises and benefits were enacted at all First Nations casinos and likely undermined Painted Hand organizers and Public Service Alliance of Canada (PSAC) attempts to organize in Yorkton the following year.

Similarly, in July 2004, the CAW and the Great Blue Heron Charity Casino, run by the Mississaugas of Scugog Island, reached an agreement on a three-year contract that provided the seven hundred casino workers with wage increases (UNI Global Union 2005). The lack of labour advocacy at First Nations casinos in Manitoba and B.C. suggests that efforts to stem labour organizing by offering workers competitive wages and benefits packages has been successful.

Several critics suggested that reserve casinos' anticipated economic benefits could potentially be offset "by increased vulnerability to the negative consequences of gambling" (Korn and Shaffer 2002: 189). Complementary research hints at the fact that First Nations individuals in Canada were more apt to developing gambling addictions, specifically that "the Canadian provincial problem gambling prevalence rate is in fact *best* predicted by proportion of the population with Aboriginal ancestry" (Williams, West and Simpson 2007). However, no rigorous responsible gambling initiatives have been implemented by First Nations, nor have before-and-after-the-establishment-of-First-Nation-casino prevalence studies been conducted (Belanger 2010). Concentrating on the negatives means that the benefits of casino job creation are often overlooked, as are the benefits gained from localized First Nations spending.

Groups such as the Council for the Advancement of Native Development Officers (CANDO) have long promoted the need for First Nations monetary retention to grow local economies. Its officers argue that for every $1 spent locally, three times the economic value can be produced locally (studies range, suggesting that $1 spent can lead to $3 to $15 returned value). Take the Tsuu T'ina First Nation, the host community of the Grey Eagle Casino and Bingo, as an example. In 2008–09, its FNDF allocation was $28,572,460, and the charity it operates brought in $19,987,644. The eighty local employees earned approximately $1.416 million, which applying a multiplier of three could potentially produce a minimum benefit of $4.248 million to the local economy. These numbers alone indicate that casinos introduced roughly $52.8 million to the Tsuu T'ina economy in 2008–09.

Certain caveats must be considered, such as the fact that the spinoff effect is unclear, for businesses have popped up that are casino-driven. We don't know exactly how many new First Nations employees have been hired at these businesses or the extent of their local spending, nor how many of the casino employees permanently reside at Tsuu T'ina. And not all First Nations casinos can boast such impressive figures. However, to reiterate, no First Nations casinos to date have closed, and all indicators suggest that First Nations casinos nationally are profitable ventures.

Much work needs to be done to improve our understanding of the positive and negative economic impacts associated with First Nations casinos in Canada. There are obvious economic benefits. Despite demonstrated success, First Nations leaders and their casino operators actively resist labour unions, undermining employee goodwill and threatening corporate stability. First Nations leaders challenging provincial legislation designed to protect both Native and non-Native casino employees indicate that First Nations governments (and American Indian tribes) are distinctly anti-worker. The print media reinforce this image by portraying First Nations casino managers as union busters playing outside the Charter of Rights and Freedoms legal framework (Belanger 2011). Such corporate strategies are counterintuitive considering that many First Nations employees are new to the casino's fast-paced work environment, where they face unique working conditions such as noise, violence and patron harassment (Dubois, Wuttunee and Loxley 2002: 58).

FIRST NATIONS CASINO ORGANIZING DRIVES

Employees frustrated with poor working conditions and inadequate wages have initiated every union organizing drive at a First Nations casino in Canada. Inviting unions to advocate was a tactically sound approach, especially considering that kinship ties meant that to do otherwise would lead workers to confront family members. Unions in this instance were considered a means of mitigating potential conflict between employees seeking improved wages and working conditions and leaders who had spent years fighting to create those jobs. Yet rather than acknowledge labour advocacy as a facet of casino operations, First Nations leaders have relied on territorial sovereignty claims to dispute non-Native agents' attempts to penetrate reserve boundaries, refusing to negotiate with union representatives prior to exhausting legal avenues to resist union certification.

First Nations leadership's resistance to labour organizing parallels recent happenings in the United States, where unions are concentrating their energies on the $26 billion tribal gaming industry after a 2004 National Labor Relations Board's (NLRB) ruling concluded that tribally owned casinos in California "appeared to be more like a commercial enterprise than a government function." Consequently, unions were granted access to tribal casino employees (Rowe 2005: 12). American Indian leaders argued, unsuccessfully, that tribal sovereignty shelters tribes from the *National Labor Relations Act*, which gives U.S. workers the right to unionize. The resulting competition among California unions led UNITE HERE, an American labour union representing hotel and restaurant workers, to sue the Communications Workers of America for violating "an AFL-CIO mandate that restricted other unions from pursuing casino workers in the state" (Nguyen 2005). American Indian leaders in California continue to fight the institution of unions, using divide-and-conquer strategies to foster worker distrust, while threatening termination for employees attending organizing meetings (Wildenthal 2007; Singel 2004).

In Canada, a host of labour unions, including the Teamsters, the Canadian Auto Workers (CAW) and the Canadian Union for Public Employees (CUPE) have attempted to organize the more than 8,700 First Nations gaming workers, of which 2,355 (27 percent) are of Aboriginal descent. First Nations leaders have responded by offering workers competitive wages and benefits packages, contesting labour union certification (claiming that reserve casinos located on crown lands fall under federal jurisdiction and, as such, are exempt from provincial labour standards) and asserting that band councils have an inherent right to determine the substance of reserve economic development and its attendant policies, including band council-established labour bylaws.

First Nations have challenged the Canadian courts on several occasions to determine the extent of their Aboriginal and treaty rights as they relate to reserve casinos. Most notable was the Shawanaga First Nation's contention that provincial (in this case, Ontario) authority for gaming did not extend to a reserve gaming house. Shawanaga leaders argued that Section 81(1) (m) of the *Indian Act* provided for band "control and prohibition of public games" and "other amusements" (Pruden 2002: 40). They demanded that the provincial and federal governments accept the First Nation's right "to control public games," which included high-stakes bingos. Shawanaga's leaders further asserted that reserve businesses, including the gaming house, were exempt from federal and provincial laws. Ontario's Eagle Lake First Nation followed suit by contesting provincial authority over its bingo operation. Both communities believed that their inherent self-governing authority and assertions of sovereignty were adequate to undermine provincial oversight on reserve, an argument the court rejected.

On appeal, the Ontario Supreme Court determined in 1994 that "the appellants had not demonstrated ... that they were acting in 'obedience' to the Shawanaga First Nation's lottery law (it did not require them to act as they did) or that the band council had *de facto* sovereignty" (*R. v. Pamajewon* 1996). Gaming was not considered to be an Aboriginal right, meaning that reserve gaming facilities were not exempt from provincial legislation according to section 35(1) of the *Constitution Act*, 1982. Provincial jurisdiction for gambling thus remained intact (Isaac 1999: 526). Two additional cases confirmed, first, that a provincial legislature has jurisdiction to enact laws in the gaming area (*R. v. Furtney* 1991) and, second, that the *Indian Act* did not supersede "the application of the criminal code to gambling on a reserve" (*R. v. Gladue* 1986).

None of these cases dealt with a First Nation's ability to restrict labour organizing in a reserve setting generally or in reserve casinos specifically. The FSIN seized upon this ambiguity to promote the organization's self-governing authority to manage labour relations. In 1999 the organization's leadership announced its intent to establish a labour code in response to the CAW's certification at the Northern Lights Casino in Prince Albert. That the FSIN challenged the encroachment of unions into reserve communities should come as no surprise, considering the organization's historical commitment to self-determination and resistance to colonial political intrusion (Belanger 2006b: 324–5).

The FSIN argued that its reserve casinos were distinct First Nations businesses that fell under federal legislation and were shielded from provincial regulation. Behind the scenes, FSIN leaders and provincial chiefs were concerned that CAW headway would inevitably lead to the unionization of band offices, tribal councils and other Native-run organizations (Parker 2001: A6). Accordingly, their proposed labour code asserted the FSIN's authority over not only reserve casinos but also all individuals represented by the province's seventy-five member bands. The FSIN's intent was to immunize member bands from federal and provincial labour laws while simultaneously empowering the Chief's Assembly to certify unions. The chiefs spoke openly of unionization's potentially compromising effect upon First Nations' jurisdiction over reserve activities and their collective financial stability.

At the centre of the controversy was the certification drive at Prince Albert's Northern Lights Casino by Canada's largest private-sector union, the CAW. In a blatant attempt at union busting, SIGA's lawyers maintained that the four casinos fell under federal jurisdiction and, as such, were exempt from provincial labour standards. Before the Saskatchewan Court of Appeal, they argued that their employees should not be permitted to form a union.

The court disagreed, ruling that the province has jurisdiction over the unionized employees at SIGA casinos. An independent mediator was appointed to produce a report as the basis for a collective bargaining agreement. The final pact was expected to raise employees' wages between $3 and $4 per hour while providing a one-time, $650 payment in lieu of retroactive pay. Prior to the ratification a new vote took place that led to the CAW's decertification that December.

By 2002, union advocacy was again in motion as Painted Hand organizers sought union certification from the PSAC in Yorkton. The PSAC applied for a certification order on November 29, 2002, albeit without majority support. A secret ballot was held January 10, 2003, and a majority of Painted Hand employees voted against the union. The PSAC's application was dismissed.

SIGA managers discouraged employee union participation by petitioning the courts, according to several workers, who also cited employee intimidation as a discouraging strategy. During the union drive of 2002, for example, an organizer who received numerous official warnings was suspended several times from work and eventually fired in January 2003. In 2001, Saskatchewan Retail, Wholesale and Department Store Union (RWDSU) organizer Gord Schmidt was temporarily banned from the Painted Hand Casino premises. He also discovered that the majority of Painted Hand workers resisted becoming involved for fear of losing their jobs. The RWDSU eventually concluded that achieving the majority support needed for certification was not possible due to workers' fears of management retribution.

In April 2003, CUPE opened a Yorkton office to organize Painted Hand Casino employees. One month later the threat of dismissals and employee suspensions came to fruition with the May 2 layoff of Trevor Lyons, who had signed a CUPE support card. Interest was soon rekindled once CUPE officials learned of the previous RWDSU drive, and the RWDSU offered their support. Organizers in Saskatchewan continue their advocacy in the hopes of establishing labour unions in the now six provincial First Nations casinos.

The implications for on-reserve workers aside, the Saskatchewan Court of Appeal's ruling upholding provincial jurisdiction over unionized employees at SIGA's casinos and the Saskatchewan Court of Queen's bench decision upholding a Saskatchewan Labour Relations Board ruling legally acknowledging a collective agreement at the Northern Lights Casino in Prince Albert represented a clear blow to the First Nations self-determination movement. Since the release of two reports, in 1977 and 1979, the FSIN has consistently demanded federal acknowledgment of traditional First Nations sovereignty, namely the most fundamental right a sovereign nation holds: the right to govern its people and territory under its own laws and customs. Expanding on these ideas, the FSIN considers the right to self-government as "inherited … from the people" and something that has never been extinguished voluntarily or by means of military defeat. This sovereignty, FSIN officials argue, has been eroded and suppressed by the legislative and administrative actions of Canada.

First Nations leaders acknowledge that section 91(24) of the *British North America Act*, 1867, gives the federal government the authority to regulate relations with First Nations but are adamant that it does not permit federal or provincial regulation of internal band affairs such as labour relations. The courts disagreed with this analysis, concluding instead that the FSIN could not enact its own labour code. It is ironic that the courts were sought out by a political organization representing self-professed, self-determining nations to determine the pith and substance of Aboriginal self-government. Such an approach arguably undermines the position that treaties reserve a complete set of rights, including self-governing rights and the right to control First Nations lands and resources without federal interference.

Three university researchers observing events as they unfolded in Saskatchewan concluded that anti-union actions had more to do with "First Nations leaders not wishing to have the authority of Chief and Council challenged" (Dubois, Wuttunee and Loxley 2002) than with defending the best interests of Aboriginal workers. University of Winnipeg professor Brock Pitawanakwat took aim at an FSIN strategy that spread the rumour that labour unions would negatively affect First Nations culture. He was especially critical of how the FSIN chiefs utilized a "false front of nationalism," described as a "red herring [employed] to maintain their power over labour relations in indigenous institutions" (Pitawanakwat 2006: 32–3). Reflecting on increasing class divisions and fluid notions of citizenship among First Nations, Pitawanakwat concluded: "The emerging capitalist class in indigenous communities has exploited ongoing and deep-seated fears of assimilation amongst our peoples. Indigenous organizations have used a nationalist and xenophobic propaganda campaign to oppose labour unions"(33). He was especially concerned with what he considered to be the FSIN's internalization and replication of traditional colonial divide-and-conquer techniques, which seek to accomplish the collective political empowerment of the FSIN and band councils at the expense of Aboriginal workers (33). Indigenous theorist Taiaiake Alfred (2008) has argued that this is a natural by-product of the *Indian Act* system, which historically frowned upon Aboriginal leaders utilizing historical societal and governing values.

Casino Rama officials responded similarly to union incursions in Ontario. On May 10, 2004, amid red and blue balloons and cabana-style tents, with the theme music to the film *Rocky*, International Brotherhood of Teamsters Union Canada president Robert Bouvier, Teamsters Local 938 president Larry McDonald and union head James P. Hoffa, son of the late union leader, held a press conference in an effort to unite Casino Rama employees seeking union certification before the Ontario Labour Relations Board. Citing management intimidation, patron disrespect and ongoing health and safety issues, the large group's goal was to install the Teamsters as their labour advocate. In an open field near the Ramara Centre, Hoffa declared before the crowd of several thousand casino workers: "This is the battle for all people. It's a battle here in Ontario about workers' rights and on-the-job dignity." With more than 1.4 million members in Canada and the U.S., including thousands of North American casino workers, the Teamsters was the sixth group to attempt to unionize the casino's estimated 3,700 employees. During the rally, Hoffa dismissed the fears of those in attendance, indicating that "this corporate giant will be brought to its knees, we're not going to take it any more" (Beech 2004: A1).

According to McDonald, a request for union support was forwarded to the Teamsters office in the spring of 2003. It is not known whether the request came from Aboriginal or non-Native employees. All the same, what McDonald described as "a group of disgruntled workers at the casino [seeking] to have us look at helping to improve their working conditions" made the request. Vowing not to "sit back and watch hard-working casino workers abused by this corporate giant," McDonald initiated a fourteen-month union drive aimed at rallying the support of Casino Rama's 1,038 table game dealers and supervisors. The Teamsters managed to generate the 40 percent support required by Ontario legislation to allow them to file for certification. The next step was a two-day, government-supervised vote, which was called for May 11–12, 2004. Following the vote, Ontario Labour Relations Board staff notified the Teamsters and casino officials that "just under 62 percent of about 900 votes cast were against joining one of the largest North American unions" (Purnell 2004: A1). Casino Rama spokesperson Sherry Lawson maintained that "the size of our victory is significant" and that "we are most pleased that our staff did not let a small minority of people make such an important decision for them." The Teamsters have maintained lobby efforts to convince casino workers to call another certification vote (e.g., McKim 2004: A3).

First Nations in Ontario also challenged outside jurisdiction as it related to labour relations at the Great Blue Heron Charity Casino, operated by the Mississaugas of Scugog Island First Nation. One of Ontario's two First Nations operating charity casinos, the First Nation sparked litigation after it established a labour code in an attempt to halt the CAW certification by casinos workers. Initially certified as bargaining agent for a unit of employees on January 23, 2003, the CAW notified the First Nation of its intent to bargain. Without responding, the band's chief, Tracy Gauthier, and two councillors approved a labour relations code at an informal band council meeting held June 6. There are no meeting minutes to draw from, and none of the involved parties or government officials were informed of the band council's intentions. Generally speaking, the code would govern labour relations both on- and off-reserve as they related to activities "involving commercial entities that stem in different ways from the First Nation." Structured along the lines of the Canada Labour Code (CLC), the band council's code set out a number of questionable provisions that do not appear in the CLC, including denying workers the right to strike or lock out; demanding unions pay a $3,000 fee to speak with workers; and subjecting workers to a $12,000 fee to file an unfair labour practices complaint to be heard before a tribunal called the Dbaaknigeniwin, based on traditional society. The code also prohibited First Nation officials from negotiating with unions not properly certified according to its regulations.

Responding to a CAW complaint of unfair practices to the Ontario Labour Relations Board (OLRB), the Mississaugas of Scugog Island First Nation refused to accept the OLRB's jurisdiction, countering that the First Nation's inherent self-governing authority shielded it from outside scrutiny. Furthermore, as leaders of a self-governing nation, the Mississaugas of Scugog Island leadership argued that they retained jurisdiction over, and a corresponding authority to develop, community bylaws related to labour relations, and that this right superseded provincial legislation.

The OLRB responded that the arguments challenging its jurisdiction were founded on baseless claims, particularly those suggesting that the management of labour was an ancestral practice, custom or tradition. It also determined that the CLC applied on-reserve, effectively overriding the newly enacted labour code. Following the ruling, approximately 850 CAW casino workers voted 92 percent in favour of a strike to support their demands for a collective agreement (Hall 2007: 1). The bargaining issues included wages and benefits, shift schedules, contracting out, seniority provisions and contract language. On July 17, 2004, the two sides agreed to a three-year contract that provided the seven hundred casino workers with wage increases ranging from $2 per hour for those at the maximum wage rate to between 15 and 30 percent for those earning below the maximum rate (UNI Global Union 2005).

The Mississaugas of Scugog Island First Nation relied on three points to defend their Aboriginal right to excise labour unions from reserve casino operations: (1) the passage of their labour relations code was an exercise of the inherent right to self-government in relation to internal affairs and access to activities in the community's territories; (2) the passage of the code was an exercise of an inherent right to regulate work-related activities in the community's territories; and (3) the Covenant Chain treaty relationship dating back to the mid-seventeenth century both confirmed and sustained the community's rights to self-determination and self-government, which were unextinguished rights. Reflecting the FSIN's position on the matter, community and organization leaders in each case asserted that passage of the labour code was an aspect or expression of Aboriginal self-government in relation to control over land, resources and community labour management. The OLRB, however, refused to accept that the Mississaugas of Scugog Island First Nation's self-governing authority extended to it being used as a check against labour organizing on reserve lands.

In response, the chief and council petitioned the Ontario Divisional Court for a judicial review seeking determination of one question: did the Mississaugas of Scugog Island First Nation have the legal right to "enact its own labour code to govern collective bargaining in relation to a commercial undertaking that operates on reserve lands" (*Mississaugas of Scugog Island First Nation v. National Automobile, Aerospace, Transportation and General Workers Union of Canada* 2007)? The petition failed and they were not granted a judicial review. The court also concluded that there is no evidence "arising from the records and conversations" that would suggest that First Nations were considered imbued with a self-determination right when they acknowledged crown sovereignty over their territories (14). Affirming the OLRB's interpretation, the court further emphasized that the "rights which might have been continued from this 'treaty' have nothing to do with and do not speak in any way to the regulation of activity as between employers and employees" (14). In sum, the Ontario Superior Court denied the Mississaugas of Scugog Island First Nation request for a judicial review of the decision. It further signalled that it did not have a constitutional right to enact it own labour codes. This decision was upheld on appeal.

CONCLUSION

In spite of modest overall returns, all First Nations casinos are revenue generators that support First Nations economic development. But casinos are more than simply economic development tools. From the very beginning they have been potent political symbols of First Nations territorial sovereignty battles. Due to their economic role as regional employers, casinos are also the catalysts driving attempts to exclude what First Nations leaders depict as neocolonial agents and their attendant policies and ideologies from reserve communities and First Nation-owned businesses. Aboriginal employees have nevertheless petitioned for union intervention, citing poor wages and working conditions, in the process becoming pawns for those seeking to halt the infiltration of state laws regardless of the economically proven employee benefits.

Resistance to labour unions has resulted in an unflattering portrait emerging that portrays First Nations leaders as anti-labour and willing to sacrifice their employees' workplace satisfaction and security in the name of vague Aboriginal and treaty rights (Belanger 2011). Yet First Nations leaders have universally resisted union incursions, utilizing threats to employment and, as in the case of the FSIN and the Lake Scugog leadership, attempting to implement localized labour codes to constrain on-reserve union activity. Such strategies have met with success in Ontario and Saskatchewan, where in the latter instance political and employer pressure arguably compelled casino employees' refusal to certify various unions. This has not stalled CUPE's efforts to partner with Aboriginal communities or from inviting the FSIN to discuss the issues. In the end, one must remain cognizant of the fact that not all employees of First Nations casinos are Aboriginal and that alienating non-Native employees is a dangerous strategy considering that their support is required to ensure workforce harmony and thus corporate stability.

How these unique events will influence reserve relations or Aboriginal/non-Native employee relations is of interest. In the process of politicizing reserve casinos, politics and economics of casino operations intersect leading inevitably to complications. First Nations leaders consider unions to be non-representative colonial manifestations challenging their political authority, a line of thinking that likely offers employees seeking job security little comfort. As well, adversarial labour negotiations and community resistance could destabilize First Nations communities demonstrating strong kinship ties, leading to family divisions.

But alliances between the CAW and the Assembly of First Nations aimed at alleviating reserve poverty by sending CAW skilled trades to First Nations demonstrate the labour movement's desire to remain relevant by embracing fresh ideas among an increasingly multi-cultural membership (e.g., Heron 1996; Palmer 1992). A burgeoning union consciousness combined with a young, educated working elite professionally trained to manage and work in First Nations casinos could also over time lead to increased First Nations/union interface. The combination of labour activists targeting First Nations casinos for certification and Aboriginal and non-Native employees seeking union protection of their rights will also likely lead to increasing moments of conflict between employer and employee.

Finally, reflecting on past legal battles, it is unlikely that First Nations in Ontario and Saskatchewan will legally contest union advocacy at reserve casinos; the courts have spoken to its problematic nature, and in each instance First Nations acquiesced. It also appears that casinos in each province will maintain their existing strategy of offering competitive wages and benefits to counter labour organizers.

However, the threat of unions is omnipresent and potentially contentious. Sixteen Grand Beach Casino employees in Manitoba were fired after participating in a community protest in March 2009 demanding band council disclose how $1.25 million in casino revenues were spent. The terminated employees subsequently contacted the Manitoba Labour Relations Board for legal advice (Bowman 2009b: 1–2). This is the only activity to occur outside of Saskatchewan and Ontario to date. The Nova Scotia First Nation VLT palaces are small operations making significant union infiltration unlikely. The same could be said of the Casino of the Rockies in British Columbia. Alberta appears to be the next testing ground as the five First Nations casinos continue to prove profitable, especially the River Cree Casino and Resort and the Grey Eagle Casino and Bingo. The various court decisions set an important precedent and should bolster outside organizing resolve. Worker triumphs resulting in improved benefits, wages and working conditions, even when union ratification did not occur, is also encouraging.

Notes

1.   The term Aboriginal peoples is used to describe any one of the following three legally defined culture groups in Canada: Métis, Inuit and Indian. The term First Nations is used to describe bands and the legal category of status Indians. The term Indian is used in legislation an policy and hence in discussions concerning legislation or policy and in its historical context whereby First Nations, Native and Aboriginal people were described within the popular and academic literature as Indians; in such cases it is used in quotations from other sources.
2.   The First Nations started in 1997 with 593 VLTs, a number that peaked at 615 in 2003. A provincial moratorium led to a reduction of VLTs, and today the First Nations control 403.

8. PRECARIOUS EMPLOYMENT AND OCCUPATIONAL HEALTH AND SAFETY IN ONTARIO

Wayne Lewchuk, Marlea Clarke and Alice de Wolff

Growing workplace insecurity and the decline of permanent full-time employment are undermining the system of occupational health and safety regulation in Ontario.[1] As a result, the health of workers is more at risk today than at any time since the early 1980s. Our research on Ontario suggests that only major changes in how we regulate workplaces will lead to fundamental improvements.

The risks that workers in insecure employment face are typified by the following two stories. A middle-aged woman we interviewed was working for a temporary employment agency and was diagnosed with carpel tunnel syndrome. She downplayed the extent of her injury and declined treatment for fear it might cause her to lose her job:

> I'm not [wearing the brace] because I'm afraid.... It does hurt but I purposely am not going to wear the brace that I have. And as I said to my mom, even if I do go to the doctor and it does require something, I'm not going to be able to do it until I'm working full-time.

Similarly, a young worker on a short-term contract decided not to apply for compensation despite suffering an injury on the job:

> I just all of a sudden realized that I had a hernia ... I thought about running it through workers comp, but I'm like, as much as they tell you that that's *not* gonna affect your employment, that's *gonna affect* your employment. ... If I took time off for any claim through workers comp, I just, I just didn't think it was gonna bode well ... I think employers see that. I know they say they don't, but I don't believe that.

These two stories typify an emerging crisis in how health and safety is regulated in Ontario and other Canadian provinces. Since the 1970s we have come to rely on a system that depends on workers being able to assert certain rights at work to protect their health. But with changes since the late 1990s in how health and safety is regulated, monitored and enforced, workers —especially those in precarious and atypical employment without union protection and collective agreements — are at risk. Many workers' job and income insecurity is causing them to hide work-related injuries and thus forego their right to compensation. This state of affairs raises serious questions about the ability of the Internal Responsibility System — the province's health and safety regulatory framework — to protect Ontario's workers and points to the need for a major shift in policy that reduces the burden on individual workers to police the safety of their own workplaces.

OCCUPATIONAL HEALTH AND SAFETY IN ONTARIO

Health and safety regulations were initially designed to minimize workplace injuries for all workers. In the 1970s, most Canadian jurisdictions moved from a regulatory framework based on government inspectors policing the workplace environment to what is known as the Internal Responsibility System (IRS). Under the IRS more emphasis was placed on workers resolving health and safety issues with their employers without the intervention of a third party, such as government inspectors. What made the shift to the IRS system unique and important was the fact that some basic rights were enshrined for workers, including the right to know about workplace risks, the right to participate in discussions at work on how to reduce these risks and the right to refuse unsafe work without fear of employer reprisals. And what made the IRS system effective was the establishment of joint health and safety committees composed of a worker-elected representative and management appointed representatives.

This shift to the Internal Responsibility Health and Safety System was the product of demands by organized workers in Canadian mines and factories for better protection from workplace hazards. Though the system fell well short of what labour was demanding, there is evidence that injury and illness rates fell significantly at workplaces where workers were represented by strong unions (Lewchuk, Robb, and Walters 1996). Led by unions who trained staff and members in health and safety and operating within a fixed institutional framework for employers and workers to address health and safety issues, the IRS system was an effective measure in giving workers a say in this critical area of workplace management and improving workers' health and safety on the job.

However, it appears that the ability of workers to use the Internal Responsibility System to protect their health has declined, particularly over

the past fifteen years. One clear indicator of this is the decline in work refusals since 2000. In 2000, the peak of the last economic cycle, the Ontario
Ministry of Labour (2009) reported 550 work refusals. By 2008, the number
of refusals had fallen to just over 200, a drop of over 60 percent. Such a dramatic falling off in work refusals reinforces anecdotal evidence that workers,
fearing retribution, are increasingly reluctant to exercise the right to refuse.
An Ontario Federation of Labour (OFL) report documented the seriousness
of this problem (McCutchen 2009).

Another sign of the reduced ability of the Internal Responsibility System
to resolve health and safety issues is evidenced in workers increasingly call-
ing in Ministry inspectors to sort out problems. The number of workplace
complaints made by workers to the Ministry has doubled since the mid-
1990s, while convictions by the Ministry are up four-fold and the dollar value
of convictions has increased nearly six-fold. At a gathering of health and
safety activists in Hamilton in 2010, the opinion was widely voiced that the
Internal Responsibility System was no longer working as it had in the 1980s
(Hall 2010). Similar views were expressed in many union submissions to the
Expert Advisory Panel to Review Ontario's Occupational Health and Safety
System (see Ontario Nurses' Association 2010)

So in this shifting regulatory environment, are workplaces in Ontario
becoming less safe? While the Workplace Safety and Insurance Board (WSIB)
claims that lost-time injuries have fallen over the last decade, no such trend
is evident in fatality rates. Given that the latter is least affected by employee
reluctance to exercise rights, this suggests that the health and safety environment in Ontario has not improved and that the drop in claims most likely
reflects increased reluctance by workers to make claims when injured. Still,
there are no precise numbers of the workers hurt at work each year. The best
estimate comes from workers' compensation data, but this is only a measure
of claims made by workers and those accepted by the Compensation Board.
Not all injuries and illnesses are reported, and not all that are reported are
approved for compensation. But there is evidence that in a weak economy
with widespread job insecurity and when unions' ability to protect the interests of workers erodes, the gap between actual injuries and compensated
injuries widens (Walters et al. 1995). Compensation data, for example, can
tell us something about the overall safety environment in Ontario. Nearly
3.5 million Ontario workers registered compensation claims between 2000
and 2009 — about 1,000 per day on average. Nearly 850,000 of these claims
resulted in lost work time equivalent to one worker every five minutes. The
average length of time off has remained steady over the past decade at
around three weeks.[2]

Moreover, workplace fatalities — which are less subject to distortions as
a result of economic conditions — have gone up. The Compensation Board

has accepted over 5,000 workplace fatality claims since 2000, well over one per day on average. During the 1990s, fatality claims accepted by the board declined by about 10 percent. But beginning in 2000, fatality claims began to rise and remained above 500 per year until 2008, and in 2009 we again see a decline, to 478, a level still higher than at the beginning of the decade. This pattern of fatality claims suggests that Ontario's occupational health and safety record is no better now than in the 1990s, and if measured by fatality rates, clearly worse. The fact of such different trajectories of lost-time injury claims and fatality claims since 2000 again supports the anecdotal evidence that workers have become increasingly reluctant to exercise their rights when injured.[3]

OCCUPATIONAL HEALTH AND SAFETY IN THE NEW ECONOMY

It is clear that current health and safety regulations and the Internal Responsibility System are inadequate in an environment of increasing employment insecurity. This is especially true for the growing number of precariously employed workers, a term that includes those employed on short-term contracts, those employed through a temporary employment agency and the self-employed.

The Canadian labour market has undergone major changes in recent decades, most notably with the growth of part-time and precarious employ-ment (Vosko, MacDonald and Campbell 2009; LaRochelle-Côté and Dionne 2009). Free trade agreements have exposed Canadian companies to more intense competition and forced them to become more export-oriented. At the same time, union density has fallen and changes in legislation and workplace organization have made it more difficult to organize workers. More and more workers are employed on short-term contracts or at workplaces that face increased competitive pressures. Workers in precarious jobs have few if any guarantees of future employment, and most are non-union and few receive benefits beyond a fixed wage. Our research suggests that this environment is putting a chill on the willingness of workers to stand up for their health and safety rights and participate in the Internal Responsibility System. Many workers fear that raising health and safety issues or making a compensation claim will reduce their chances of keeping an existing job or finding more work. When injuries do occur, some employers are using the precariousness of their employees to avoid their responsibilities. One worker described the lack of action when an employee is injured: "I've hurt myself a few times. Like I whacked my face off a shelf, I could barely see, but no report's writ-ten up. I don't know, its just kinda weird how they handle stuff over there."

In this new world of work, complaining about health and safety condi-tions or making a claim for an injury can spell the end of a job. The Ontario Federation of Labour documented the extent of this problem and the difficulty workers have using existing mechanism to seek redress (McCutchen 2009). As we have found in Ontario, this situation makes the existing system of health and safety regulation increasingly unworkable.

THE INTERNAL RESPONSIBILITY SYSTEM AND THE NEW ECONOMY

The Internal Responsibility System for worker health and safety emerged in Ontario in the 1970s primarily in response to the concerns of unionized, male workers in full-time permanent employment relationships. The demand for change came from unions such as the United Steel Workers, which was particularly concerned about conditions in northern mines and in steel mills in southern Ontario. Its focus was the male full-time workers exposed to toxins and physically hazardous work in these establishments. Smaller workplaces, women workers and those in part-time and precarious employment were not explicitly excluded, though over time it has become clear that the system did not serve their interests as effectively as it did workers in permanent full-time unionized work. As precarious employment and fragmented work arrangements have increasingly become the norm, the inadequacies of health and safety regulations established in the 1970s have become increasingly apparent.

Part-time employment now represents about one-fifth of all employment, twice the proportion as when the Internal Responsibility System was first introduced (Statistics Canada 2008). The percentage of workers in temporary employment, meanwhile, has increased by 50 percent since 1970 and now represents more than one in five Canadian workers (Vosko, MacDonald and Campbell 2009: 30; Lowe 2007; Kapsalis and Tourigny 2004: 6). By 2007, over one million Canadian workers were in temporary full-time jobs. Another 700,000 were in temporary part-time jobs and over 1.5 million were classified as self-employed but without employees (Vosko, MacDonald and Campbell 2009: 30). Precarious employment has spread to all sectors, from manufacturing to service and from blue-collar to white-collar work. This is no longer just a women's issue or a concern of new immigrants, although both groups are more likely to be precariously employed. Precarious employment and low-wage work now affects a majority of the Canadian workforce.

Even workers still employed in so-called permanent jobs are experiencing an increase in employment insecurity. At one time, workers in permanent full-time positions were subject to layoffs mainly as a result of slumps in demand. Seniority brought a degree of security. Recent research, though, has found that even permanent full-time workers are increasingly at risk of losing their jobs as companies shed workers in search of higher profits. Hallock (2009) concludes that the implicit contract by which employers guarded senior workers from unnecessary layoffs and workers returned the favour by showing loyalty to their employers has frayed.

These changes reflect a general increase in employment insecurity for most workers and mark the end of a brief period when employment was becoming more permanent and secure (Cappelli 1999; Vosko, MacDonald and Campbell 2009). Terms such as the "great risk shift," the "risk society" and "flexible capitalism" describe this new world of work (Beck 2000; Hacker 2006). Sennett (1998: 9) refers a set of economic relations in which "workers are asked to behave nimbly, to be open to change on short notice, to take risks continually, to become ever less dependent on regulations and formal procedures." Several authors have come to the conclusion that the system of lifetime jobs, internal career ladders and regular advancement through the ranks is "dead" (Cappelli 1999; Farber 2008).

The continuing internationalization of markets for Canadian goods and services and of corporate ownership structures for companies operating in Canada is exposing Canadian workers to additional insecurity (see Peters, this volume). Canadian markets have been opened to foreign competition as a consequence of free trade agreements, and this has forced Canadian companies to become more export-oriented. In 1970, less than one-fifth of Canadian GNP was destined for export. By 2000, this share had climbed to over 45 percent of GNP (Statistics Canada 2007b). Protections such as the Auto Pact, which once shielded an important component of the Canadian manufacturing sector from unrestricted foreign competition, have been gutted. Foreign takeovers of major Canadian employers have left decisions about Canadian employment in the hands of large transnational companies with the ability to play workers in one country off those in another.[4] At the same time, union density has fallen and changes in labour legislation and workplace organization are making it more difficult for unions to organize and represent workers.

People working in insecure and precarious employment are facing a number of factors that increase their risk of injury and illness, at the same time as existing regulatory frameworks are becoming ineffective in protecting their health at work (Keegel 2009; Walters 2000; Quinlan 2000). An important predictor of lower injury rates is a stable and experienced workforce (Shannon et al. 1996). As employment becomes less permanent, tenure and experience with a given employer declines, thereby increasing the risk of injury and illness. Precarious employment often means employment at multiple worksites and constantly changing tasks and working environments. Legislation regulating exposure to toxic substances assumes a single employer and does not deal effectively with exposures accumulated at multiple workplaces. Perhaps even more problematic are the weaker levels of health and safety protection extended to workers in precarious employment relationships (Lippel 2006; Bernstein et al. 2006). In some cases, entire classes of workers, such as the self-employed, are excluded from health and safety legislation, while sectors in which precarious employment is particularly prevalent, such as agriculture or domestic work, provide no protection.

A rights-based framework like the Internal Responsibility System is only effective in safeguarding workers if it has teeth and is widely used in all workplaces, both union and non-union alike. Under the IRS, only unions and solidarity among workers make it possible for workers to fully exercise their limited rights, including the right to refuse dangerous work and the right to take advantage of employee representatives in health and safety matters, without fear of retribution (Lewchuk, Robb and Walters 1996). Lower rates of unionization and weaker ongoing links to co-workers make those in precarious employment relationships more vulnerable to retribution for asserting the rights granted by legislation (O'Grady 2000).

We can see this clearly in Ontario, where workers in precarious employment are commonly less well served by the Internal Responsibility System. Using survey and interview data,[5] we provide evidence of the extent to which the system is failing to protect workers in atypical employment. We show that workers in precarious employment face increased workplace risks, receive less training in how to work safely, are unable to assert their right to know and are unable to effectively participate in workplace-based efforts to make work safer. These failings help us understand how it is that officially, lost-time injury rates are falling, but workers are still being injured and killed on the job.

DO WORKERS IN PRECARIOUS EMPLOYMENT FACE DIFFERENT WORK-RELATED HEALTH AND SAFETY RISKS?

Regardless of the form of the employment relationship, work continues to expose all Canadians to health risks. Our study of a sample of Ontario workers found that about one in five workers report poor air quality, working in noisy environments or uncomfortable temperatures, working with toxic substances or working in pain. Women were less likely to report working with toxic substances or in noisy environments, while workers from racialized groups were more likely to report working in noisy environments. About 40 percent reported being tense at work at least half the time and about one-quarter reported being harassed at work. Women and white workers were both less likely to report being harassed at work.

Similar to research findings reported by Quinlan (2000), our findings suggest that those in precarious employment relationships face greater work-related health and safety risks than their counterparts in permanent employment relationships. Quinlan argues that the shift to precarious employment creates new workplace risks associated with a greater sense of workplace disorganization, including the lack of training, worker unfamiliarity with work processes and less experienced managers, who are themselves often employed precariously. Several of the workers in precarious employment who we interviewed spoke of their lack of knowledge or access to safety equipment, a lack of specific training on workplace hazards and fragmented levels of authority or supervision. A contract worker in his twenties employed through a subcontracting arrangement with an internet cable company told us that he frequently worked without adequate safety equipment or knowledge of safety issues:

> I needed ladder hooks to hook onto cables on the poles. They didn't have the hooks for the ladders. And they were supposed to have a safety harness for climbing up the poles and they didn't provide that either. There was a lot of safety equipment they didn't really provide.... So, I had my ladder up against a cable strand on the poles and one of the cables broke and I almost fell. So that was very scary.... It would have been a thirty-foot fall.

In our study, the men in precarious employment consistently reported the most frequent exposure to physical risks of any group. Men in permanent part-time employment generally reported more physical risks than permanent full-time workers, but fewer than the precariously employed.

Women often faced physical hazards regardless of the employment relationship. Women in precarious employment were more likely to report working in pain, while women in permanent part-time employment were more likely to report working with toxic substances. There were no significant differences for women in different employment relationships in the frequency of noisy environments, poor air quality or uncomfortable temperatures.

Workers in precarious employment also face higher levels of stress, although the differences relative to the permanently employed are less pronounced than with physical risks. Men in precarious employment were as likely to report being tense at work as the permanent full-time employees, but more likely to report being harassed at work and more likely to report conflicting demands due to multiple employers. Women in precarious employment actually reported less tension at work, but were somewhat more likely to report being harassed and experiencing conflict due to multiple employers.

Overall, the findings reported in Table 8.1 suggest that men and women in precarious employment relationships face hazardous working conditions more frequently than men or women in permanent full-time employment. For men, the most serious risks appear to be physical risks, harassment and disorganization, while women report a high frequency of pain at work and greater disorganization. Those in permanent part-time relationships generally report more workplace risks than those in permanent full-time employment, but fewer than those in precarious employment. These findings suggest that the shift to precarious employment may be increasing exposure to physical risks most dramatically for men, who had previously been best-served by the Internal Responsibility System.

Table 8.1 Exposure to Physical Hazards by Employment Relationship and Sex (% of Surveyed Workers)

		Precarious Employment	Permanent Part-time	Permanent Full-time
Used toxic substances at least ¼ the time	Male	29.8	26.2	16.2
	Female	10.4	22.6	12.6
Work in noisy environments at least ½ the time	Male	25.2	23.8	14.4
	Female	15.9	20.8	14.1
Experience discomfort due to air quality as least ½ the time	Male	28.5	21.4	21.7
	Female	23.2	17.0	20.1
Work in uncomfortable temperature at least ½ the time	Male	33.8	16.7	20.8
	Female	29.9	27.4	25.2
Work in pain at least ½ the days last month	Male	26.5	21.4	16.9
	Female	25.6	14.2	17.0
Tense at work at least ½ the days last month	Male	41.1	31.0	39.9
	Female	34.2	38.7	43.4
Harassed at work in the last month	Male	35.8	16.7	26.7
	Female	26.2	26.7	22.1
Multiple employers create conflicting demands	Male	37.8	23.8	10.0
	Female	30.5	27.4	11.7

CAN WORKERS IN PRECARIOUS EMPLOYMENT ASSERT THEIR RIGHT TO KNOW THROUGH HEALTH AND SAFETY TRAINING AND ACCESS TO INFORMATION?

One of the central pillars of the Internal Responsibility System for health and safety is a worker's right to know about the risks at work and the hazards associated with the materials they work with. Workers learn about risks through workplace training and through access to hazardous materials data sheets, which are supposed to be prominently posted in all workplaces. Table 8.2 suggests, however, that many Ontario workers are not receiving health and safety training, nor are they receiving safety information about the materials they are using. This was especially true for workers in precarious employment. But all workers are currently being failed by the IRS.

Barely half of the men and women we surveyed in permanent full-time positions reported receiving health and safety training at work. Even fewer of the men and women in precarious employment received training. Survey respondents were also poorly informed about the toxic substances used at work. Just over half of those employed in permanent full-time positions and who regularly use toxic substances had received basic information. Only one-third of the men in precarious employment received such information. Men and women in permanent part-time employment reported less frequent training sessions than those in permanent full-time employment, but more frequent than those in precarious employment. Workers from racialized groups were marginally less likely to receive health and safety training or information about the toxic substances they employ.

Table 8.2 Health and Safety Training by Employment Relationship and Sex (% of surveyed workers)

		Precarious Employment	Permanent Part-time	Permanent Full-time
Received H&S training at work	Male	37.8	40.5	52.8
	Female	25.2	39.6	51.5
Received information on toxic substances at work (If working with toxic substances)	Male	37.8	45.5	55.6
	Female	50.0	45.8	59.1

These findings suggest a major failure of the Internal Responsibility System to provide the information workers need to be active participants in the process. Without exercising their right to know, they are unlikely to exercise the corresponding right to participate or refuse. This problem is particularly severe for those in precarious employment.

CAN WORKERS IN PRECARIOUS EMPLOYMENT EXERCISE THEIR RIGHT TO PARTICIPATE IN HEALTH AND SAFETY MATTERS?

A second pillar of the Internal Responsibility System is the right to participate in health and safety discussions at work. The main forum for such discussions is the mandated joint health and safety committees that bring together representatives of workers and managers. Committees are empowered to act on workers' concerns, investigate accidents and discuss initiatives that will reduce health and safety risks. Our findings suggest that the ability of workers to exercise this right is constrained for a large number of workers, particularly for men and women in precarious employment relationships. Given the importance of worker participation for the effective functioning of the system, the limited ability to raise safety concerns or participate in a meaningful way in health and safety discussions at work certainly weakens the efficacy of the entire system.

About one-third of the workers we surveyed believed that raising a health and safety issue or making an injury compensation claim would at least somewhat affect their future employment. Workers in precarious employment were almost twice as likely as workers in permanent employment to report that taking such actions would negatively affect their chances of future employment. Nearly half of all workers believed that raising the subject of employment rights with their employer would affect future employment. Men and women in precarious employment were the most likely to express such a belief, with three out of four precariously employed men believing there would be repercussions if they asserted their employment rights. Men and women in permanent part-time employment and permanent full-time employment were about equally likely to believe that raising a health and safety issue would negatively affect their job prospects.

Table 8.3 Right to Participate by Employment Relationship and Sex (% of total surveyed)

		Precarious Employment	Permanent Part-time	Permanent Full-time
Raising H&S concern at least somewhat likely to affect negatively future employment	Male	49.7	26.2	30.3
	Female	42.7	24.5	24.0
Making WSIB claim at least somewhat likely to affect negatively future employment	Male	67.6	35.7	34.6
	Female	51.2	36.8	31.0
Raising employment rights at least somewhat likely to affect negatively future employment	Male	73.5	52.4	45.9
	Female	57.9	41.5	41.9
Raising H&S will lead to change at least ½ the time	Male	31.8	35.7	43.8
	Female	29.9	30.2	40.1

The survey findings also indicate that workers have significant doubts that raising health and safety concerns at work will lead to change. Less than half of the entire sample believed that raising a health and safety issue would result in change half the time or more. Nearly 70 percent of precarious workers had doubts that raising health and safety issues would lead to change. Combined with the concerns reported above that raising health and safety issues would negatively affect future employment prospects, this finding raises further doubts about the overall ability of workers, particularly for those in precarious employment, to participate in improving workplace health and safety in Canada. Barely one in five workers in precarious employment believed that raising a health and safety concern would lead to change most of the time.

On the issue of participation in the Internal Responsibility System, race had a consistent negative effect. Workers from racialized groups were less likely to receive health and safety training than white workers. They were also more likely to believe that raising a health and safety issue at work, making a compensation claim or complaining about labour standards would affect future employment prospects. They were also less likely to believe that raising a health and safety issue would lead to significant change.

Given their high level of concern regarding the implications of such actions on future employment, it is hard to imagine precariously employed men and women effectively exercising their right to raise health and safety concerns at work, seek compensation for an injury or defend their employment rights. The effects of such a chill on workers' ability to raise health and safety concerns or to refuse unsafe work are entirely predictable. This is even more of a concern for workers from racialized groups.

Table 8.4 reports findings on levels of support at work. It is generally accepted that the rights associated with the Internal Responsibility System are most effectively exercised when workers have the backing of a union and co-workers. But as union density rates in Canada have fallen in the last two decades, legislative changes and competitive pressures have limited the capacity of unions to act on behalf of their members. Less than one-fifth of workers in the study reported being union members at all their places of employment. Men in precarious employment were marginally less likely to report having a union than men in permanent full-time employment. The difference in unionization rates of women in precarious employment and those in permanent full-time employment was larger.

Table 8.4 Support to Defend Rights under the Internal Responsibility System by Employment Relationship and Sex (% of total surveyed)

		Precarious Employment	Permanent Part-time	Permanent Full-time
Union member all workplaces	Male	14.6	14.3	19.6
	Female	4.9	19.1	19.4
Union help at least ½ the time if needed	Male	22.7	14.6	22.4
	Female	14.6	31.4	24.9
Help with job available	Male	32.5	31.0	42.4
	Female	40.9	48.1	40.5

Unions are still able to help workers who are not members. Interestingly, men in precarious employment and in permanent full-time employment were equally likely to report that a union would help them. However, in both cases, less than one in four survey respondents reported that a union was there to help them if they needed it. There is also evidence that men in precarious employment were less likely to be able to call on the help of co-workers if needed. Men in permanent part-time employment were as likely to report being union members as those in precarious employment but less likely to report that a union would help them if they needed it. Women in precarious employment were less likely than women in permanent full-time employment to report that a union would help them if needed but as likely to report they could get help with their job if they need it.

CONCLUSIONS

Regular exposure to hazardous working conditions and toxic substances remains a reality for many Canadian workers. Thirty-five years after the introduction of the Internal Responsibility System in Ontario and the formal recognition of worker health and safety representatives, there remain major gaps in the health and safety regulatory system for all workers. Those in precarious employment are particularly ill-served by the current system.

In Ontario as well as across Canada, exposure to workplace health and safety risks falls disproportionately on those who lack job security for one reason or another. Precarious workers in Ontario generally faced the most risks and were least able to effect change through the Internal Responsibility System. Workers in permanent part-time employment faced the second highest frequency of risks and were the second least likely to be able to exploit the mechanisms of the Internal Responsibility System. Workers in permanent full-time employment faced the fewest risks and were the most effective in using the Internal Responsibility System to raise health and safety issues and effect change.

Relative to men in permanent full-time employment, men in precarious employment relationships reported much higher levels of workplace health and safety risks. There was less difference in the risks reported by women in permanent full-time employment and those in precarious employment. This suggests that men who have moved from permanent to precarious employment have been the most negatively affected by the erosion of secure employment and workplace rights over the last fifteen years. This is not surprising given that the push to implement improved health and safety regulations thirty years ago came mainly from men in permanent full-time employment. There is also some evidence that workers from racialized groups are at a particular disadvantage in making use of the Internal Responsibility System.

In short, the Canadian regulatory system is flawed. Changes in the structure of the Canadian labour market and increasing global competition and deregulation in the thirty years since the introduction of the Internal Responsibility System have acted to limit its effectiveness. The emerging pattern of weaker health and safety protection for those in precarious employment and for workers from racialized groups is a concern given the growth in precarious employment, the decline in union density and the increasing racial diversity of Ontario's workforce. Given these trends, it seems unrealistic to expect worker health and safety representatives and joint health and safety committees, as currently structured, to be effective.

In a climate of growing job insecurity and limited worker power, relying on workers themselves to protect their health at work is not working. Ultimately, the vulnerability of those in precarious employment needs to be faced if we are to continue to rely on employee voice and participation at work to move the health and safety agenda forward. As cautioned by others, reducing worker insecurity and improving health and safety outcomes will not be an easy matter (see Walters 2000: 55–56). But there are a range of strategies that could work. (Lewchuk, Clarke, and de Wolff 2011). Policies that encourage unions to organize workers in precarious employment would enhance the ability of workers to exercise existing rights under the Internal Responsibility System and could lead to improved health and safety outcomes. Existing unions could be mandated to appoint trained health and safety representatives to assist workers in non-union companies. There is a growing need to enhance the level of external regulation and increase the number of inspectors and expand their role in guarding the health of workers (Storey and Tucker 2006: 178). There is also a need to change how joint health and safety committees function. This could include imposing on employers a duty to bargain with these committees in health and safety matters (O'Grady 2000) or giving them new authority to deal with health and safety issues at work rather than simply advising management (Digby and Riddell 1985). The report of the Expert Advisory Panel to Review Ontario's Occupational Health and Safety System (2010) goes some way to recognizing the need for such changes.

Ultimately, the surest route to improving the health of workers is through reducing their level of economic insecurity. Various countries have taken steps to protect workers on temporary employment contracts, including requiring employers to offer workers permanent status after a given number of short-term contracts. Others have reduced employment and income insecurity of those without permanent employment by enhancing unemployment insurance provisions and providing improved access to job retraining and job search assistance. While such policies are often framed as strategies to improve the function of labour markets, our research has shown that they could also significantly improve worker health outcomes.

Notes

1. This research is drawn from a set of surveys and interviews done by the authors in southern Ontario in 2005 and 2006. We would like to thank Ashley Robertson for research assistance and Andy King for helping inspire the original project. We acknowledge the financial support of the Ontario Workplace Safety and Insurance Board, the Social Sciences and Humanities Research Council and

the Lupina Foundation.

2.   This figure excludes injuries that result in long-term absences from work (greater than twelve weeks).

3.   The estimates of workplace injuries and fatalities in this section are found in Workplace Safety and Insurance Board 2009, 1997.

4.   In the last few years much of Canada's steel making capacity (STELCO and DOFASCO), mining (ALCAN, INCO, Falconbridge), high tech (NORTEL), retail (Hudson's Bay), services (Four Seasons Hotel) and large sections of Western Canada's tar sands capacity have fallen into foreign hands.

5.   The data used in this chapter was collected through a fixed response, self-administered questionnaire conducted between September and December of 2005 (Lewchuk, Clarke and de Wolff 2008). The questionnaire measured the physical conditions of work, the characteristics of the employment relationship and health outcomes of workers. In addition, the researchers conducted approximately a hundred interviews with a random selection of survey participants in precarious employment relationships.

REFERENCES

Alberta Federation of Labour. 2010. "Alternative Fiscal Update. At <http://afl.org/index.php/View-document/215-2010Aug25_Alternative-Fiscal-Update.html>.

Alberta Government. 2008. "Industry and Economy. Edmonton, AB. At <http://www.alberta.ca/home/181.cfm>.

Albo, Greg, Sam Gindin and Leo Panitch. 2010. *In and Out of Crisis: The Global Financial Meltdown and Left Alternatives*. Oakland, CA: PM Press.

Alfred, Taiaiake. 2008. *Peace, Power, Righteousness: An Indigenous Manifesto*. Toronto: Oxford University Press.

Allemang, John. 2012. "The sorry state of our unions." *Globe and Mail* March 24.

Amable, Bruno. 2003. *The Diversity of Modern Capitalism*. New York: Oxford University Press.

Anderson, John, James Beaton and Kate Laxer. 2006. "The Union Dimension: Mitigating Precarious Employment." In L. Vosko (ed.), *Precarious Employment: Understanding Labour Market Insecurity in Canada*. Montreal and Kingston: McGill-Queen's University Press.

Arnold, Stephen. 2007a. "Dofasco will stay true to Hamilton." *Hamilton Spectator* October 15.

____. 2007b. "Dofasco cutting summer positions, offering buyouts." *Hamilton Spectator* November 1.

____. 2011a. "Personal Interview with Leo Gerard." *Hamilton Spectator* January 29

____. 2011b. "Interview with Rolf Gerstenberger." *Hamilton Spectator* January 29.

____. 2011c. "$253m bolsters Dofasco's future." *Hamilton Spectator* Janueary 19.

____. 2011d. "Dofasco's new money-saving move." *Hamilton Spectator* November 3.

____. 2011e. "Picket line buoyed by CUPE visitors." *Hamilton Spectator* January 5.

____. 2011f. "Thousands protest U.S. Steel." *Hamilton Spectator* January 31.

Arthurs, H. W. 1969. "Collective Bargaining in the Public Service of Canada: Bold Experiment or Act of Folly?" *Michigan Law Review* 67, 5.

Aseneskak Casino: The Pas/Opaskwayak Cree Nation. 2007. *2007 Annual Report* . Manitoba.

Bacon, Nicolas, and Paul Blyton. 2000. "Meeting the Challenge of Globalisation — Steel Industry Restructuring and Trade Union Strategy." *International Metalworker's Federation*. At <http://imfmetal.org/files/REP_2000_ENGLISH.pdf>.

Baird, Moira 2001. "Employment numbers up: Percentage of people without jobs also rises." *Telegram*, St. John's, May 12.

Baker, Dean. 2009. *Plunder and Blunder: The Rise and Fall of the Bubble Economy*. Sausalito, CA: PoliPointPress.

Bank of Canada. 2004. "Financial System Review June 2004."

____. 2009. "Financial System Review December 2009."

Barnett, Julia, and Carlos Fanelli. 2010. "Lessons Learned: Assessing the 2009 City of Toronto Strike." *Bullet — Socialist Project*.

Bartlett, David. 2009. "Immigrants could help fill voids in labour market: Employers council." *Western Star*, Corner Brook, March 10.

Basok, Tanya. 2009. *Tortillas and Tomatoes: Transmigrant Mexican Harvesters in Canada*. Montreal/Kingston: McGill-Queen's University Press.

BC Campaign 2000. 2010. "2010 Child Poverty Report Card. Vancouver. At <http://www.firstcallbc.org/pdfs/economicequality/3-reportcard2010.pdf>.

BC Ministry of Skills Development and Labour. 2002a. "2002/03-2004/05 Service Plan Summary." Victoria: Queen's Printer.

____. 2002b. "Employment Standards Changes Come into Effect November 30." Victoria: Queen's Printer.

____. 2004. *A Human Resource Strategy for British Columbia.* Victoria: Queen's Printer.

BC Stats. 2010. "British Columbia Employment by Detailed Industry, Annual Averages."

Beauchesne, Eric. 2004. "Jobs, wealth, not always connected, says report: Newfoundland's growth leads, but unemployment rate is tops." *Telegram*, St. John's, May 11.

Beaulne, Pierre 2009. "L'impact de la financiarisation au Québec." *Nouveaux cahiers du socialisme* 2.

Beck, Ulrich. 2000. *The Brave New World of Work.* Cambridge: Polity Press.

Beech, Monique. 2004. "Hoffa's son pays a visit to Ramara: Says Teamsters would hold dealers' interests high." *Orillia Packet and Times* May 11.

Beine, Michel A.R., Charles S. Bos and Serge Coulombe. 2009. "Does the Canadian Economy Suffer from Dutch Disease?" *Tinbergen Institute Discussion Paper* 09-096/4: 36.

Belanger, Yale D. 2006a. *Gambling with the Future: The Evolution of Aboriginal Gaming in Canada.* Saskatoon: Purich Publishing.

____. 2006b. *Seeking a Seat at the Table: A Brief History of Indian Political Organizing in Canada, 1870–1951.* Peterborough: Trent University.

____. 2010. "First Nations Gaming as a Self-Government Imperative: Ensuring the Health of First Nations Problem Gamblers." *International Journal of Canadian Studies / Revue internationale d'études canadiennes* 41, 1.

____. 2011. "Labour Unions and First Nations Casinos: An Uneasy Relationship." In Y.D. Belanger (ed.), *First Nations Gaming in Canada: Perspectives.* Winnipeg: University of Manitoba Press.

Bernard, Elaine, and Christopher Schenk. 1992. "Social Unionism: Labor as a Political Force." *Social Policy* 23, 1.

Bernstein, Stephanie, Katherine Lippel, Eric Tucker and Leah Vosko. 2006. "Precarious Employment and the Law's Flaws: Identifying Regulatory Failure and Securing Effective Protection for Workers." In L.F. Vosko (ed.), *Precarious Employment: Understanding Labour Market Insecurity in Canada.* Montreal: McGill Queen's University Press.

Black, Jill, and Richard Shillington. 2005. "Employment Insurance: Research Summary for the Task Force for Modernizing Income Security for Working Age Adults." Toronto: St. Christopher's House. At <http://www.stchrishouse.org/get-involved/community-dev/modernizing-income-work-adults/m-i-s-w-a-a-reading-mat/>.

Bowman, Bill 2009a. "Harvest is great but labourers few, Young people continue to leave despite improved local job market." *Compass*, Carbonear, NL, August 25.

Bowman, Brian. 2009b. "Beef at Brokenhead. Participating demonstrators fired, suspended by First Nation." *Drum* April 7.

Boychuk, Regan. 2010. *Misplaced Generosity: Extraordinary Profits in Alberta's Oil and Gas Industry.* Edmonton: Parkland Institute. At <http://www.parklandinstitute.ca/research/summary/misplaced_generosity/>.

Brake, Michael. 2007. "Taking on the system." *Western Star*, Corner Brook, November 15.

Brautigam, Tara 2007. "Province braces for prosperous future — and its consequences." *Western Star*, Corner Brook, December 28.

Breen, Kerri 2009. "Employers' council defends poll. Federation of labour calls survey an attack on workers' comp, EI." *Telegram*, St. John's, November 27.

Brenner, Robert. 2006. *The Economics of Global Turbulence.* New York: Verso.

Bronfenbrenner, Kate. 2007. *Global Unions: Challenging Transnational Capital Through Cross-Border Campaigns.* Ithaca: Cornell University Press.

Bronfenbrenner, Kate, Sheldon Friedman, Richard W. Hurd, Rudolph Oswald and Ronald L. Seeber (eds.). 1998. *Organizing to Win: New Research on Union Strategies.* Ithaca: Cornell University Press.

Brownlee, Jamie. 2005. *Ruling Canada: Corporate Cohesion and Democracy.* Halifax, NS: Fernwood Publishing.

Bruce, Peter. 1988. "Political Parties and the Evolution of Labor Law in Canada and the United States," PhD dissertation, MIT.

Bruno, Robert. 2005. "USWA Bargained and State Responses to the Recurrent Steel Crisis." *Labor Studies Journal* 30, 1.

Burton, Randy. 2002. "Casinos at heart of power struggle: Native opponents in agreement, however that casinos provide good jobs." *Saskatoon Star-Phoenix*, November 16.

Cadigan, Sean T. 2002. "The Moral Economy of Retrenchment and Regeneration in the History of Rural Newfoundland." In R. Byron (ed.), *Retrenchment and Regeneration in Rural Newfoundland.* Toronto: University of Toronto Press.

Camfield, David. 2006. "Neoliberalism and Working-Class Resistance in British Columbia: The Hospital Employees' Union Struggle, 2002–2004." *Labour/Le Travail* 57, 1.

_____. 2011a. *Canadian Labour in Crisis: Reinventing the Workers' Movement.* Halifax: Fernwood Publishing.

_____. 2011b. "The 'Great Recession', the Employers' Offensive and Canadian Public Sector Unions." *Socialist Studies/Etudes Socialistes* 7, 1/2.

_____. Forthcoming. "Labour's Response to the Crisis and the Future of Working Class Politics." In T. Fowler (ed.), *Canadian Labour, the Canadian State, and the Crises of Capitalism.* Ottawa: Red Quill.

Canada NewsWire. 2000. "Newfoundland & Labrador economy poised for continued strong growth, says Bank of Montreal." September 6.

_____. 2001. "Growth in Newfoundland will continue to outpace the national average, say Bank of Montreal economists." April 25.

_____. 2002. "Newfoundland & Labrador leading the nation in growth, says BMC Financial Group." November 7.

_____. 2007. "Newfoundland and Labrador's Economy is expected to be the country's growth leader this year, says RBC Economics." June 22.

Canadian Chamber of Commerce. 2011. "Federal Budget Aligns with Canadian Chamber's Call for Action." At <http://www.chamber.ca/index.php/en/

policy-wins/C156/federal-budget-aligns-with-canadian-chambers-call-for-action/>.

Canadian Gaming Association. 2008. *Economic Impact of the Canadian Gaming Industry: Key Findings Report.* Toronto: HLT Advisory.

Canadian Steel Producers Association. 2010. "'Steel Days' promotes Canadian steel industry impact and sustainability." *Algoma News*, Wawa, June 1.

Cappelli, Peter. 1999. *The New Deal at Work: Managing the Market-Driven Workforce.* Boston: Harvard Business Press.

Carroll, William K. 2004. *Corporate Power in a Globalizing World.* Toronto: Oxford University Press.

____. 2007. "From Canadian Corporate Elite to Transnational Capitalist Class: Transitions in the Organization of Corporate Power." *Canadian Review of Sociology/Revue de Sociologie* 44, 3.

Carroll, Wiliam K., and R.S. Ratner (eds.). 2005. *Challenges and Perils: Social Democracy in Neoliberal Times.* Black Point, NS: Fernwood Publishing.

Carter, Angela. 2011. "Environmental Policy in a Petro-State: The Resource Curse and Political Ecology in Canada's Oil Frontier." PhD dissertation, Cornell University.

CAW-CEP. 2012. *A Moment of Truth.* Toronto: New Union Project. At <http://www.newunionproject.ca>.

CBC News. 2010a. "B.C. Natives seek gambling revenue." June 28. At <http://www.cbc.ca/news/canada/british-columbia/story/2010/06/28/bc-first-nations-gaming-commission.html>.

CBC News. 2010b. "First Nations propose Aboriginal gaming body." July 21. At <http://cbc.ca/canada/story/2010/07/21/afn-gaming-commission.html>.

CCPA (Canadian Centre for Policy Alternatives). 2010. *Getting the Job Done Right: Alternative Federal Budget 2010.* Ottawa.

____. 2011. *Alternative Federal Budget 2011: Rethink, Renew, Rebuild.* Ottawa.

Charest, René 2009. "Le mouvement syndical québécois à la croisée des chemins : se battre ou subsister?" *Nouveaux Cahiers du socialisme* 2.

Chronicle Herald. 2008. "Hebron offshore deal worth 3,500 jobs, $20 billion; Williams: "Bold steps' for N.L." Halifax, NS, August 21.

Clancy, Peter. 2004. *Micropolitics and Canadian Business: Paper, Steel, and the Airlines* Peterborough: Broadview Press.

Clark, Dale, and Rosemary Warskett. 2010. "Labour Fragmentation and New Forms of Organizing and Bargaining in the Service Sector." In N. Pupo and M. Thomas (eds.), *Interrogating the New Economy: Restructuring Work in the 21st Century.* Toronto: University of Toronto Press.

Clarkson, Stephen. 2008. *Does North America Exist? Governing the Continent After NAFTA and 9/11.* Toronto: University of Toronto Press.

CLC (Canadian Labour Congress). 2009a. *Recession Watch Volume 1: A Bulletin About our Economy.* Ottawa: Social & Economic Policy Department. At <http://www.canadianlabour.ca/sites/default/files/RecessionWatch-01_EN.pdf>.

____. 2009b. *Recession Watch Volume 2: A Bulletin About our Economy.* Ottawa: Social & Economic Policy Department. At <http://www.canadianlabour.ca/sites/default/files/RecessionWatch-02_EN.pdf>.

____. 2009c. *Recession Watch Issue 3.* Ottawa: Social & Economic Policy Department.

At <http://www.canadianlabour.ca/sites/default/files/Recession-Watch-03-Fall-2009-EN.pdf>.

CMHC. 2009, 2010. *Canadian Housing Observer*. Ottawa.

Cohen, Marjorie Griffin, and Marcy Cohen. 2004. *A Return to Wage Discrimination: Pay Equity Losses Through the Privatization of Health Care*. Vancouver: Canadian Centre for Policy Alternatives B.C. Office.

Community Resource Services Ltd. 2003. *Socio-Economic Benefits from Petroleum Industry Activity in Newfoundland and Labrador*. St. John's. At <http://empr. gov.bc.ca/OG/offshoreoilandgas/ContributionAgreements/Documents/ BENEFITSREPORT200325-11.pdf>.

ConocoPhillips. 2007. "Royalty Review submission." At <http://albertaroyaltyre-view.ca/public_meetings/submissions/2007_0619_kevin_myers_conocophil-lips.pdf>.

Cordeiro, Eduardo E. 1989. "The Economics of Bingo: Factors Influencing the Success of Bingo Operations on American Indian Reservations." In Stephen Cornell and Joseph P. Kalt (eds.), *What Can Tribes Do? Strategies and Institutions in American Indian Economic Development*. Los Angeles: University of California Press.

Corman, June Shirley, Meg Luxton and David Livingstone. 1993. *Recasting Steel Labour: The Stelco Story*. Halifax: Fernwood Publishing.

Cornell, Stephen E., and Joseph P. Kalt. 2006. *Two Approaches to Economic Development on American Indian Reservations: One Works, the Other Doesn't*. MA: Native Nations Institute for Leadership, Management, and Policy.

Couturier, Eve-Lyne, and Bertrand Schepper. 2010. *Who Is Getting Richer, Who Is Getting Poorer: Quebec 1976–2006*. Ottawa: Canadian Centre for Policy Alternatives. At <http://www.policyalternatives.ca/publications/reports/who-getting-richer-who-getting-poorer>.

Cross, P. 2008. "The Role of Natural Resources in Canada's Economy." *Canadian Economic Observer* Catalog no. 11-010-X (November).

Cross, Philip. 2010. *Year-End Review of 2009*. Statistics Canada. At <http://www. statcan.gc.ca/pub/11-010-x/2010004/part-partie3-eng.htm>.

Cross, Philip, and Geoff Bowlby. 2006. "The Alberta economic juggernaut: The boom on the rose." *Canadian Economic Observer*, September.

Dark, Taylor E. 2011. "The Economic Crisis and Organized Labor: Resentment over Solidarity." *New Political Science* 33, 4.

Dembicki, Geoff. 2010. "Oil Sands Workers Don't Cry: Toughing it out in the cold, isolated, male world of mobile workers in Alberta's oil patch." *Tyee*. At <http:// thetyee.ca/News/2010/08/16/OilWorkersDontCry/print.html>.

Democracy Watch. 2011. *Join the 'Government Ethics Coalition' to help push for stronger lobbying and ethics rules and ethics enforcement in Canada*. Ottawa. At <http://dwatch. ca/camp/ethicscoal.html>.

Dickie, Patrick. 2005. "The Crisis in Union Organizing under the B.C. Liberals." Vancouver: Hastings Labour Law Office. At <http://www.labourlawoffice. com/_.../4 The_Crisis_in_Union_Organizing_under_the_B.C._Liberals (nov 2005).pdf>.

Digby, Caroline, and Craig Riddell. 1985. "Occupational Health and Safety in Canada." In C. Riddell (eds.), *Canadian Labour Relations*. Toronto: University of

Toronto Press and Royal Commission on the Economic Union and Development Prospects for Canada.

Dubois, Alison, Wanda A. Wuttunee and John Loxley. 2002. "Gambling on Casinos." *Journal of Aboriginal Economic Development* 2, 2.

Duménil, Gérard, and Dominique Lévy. 2011. *The Crisis of Neoliberalism*. Cambridge, MA: Harvard University Press.

Dyer, Simon. 2006. "Alberta's Perceptions of Oilsands Development Poll." Edmonton: Pembina Institute. At <http://www.pembina.org/pub/1233>.

Economist. 2008. "The World Economy: Capitalism at Bay." October 18.

____. 2009. "Sliding off piste: Anxieties Mount over the Games." September 3.

Edmonton Social Planning Council and Public Interest Alberta. 2009. *We Must Do Better: It's Time to Make Alberta Poverty-Free*. At <http://edmontonsocialplanning. ca/images/stories/pdf/We_Must_Do_Better_Final.pdf>.

Elections Newfoundland and Labrador. 1996–2010. *Annual Reports — Political Party*. St. John's. At <http://www.elections.gov.nl.ca/elections/PoliticalFinanceReports/index.asp>.

Emmenger, Patrick, Silja Hausermann, Bruno Palier and Martin Seeleib-Kaiser (eds.). 2011. *The Age of Dualization: How European Societies Adapt to Deindustrialization*. New York: Oxford University Press.

Emter, Nicholas. 2010. *Weathering the storm: Recession in Review: The Alberta economy and employment*. University of Alberta Western Centre for Economic Research. At <http://business.ualberta.ca/en/Centres~/media/University20of20Alberta/Faculties/Business/Faculty20Site/Centres/WCER/Documents/Publications/InformationBulletins/139electronic/139_electronic2.ashx>.

Expert Advisory Panel on Occupational Health and Safety. 2010. *Report and Recommendations to the Minster of Labour*. Toronto. At <http://labour.gov.on.ca/english/hs/pdf/eap_report.pdf>.

Fairbrother, Peter, Dean Stroud and Amanda Coffey. 2004. *Paper 54 — The European Union Steel Industry: From a National to a Regional Industry*. Cardiff University, School of Social Sciences. At <cardiff.ac.uk/socsi/research/publications/workingpa-pers/paper-54.html>.

Fairbrother, Peter, and Charlotte A.B. Yates (eds.). 2003. *Trade Unions in Renewal: A Comparative Study*. New York: Continuum.

Fairey, David. 2005. *Eroding Worker Protections: British Columbia's New "Flexible" Employment Standards*. Vancouver: Canadian Centre Policy Alternatives B.C. Office.

Farber, Henry S. 2008. *Job Loss and the Decline of Job Security in the United States*. Princeton University, Idustrial Relations Section. At <http://irs.princeton.edu/pubs/pdfs/520revised.pdf>.

Fekete, Jason. 2006. "Klein admits Tories goofed on growth." *Calgary Herald*, September 1.

Ferguson, Rob, Robert Benzie, and Tanya Talaga. 2012. "Caterpillar Closes Electro-Motive Plant in London." *Toronto Star* February 3.

Flanagan, Greg, and Diana Gibson. 2009. *Breaking the Cycle: Stimulus with Responsibility, Stewardship, and Sustainability*. Edmonton: Parkland Institute. At <http://parklan-dinstitute.ca/downloads/reports/BreakingTheCycleweb.pdf>.

Food Banks Canada. 2009. *Hunger Count 2009*. At <http://cafb-acba.ca/documents/HungerCount2009NOV16.pdf>.

Fort McMurray Today. 2006. "Ralph Klein Out of Step: Pembina Director." Fort McMurray, AB, April 8.

Freeman, Richard. 2008. "Labor Market Institutions Around the World." London, UK: London School of Economic and Political Science, Centre for Economic Performance.

Galabuzi, Grace-Edward. 2006. *Canada's Economic Apartheid: The Social Exclusion of Racialized Groups in the New Country*. Toronto: Canadian Scholars' Press.

Gates-Gasse, Erika. 2010. "'Two Step' Immigration: Canada's New Immigration System Raises Troubling Issues." *Monitor* October 1.

Gerstenberger, Rolf. 2007. "Union braces to 'defend' steelworkers." *Hamilton Spectator* September 10.

Gibson, Diana. 2007a. *Taming the Tempest: An Alternate Development Strategy for Alberta*. Edmonton: Parkland Institute. At <http://policy.ca/policy-directory/Detailed/Taming-the-Tempest_-An-Alternate-Development-Strategy-for-Alberta-1863.html>.

_____. 2007b. *The Spoils of the Boom: Income, Profits and Poverty in Alberta*. Edmonton: Parkland Institute. At <http://parklandinstitute.ca/downloads/reports/Spoilsboomreport.pdf>.

Gibson, Diana, and Ricardo Acuña. 2011. *Tories' Gross Fiscal Mismanagement Sells Albertans Short*. Edmonton: Parkland Institute. At <http://parklandinstitute.ca/media/comments/tories_gross_fiscal_mismanagement_sells_albertans_short/>.

Gindin, Sam. 1995. *The Canadian Auto Workers: The Birth and Transformation of a Union*. Toronto: James Lorimer and Company.

_____. 2011. "Unionism, Austerity, and the Left." *Bullet*, Toronto. At <http://www.socialistproject.ca/bullet/500.php>.

Gindin, Sam, and Michael Hurley. 2010. "The Public Sector: Searching for a Focus." *Bullet*, Toronto.

Gordon Campbell and the B.C. Liberals. 2001. *A New Era for British Columbia: A Vision for Hope and Prosperity for the Next Decade and Beyond*. Victoria.

Gordon, Terry Weber. 2003. "Newfoundland Economy Soars." *Globe and Mail* April 28.

Graefe, Peter. 2000. "The High Value-Added, Low-Wage Model: Progressive Competiveness in Quebec from Bourassa to Bouchard." *Studies in Political Economy* 61 (Spring).

_____. 2003. "Trade Unions and Competitive Nationalism: A House of Mirrors." In M. Griffin Cohen and S. McBride(eds.), *Global Turbulence: Social Activists and State Responses to Globalization*. Aldershot, UK: Ashgate.

Grant Thornton. 2007. "South Beach Casino Limited Partnership Financial Statements." Winnipeg: Grant Thornton International.

Grenier, Eric. 2012. "Conservative Fundraising: Lead on Other Canadian Parties Narrows." *Huffington Post Canada*, Ottawa, February 3.

Gulf News. 2006. "Newfoundland Workers Help Ease Alberta Labour Crunch. Atlantic Migration Up 300 Percent." *Gulf News*, Channel-Port-Aux Basques, July 10.

Gutstein, Donald. 2009. *Not a Conspiracy Theory: How Business Propaganda Hijacks Democracy*. Toronto: Key Porter Books.

Hacker, Jacob, and Paul Pierson. 2010. *Winner-Take-All Politics: How Washington Made the Rich Richer — And Turned Its Back on the Middle Class*. New York: Simon & Schuster.

Hacker, Jacob S. 2006. *The Great Risk Shift: The Assault on American jobs, Families, Health Care, and Retirement and How You Can Fight Back*. Oxford: Oxford University Press.

Hall, Alan, 2010. "To Report or Not to Report Injuries: Worker Rationales and Workplace Constraints." Paper Presented at Labour OHCOW Academic Research Collaboration (LOARC) Teach-in, "Internal Responsibility Thirty Years Later: Not Yet Healthy and Still Not Safe." McMaster University, May 25.

Hall, Chris. 2007. "Contract talks to begin between Great Blue Heron Casino, union." *This Week* August 14.

Hallock, Kevin F. 2009. "Job Loss and the Fraying of the Implicit Employment Contract." *The Journal of Economic Perspectives* 23, 4.

Handler, Joel. 2004. *Social Citizenship and Workfare in the United States and Western Europe*. New York: Cambridge University Press.

Harris, Kathleen. 2011. "Gerstein credits donors and details for CPC fundraising breakthroughs." *Ipolitics*, Ottawa, June 11.

Health Services and Support — Facilities Subsector Bargaining Assn. v. British Columbia. 2007. S.C.C.

Heisz, Andrew, and Sébastien LaRochelle-Côté. 2006. *Work Hours Instability in Canada*. Ottawa: Business and Labour Market Analysis Division Statistics Canada. At <http://publications.gc.ca/Collection/Statcan/.../11F0019MIE2006278. pdf>.

Heron, Craig. 1996. *The Canadian Labour Movement: A Short History*. Second edition. Toronto: James Lorimer.

Hickey, Sue 2008. "Province showing lowest unemployment rate in 25 years: Chamber says central businesses adapting to labour market." *Advertiser*, Grand Falls-Windsor, NL, January 21.

Hogan, William Thomas 1994. *Steel in the 21st century: Competition Forges a New World Order*. New York: Maxwell Macmillan International.

Holmes, John, and Austin Hracs. 2010. "The Transportation Equipment Industry." In C. Lipsig-Mumme (ed.), *What Do We Know? What Do We Need to Know? The State of Canadian Research on Work, Employment, and Climate Change*. Toronto: York University.

Humphreys, Macartan, Jeffrey D. Sachs and Joseph E. Stiglitz. (eds.). 2007. *Escaping the Resource Curse*. New York: Colombia University Press.

ILO. 2011. "Global Employment Trends 2011: The Challenge of a Jobs Recovery." Geneva: International Labour Organisation. At <http://www.ilo.org/global/publications/books/WCMS_150440/lang--en/index.htm>.

Imperial Oil. 2007. "Alberta Royalty Review Panel written submission." At <http://albertaroyaltyreview.ca/public_meetings/submissions/2007_0524_george_bezaire_imperial_oil.pdf>.

Institut de la statistique du Québec. 2010a. "Nombre d'emplois, 2001-2009." Quebec City, PQ.

_____. 2010b. "Nombre d'emplois et répartition selon le niveau de qualité, 2001-2009." Quebec City, PQ.

Isaac, Thomas. 1999. *Aboriginal Law: Cases, Materials, and Commentary*. Saskatoon: Purich Publishing.

Ivanova, Iglika. 2009. *B.C.'s Growing Gap: Family Income Inequality 1976–2006*. Canadian Centre for Policy Alternatives B.C. Office.

Iversen, Torben, and David Soskice. 2008. "Electoral Institutions, Parties, and the Politics of Class: Explaining the Formation of Redistributive Coalitions." In P. Beramendi and C.J. Anderson (eds.), *Democracy, Inequality, and Representation*. New York: Russell Sage Foundation.

Jackson, Andrew. 2010. *Work and Labour in Canada: Critical Issues*. Second ed. Toronto: Canadian Scholars' Press.

Jackson, Andrew, and Sylvain Schetagne. 2010. *Is EI Working for Canada's Unemployed?* Ottawa: Canadian Centre for Policy Alternatives. At <http://www.policyalter-natives.ca/publications/reports/ei-working-canadas-unemployed>.

Jalette, Patrice, Reynald Bourque and Mélanie Laroche. 2008. "Les relations du travail au Québec : évolution récente et perspectives." *Effectif* 11, 2.

Jalette, Patrice, and Natasha Prudent. 2010. "Le secteur manufacturier la tête sous l'eau." In *L'état du Québec 2010*. Montréal: Boréal, Institut du Nouveau Monde.

Jenson, Jane. 2010. "Rolling Out or Backtracking on Quebec's Child Care System? Ideology Matters." In M. Griffin Cohen and J. Pulkingham (eds.), *Public Policy for Women*. University of Toronto Press.

Jha, Veena. 2009. *Employment Sector: Employment Working Paper No. 34: The Effects of Fiscal Stimulus Packages on Employment*. International Labour Office. At <ilo.org/public/libdoc/ilo/2009/109B09_128_engl.pdf>.

Joanis, Marcelin, and Luc Godbout. 2009. *Le Québec économique 2009. Le chemin parcouru depuis 40 ans*. Le Presses de l'Université Laval.

Jones, Jeffrey. 2006. "Outgoing Alberta leader wants industry to set pace." *Reuters* August 31.

Kapsalis, Costa, and Pierre Tourigny. 2004. "Duration of Non-Standard Employment." *Perspectives on Labour and Income* 5, 12.

Katz-Rosene, Ryan. 2003. *Union Organizing: A Look at Recent Organizing Activity Through Analysis of Certification Across Canadian Jurisdictions*. Ottawa: Canadian Labour Congress.

Keegel, Tessa Germaine. 2009. *"Tell me about it": Worker Participation in Occupational Health and Safety and Hazard Communication in the Workplace*. Victoria: University of Melbourne.

Kelly, Erin, David Schindler, Peter Hodson, Jeffrey Short, Roseanna Radmanovich and Charlene Nielsen. 2010. "Oil sands development contributes elements toxic at low concentrations to the Athabsca River and its tributaries." Proceedings of the National Academy of Sciences Early Edition. At <http://pnas.org/content/early/2010/08/24/1008754107.full.pdf+html>.

Kelly, Nancy. 2009. "Danny Williams hopes to lead country in labour force participation." *Western Star*, Corner Brook, June 24.

Kent Baker, H., Samir Saadi, Devinder Ghandi and Shantanu Dutta. 2007. "The Perceptions of Dividends by Canadian Managers: New Survey Evidence." *International Journal of Managerial Finance* 3, 1.

Kerstetter, Steve. 2001. *B.C. Home to Greatest Wealth Gap in Canada*. Vancouver:

Canadian Centre for Policy Alternatives. At <http://policyalternatives.ca/sites/default/files/uploads/publications/B.C._Office_Pubs/btn_bcwealthgap.pdf>.

Korn, David A., and Howard J. Shaffer. 2002. "Gambling and Related Mental Disorders: A Public Health Analysis." *Public Health* 23, 1.

Koustas, Alex. 2010. "Provincial Trends." Toronto: Scotiacapital. At <http://www.scotiacapital.com/English/bns_econ/ptrends.pdf>.

Krogman, Naomi, Sara O'Shaughnessy, Angela Angell, Sara Dorow, Goze Dogu, Mike Haan and Adriko Lozowy. 2010. *Social Impacts of Resource Development in Ft. McMurray: Examining Lived Experiences.* Edmonton, AB. At: www.see.ualberta.ca/

La Botz, Dan. 2005. "Strikes." In J. Slaughter (ed.), *A Troublemaker's Handbook.* Detroit: Labor Education and Research Project.

Labrosse, Alexis. 2006. *Présence syndicale au Québec en 2005.* Québec: Ministère du Travail. At <http://travail.gouv.qc.ca/publications/rapports/bilanrt/pres_synd2005.pdf>.

LaRochelle-Côté, Sébastien, and Claude Dionne. 2009. "International Differences in Low-Paid Work." *Statistics Canada: Perspectives on Labour and Income.* Ottawa. At <http://www.statcan.gc.ca/pub/75-001-x/2009106/article/10894-eng.htm>.

Lemphers, Nathan, Simon Dyer and Jennifer Grant. 2010. *Toxic Liability: How Albertans Could End Up Paying for Oilsands Mine Reclamation.* Calgary: Pembina Institute. At <http://pubs.pembina.org/reports/toxic-liability-report.pdf>.

Lévesque, Kathleen. 2010. "Des festins pour l'avocat de la FTQ-Construction." *Le Devoir* May 4.

Lewchuk, Wayne, Marlea Clarke and Alice de Wolff. 2008. "Working Without Commitments: Precarious Employment and Health." *Work, Employment & Society* 22, 3.

_____. 2011. *Working Without Commitments: The Health Effects of Precarious Employment.* Montreal: McGill Queen's University Press.

Lewchuk, Wayne, Leslie A. Robb, and Vivienne Walters. 1996. "The Effectiveness of Bill 70 and Joint Health and Safety Committees in Reducing Injuries in the Workplace: The Case of Ontario." *Canadian Public Policy* 22, 3.

Lippel, Katherine. 2006. "Precarious Employment and Occupational Health and Safety Regulation in Quebec." In L.F. Vosko (ed.), *Precarious Employment: Understanding Labour Market Insecurity in Canada.* Montreal: McGill Queen's University Press.

Livingstone, D.W., and Warren Smith. 2011. "A future for steel in Canada?" *Hamilton Spectator* February 26.

Livingstone, D.W., Warren Smith, and Dorothy E. Smith. 2011. *Manufacturing Meltdown: Reshaping Steel Work.* Halifax, NS: Fernwood Publishing.

Locke, Wade. 1999. *Harnessing the Potential: Atlantic Canada's Oil and Gas Industry.* St. John's, NL: Strategic Concepts, Inc., Community Resource Services.

_____. 2008. *Implications of Energy Developments in Atlantic Canada for Public Policy.* Unpublished research paper. Department of Economics, Memorial University, St. John's NL.

_____. 2009. *Oil and Gas: The Economic Crisis and The Local Economy.* St. John's, Unpublished research paper. Department of Economics, Memorial University,

St. John's NL

Lowe, Graham. 2007. *21st Century Job Quality: Achieving What Canadians Want: Research Report W/37 Work and Learning.* Ottawa: Canadian Policy Research Networks.

Lucifora, Claudio, and Weimar Salverda. 2009. "Low-Pay." In W. Salverda, B. Nolan and T.M. Smeeding (eds.), *The Oxford Handbook of Economic Inequality.* New York: Oxford University Press.

Mackenzie, Hugh. 2012. *Canada's CEO Elite 100: The 0.01%.* Ottawa: Canadian Centre for Policy Alternatives. At <http://www.policyalternatives.ca/publications/reports/canada%E2%80%99s-ceo-elite-100>.

Mandel, David 2010. "Fighting Austerity? The Public Sector and the Common Front in Quebec." *Bullet* July 25.

Manitowabi, Darryl. 2007. *From Fish Weirs to Casinos: Negotiating Neoliberalism in Mnjikaning.* Toronto: University of Toronto.

Marland, Alex. 2007. "The Provincial Election in Newfoundland and Labrador." *Canadian Political Science Review* 1, 2.

Marshall, Dale, and Jodi-Lyn Newnham. 2004. *Running on Empty: Shifting to a Sustainable Energy Pan for B.C.* Vancouver: Canadian Centre Policy Alternatives B.C. Office and David Suzuki Foundation.

Marshall, Katherine. 2009. "The Family Work Week." *Perspectives on Labour and Income Statistics Canada.* Ottawa. At <http://www.statcan.gc.ca/pub/75-001-x/2009104/article/10837-eng.htm>.

McBride, Stephen. 2005. *Paradigm Shift: Globalization and the Canadian State.* Halifax, NS: Fernwood Publishing.

Mcbride, Stephen, and Kathleen Mcnutt. 2007. "Devolution and Neoliberalism in the Canadian Welfare State: Ideology, National and International Conditioning Frameworks, and Policy Change in British Columbia." *Global Social Policy* 7, 2.

Mcbride, Stephen, and John Shields. 2004. *Dismantling a Nation: The Transition to Corporate Rule in Canada.* Second ed. Halifax, NS: Fernwood Publishing.

McCutchen, Brendan 2009. "Culture of Fear: A Report on the Status of the Enforcement of Reprisal Protection for Workers Under the Ontario Occupational Health and Safety Act." *Ontario Federation of Labour.*

McKim, Colin. 2004. "Union drive not stalled: Teamsters." *Orillia Packet and Times* July 29.

____. 2008. "Report: Canadian casinos job giants; 400,000 people directly or indirectly supported by gaming industry." *Orillia Packet and Times* n.d.

McLean, Everton. 2009a. "Looking to foreign shores. Enticing immigrant workers part of dealing with labour shortage: NLEC." *Telegram*, St. John's, March 12.

____. 2009b. "Oil and gas: One billion barrels and counting." *Telegram*, St. John's, January 27.

McMahon, Fred, and Miguel Cervantes. 2009. *Fraser Institute Annual Survey of Mining Companies 2008/2009.* Vancouver: Fraser Institute. At <http://www.fraserinstitute.org.

Mississaugas of Scugog Island First Nation v. National Automobile, Aerospace, Transportation and General Workers Union of Canada. 2007.

Morrissey, Alisha. 2006. "Fault-line job market. Province's job market mediocre: Economist." *Telegram*, St. John's, July 12.

____. 2007. "Unemployment Rate 13.2%. National Average 5.9%. A number for all seasons." *Telegram*, St. John's, December 17.

Murnighan, Bill, and Jim Stanford. Forthcoming. "'We Will Fight This Crisis': Auto Workers Resist an Industrial Meltdown." In T. Fowler (ed.), *Canadian Labour, the Canadian State, and the Crisis of Capitalism*. Ottawa: Red Quill.

Murray, Grant, Barbara Neis and Johan P. Johnsen. 2006. "Lessons Learned from Reconstructing Interactions between Local Ecological Knowledge, Fisheries Science, and Fisheries Management in the Commercial Fisheries of Newfoundland and Labrador, Canada." *Human Ecology* 34, 4.

Murray, Gregor, and Joelle Cuillerier. 2009. "The Sky Is Not Falling: Unionization, Wal-Mart, and First-Contract Arbitration in Canada." *Just Labour: A Canadian Journal of Work and Society* 15 (Special Edition).

Murray, Stuart, and Hugh Mackenzie. 2007. *Bringing Minimum Wages Above the Poverty Line*. Ottawa: Canadian Centre for Policy Alternatives. At <http://www.policyalternatives.ca/sites/default/files/uploads/publications/National_Office_Pubs/2007/minimum_wage_above_poverty_line.pdf>.

National Council of Welfare. 2008a. *Welfare Incomes 2008: Bulletin No. 1*. Ottawa: National Council of Welfare. At <http://www.ncw.gc.ca/l.3bd.2t.1ils@-eng.jsp?lid=82>.

_____. 2008b. *Welfare Incomes 2008: Bulletin No. 4*. Ottawa: National Council of Welfare. At <http://www.ncw.gc.ca/l.3bd.2t.1ils@-eng.jsp?lid=86>.

National Task Force on Oil Sands Strategy. 1995. *Fiscal Report: A Recommended Fiscal Regime for Canada's Oil Sands Industry: Appendix C*. Edmonton: Alberta Chamber of Resources.

_____. 1996. *A New Era of Opportunity for Canada's Oil Sands*. Edmonton: Alberta Chamber of Resources.

Natural Resources Canada. 2011. *Important Facts on Canada's Natural Resources*. Ottawa: Queen's Printer.

_____. 2010. "Table #4 — Features of Canadian Provincial/Territorial Mining Tax Regimes." Ottawa: Queen's Printer.

Naumetz, Tim. 2011. "Tories raise whopping $17.3 million, parties question 'Republican-Style' tactics." *Hill Times online*, Ottawa, ON.

Neis, Barbara , and Robert Kean. 2003. "Why Fish Stocks Collapse: An Interdisicplinary Approach to the Problem of 'Fishing Up'." In R. Byron (ed.), *Retrenchment and Regeneration in Rural Newfoundland*. Toronto: University of Toronto Press.

Newfoundland and Labrador Statistics Agency. 1996, 2001, 2006. *Community Accounts*. St. John's, NL. At <http://www.stats.gov.nl.ca/>.

Nguyen, Chris T. 2005. "One union sues another over California tribal casino workers." *North County Times* May 5. At <http://nctimes.com/business/article_728d6c54-97f6-543b-9a3a-39ec5d6615a5.html>.

Nicholls, Christopher. 2006. "The Characteristics of Canada's Capital Markets and the Illustrative Case of Canada's Legislative Response to Sarbanes-Oxley." *The Task Force to Modernize Securities Legislation in Canada. Vol. 4, Maintaining a Competitive Capital Market in Canada*. Toronto. At <http://www.tfmsl.ca/>.

NIGA (National Indian Gaming Association). N.d. *Economic Impact Report* 2008. At <indiangaming.org/info/pr/press-releases-2009/NIGA_08_Econ_Impact_Report.pdf>.

NL Department of Finance 2002. "The Economic Review: 2002." NL: Government of Newfoundland and Labrador.

_____. 2005. "The Economic Review: 2005." NL: Government of Newfoundland and Labrador.

_____. 2006. "The Economic Review: 2006." NL: Government of Newfoundland and Labrador.

_____. 2007. "The Economic Review: 2007." NL: Government of Newfoundland and Labrador.

_____. 2008. "The Economic Review: 2008." NL: Government of Newfoundland and Labrador.

_____. 2009. "The Economic Review." Government of Newfoundland and Labrador.

NL Labour Relations Agency. Online. "Paid Employees and Union Coverage by Industry, Canada and Provinces." St. John's, NL. At <http://www.gov.nl.ca/lra/stats/unionization.html>.

NLFL (Newfoundland and Labrador Federation of Labour). 2011. "Protecting the Labour Rights of Newfoundlanders and Labradorians in a Globalized World." St. John's, NL.

Norcliffe, Glen B. 2005. *Global Game, Local Arena: Restructuring in Corner Brook, Newfoundland.* St. John's: Inst. of Social & Economic Research Press.

Northern Pen. 2008. "Agreements aimed at preparing people for future jobs." St. Anthony, NL, September 15.

_____. 2009a. "Addressing recruitment, retention, skills development issues." St. Anthony, NL, July 20

_____. 2009b. "Province gearing up to enhance labour market." St. Anthony's, NL, August 10.

O'Grady, John. 2000. "Joint Health and Safety Committees: Finding a Balance." In T. Sullivan (ed.), *Injury and the New World of Work.* Vancouver: UBC Press.

OECD. 2008. *Growing Unequal.* Paris.

_____. 2010a. *OECD Economic Outlook: Issue 1.* 1, 87, May. Paris.

_____. 2011a. *Divided We Stand: Why Inequality Keeps Rising.* Paris.

_____. 2011b. *OECD Employment Outlook 2011.* Paris.

OFL (Ontario Federation of Labour). 2010. "Anti-Scab Speaking Notes." Toronto. At <http://ofl.ca/index.php/html/index_in/some_lines_shouldnt_be_crossed>.

_____. 2011. "Closing of Brantford's ECP Factory the Disgracful Result of Premier's Inaction." Toronto. At <http://ofl.ca/index.php/news/index_in/ontario_federation_of_labour_closing_of_brantfords_ecp_factory_the_disgrace/>.

OLRB (Ontario Labour Relations Board). 2009. *Ontario Labour Relations Board 2009.* Toronto.

Ommer, Rosemary E., and the Coasts under Stress Research Project Team. 2007. *Coasts Under Stress: Restructuring and Social-Ecological Health.* Kingston/Montreal: McGill-Queen's University Press.

Ontario Ministry of Labour. 2009. "Enforcement Statistics." Toronto. At <http://www.labour.gov.on.ca/english/hs/pubs/enforcement/index.php>.

Ontario Nurses' Association. 2010. "Submission to the Expert Advisory Panel to Review Ontario's Occupational Health and Safety System." At <http://ona.

org/documents/File/politicalaction/ONASubmission_xpertAdvisoryPanel-ToReviewOntarioOccupationalHealthAndSafetySystem_201006.pdf>.

Ontario, Office of the Integrity Commissioner of. 2001. *Lobbyist Registration Act 1998 Annual Report April 1, 2000–March 31, 2001*. Toronto: Publications Ontario.

_____. 2011. *Office of the Integrity Commissioner of Ontario Annual Report 2010–2011*. Toronto: Publications Ontario.

Osberg, Lars. 2008. *A Quarter Century of Economic Inequality: 1981–2006*. Ottawa: Canadian Centre for Policy Alternatives.

Osberg, Lars, and Pierre Fortin. 1998. *Hard Money, Hard Times: Why Zero Inflation Hurts Canadians*. Toronto, ON: James Lorimer.

Palier, Bruno, and Kathleen Thelen. 2008. "Institutionalizing Dualism: Complementarities and Change in France and Germany." *Politics and Society* 38, 1.

Palmer, Bryan D. 1992. *Working-Class Experience: Rethinking the History of Canadian Labour, 1800–1991*. Toronto: McClelland & Stewart.

Panitch, Leo, and Donald Swartz. 2003. *From Consent to Coercion: The Assault on Trade Union Freedoms*. Third ed. Aurora, ON: Garamond Press.

Parker, James. 2001. "Top court slams door on SIGA appeal of casino union: Rights of P.A. workers to unionize upheld; sides eye first collective agreement." *Saskatoon Star-Phoenix*, August 31.

Parkland Institute. 2009. *Giving Away the Golden Egg*. Edmonton. At <http://parklandinstitute.ca/downloads/reports/givingawaythegoldenegg-factsheet.pdf>.

_____. 2011. *The Lion's Share: Corporate Profits and Taxes in Alberta*. Edmonton. At <http://parklandinstitute.ca/research/summary/the_lions_share/>.

Penner, Devin. 2010. "Canada's 'Long Downturn'? A Critical Assessment of Robert Brenner's Recent Writings on the World Economy." Paper presented at Canadian Political Science Association 82nd Annual Conference, June 1-3. Concordia University, Montreal.

Peters, John. 2010. "Down in the Vale: Corporate Globalization, Unions on the Defensive, and the USW Local 6500 Strike in Sudbury, 2009–2010." *Labour/Le Travail* 66. Fall.

_____. 2011. "The Rise of Finance and the Decline of Organised Labour in the Advanced Capitalist Countries." *New Political Economy* 16, 1.

_____. Forthcoming. "The End of the Road? or the Rise of a 'New' Economy? The Ontario Growth Model." In G. Albo and C.W. Smith (eds.), *Divided Province: Ontario Politics in the Age of Neoliberalism*. Toronto: University of Toronto Press.

Phillips, Shannon. 2010. *Women's Equality a Long Way Off in Alberta*. Edmonton: Parkland Institute. At <http://parklandinstitute.ca/research/summary/womens_equality_a_long_way_off_in_alberta/>.

Pinet, David, and Peter Weltman. 2010. *Update — Infrastructure Stimulus Fund*. Ottawa: Office of the Parliamentary Budget Officer. At <http://www.parl.gc.ca/PBO-DPB/documents/isf_performance_update.pdf>.

Pitawanakwat, Brock. 2006. "Indigenous Labour Organizing in Saskatchewan: Red Baiting and Red Herrings." *New Socialist* 58 (Sept.–Oct.).

Powell, Naomi 2006. "'We Have a Deal' Mittal." *Hamilton Spectator* June 27.

_____. 2007. "Company pays premium for Stelco." *Hamilton Spectator* August 27.

Pricewaterhousecoopers. 2010b. "Perspectives on the Canadian Banking Industry."

At <http://www.pwc.com/en_CA/ca/banking-capital-markets/publications/perspectives-canadian-banking-industry-2010-12-en-2.pdf>.

_____. 2010c. "Canadian Annual Energy Survey 2010 Edition: Survey of 2009 Results." Toronto. At <http://www.pwc.com/ca/en/energy-utilities/publications/canadian-energy-survey-2010-en.pdf>.

Pruden, Hal. 2002. "An Overview of the Gambling Provisions in Canadian Criminal Law and First Nations Gambling." *Journal of Aboriginal Economic Development* 2, 2.

Purnell, Jim. 2004. "Casino dealers spurn union embrace: 14-month unionizing drive falls flat; about 62% of voters said no to joining Teamsters." *Orillia Packet and Times*, Orillia, May 14.

Quinlan, Michael. 2000. "Precarious Employment, Work Re- Organization and the Fracturing of OHS Management." In K. Frick, P. L. Jensen, M. Quinlan and T. Wilthagen (eds.), *Systematic Occupational Health and Safety Management: Perspectives on an International Development*. Oxford: Pergamon Science.

R. v. Furtney. 1991.

R. v. Gladue. 1986. (Alta. Prov. Ct.).

R. v. Pamajewon. 1996.

Reid, Harry. 1990. "The Indian Gaming Act and the Political Process." In W.R. Eadington (ed.), *Indian Gaming and the Law*. Reno: University of Nevada.

Richards, Tim, Marcy Cohen and Seth Klein. 2011. *Working for a Living Wage 2010: Making Paid Work Meet Basic Family Needs in Metro Vancouver*. Canadian Centre for Policy Alternatives–BC Office. At <www.policyalternatives.ca/livingwage2010>.

Report on Business. 2008. "Canada's New Provincial Powerhouses." *Globe and Mail* May 16.

Roberts, Dexter. 2010. "For China, too much steel isn't enough," *Bloomberg Business Week*. At <http://www.businessweek.com/articles/2012-06-28/for-china-too-much-steel-isnt-enough>.

Roberts, Terry. 2008. "Forestry: New operator possible: Union." *Telegram*, St. John's, December 9.

Robertson, Grant. 2011a. "CIBC's McGaughey gets 50% Raise." *Globe and Mail* March 17.

_____. 2011b. "Scotiabank's Rick Waugh Earns $10.7 Million." *Globe and Mail* March 4.

Rose, Joseph B. 2007. "Canadian Public Sector Unions at the Crossroads." *Journal of Collective Negotiations* 31, 7.

Rosenfeld, Herman. 2009. "The North American Auto Industry in Crisis." *Monthly Review* 61, 2.

Ross, Stephanie, and Larry Savage (eds.). 2012. *Rethinking the Politics of Labour in Canada*. Halifax, NS: Fernwood Publishing.

Rowe, Randi Hicks. 2005. "Targeted: Unions set their sights on tribal casinos." *American Indian Report*.

Roy, Noel, Ragnar Arnason, and William E. Schrank. 2009. "The Identification of Economic Base Industries, with an Application to the Newfoundland Fishing Industry." *Land Economics* 85, 4.

Sachs, Jeffrey D., and Andrew M. Warner. 2001. "The Curse of Natural Resources." *European Economic Review* 45, 4–6.

Sandborn, Tom. 2006a. "Canadian Ironworkers Shut out of Big Bridge Job, Say Unions, Contractors." *Tyee*, Vancouver, September 1.

____. 2006b. "Costa Rican Tunnellers Told Strike Would Kill Project." *Tyee*, Vancouver, November 20.

____. 2008. "Foreign Farm Workers Unionize: A First in B.C." *Tyee*, Vancouver, August 21.

____. 2010a. "The Decades Top Ten Labour Stories in B.C." *Tyee*, Vancouver, August 8.

____. 2010b. "The Biggest Rollback of Worker Rights in Canadian History." *Tyee*, Vancouver, September 7.

Saskatchewan Indian Gaming Authority. 2008. *Sharing Success, 2007-2008*. At <SIGA. sk.ca/News%20Releases/2007-2008%20Annual%20Report.pdf>.

Saskatoon Star-Phoenix. 2002. "Labour board imposed deal at P.A. casino." January 24.

Savage, Larry. 2010. "Contemporary Party-Union Relations in Canada." *Labor Studies Journal* 35, 1.

Sayers, Anthony D., and David K. Stewart. 2011. "Is This the End of the Tory Dynasty? The Wildrose Alliance in Alberta Politics." *School of Public Policy SPP Research Papers University of Calgary* 4, 6.

Schrank, William E. 2005. "The Newfoundland Fishery: Ten Years after the Moratorium." *Marine Policy* 29, 5.

Sennett, Richard. 1998. *The Corrosion of Character: The Personal Consequences of Work in the New Capitalism*. New York: W.W Norton.

Shannon, Harry S., Vivienne Walters, Wayne Lewchuk, Jack Richardson, Lea Anne Moran, Ted Haines and Dave Verma. 1996. "Workplace Organizational Correlates of Lost-Time Accident Rates in Manufacturing." *American Journal of Industrial Medicine* 29.

Shantz, Jeff. 2009. "The Limits of Social Unionism in Canada." *Working USA The Journal of Labor and Society* 12, 1.

Sharpe, Andrew, Jean-Francois Arsenault and Peter Harrison. 2008. *The Relationship between Labour Productivity and Real Wage Growth in Canada and OECD Countries*. Ottawa: Centre for the Study of Living Standards. At <http://www.csls.ca/sectors/labourmarkets.asp>.

Shell Canada Energy. 2007. "Alberta Royalty Review Submission. At <http://albertaroyaltyreview.ca/public_meetings/submissions/2007_0514_brian_straub_shell_canada02.pdf>.

Shepell•fgi Research Group. 2009. "Health and Wellness Trends in the Oil and Gas Sector. At <http://shepellfgi.com/EN-CA/AboutUs/News/Research Report/pdf/Oil and Gas Report_2009.pdf>.

Shrimpton, Mark, and Keith Storey. 2001. "The Effect of Offshore Employment in the Petroleum Industry: A Cross-National Perspective." Herndon: U.S. Dept. of the Interior, Minerals Management Service, Environmental Studies Program.

Simon, Bernard. 2007. "Alberta oilsands frenzy slows to a more sustainable pace." *Financial Times*, London, May 8.

Sinclair, Peter R. 2008. "An Ill Wind Is Blowing Some Good: Dispute over Development of the Hebron Oilfield off Newfoundland. At <http://ucs.mun.ca/~oilpower/documents/illwind.pdf>.

Sinclair, Peter R., Martha MacDonald and Barbara Neis. 2006. "The Changing

World of Andy Gibson: Restructuring Forestry on Newfoundland's Great Northern Peninsula." *Studies in Political Economy* 78, 0.

Singel, Wenona T. 2004. "Labor Relations and Tribal Self-Governance." *North Dakota Law Review* 80.

Slinn, Sara. 2008. "No Right (to Organize) Without a Remedy: Evidence and Consequences of the Failure to Provide Compensatory Remedies for Unfair Labour Practices in British Columbia." *McGill Law Journal* 53.

Slinn, Sara, and Richard Hurd. 2009. "Fairness and Opportunity for Choice: The Employee Free Choice Act and the Canadian Model." *Just Labour* 15 (November).

Smith, Garry J., and Harold J. Wynne. 2000. *Review of the Gambling Literature in the Economic and Policy Domains.* Edmonton: Alberta Gaming Research Institute.

Snyder, Linda. 2006. "Workfare: Ten Years of Pickin' on the Poor." In A. Westhues (ed.), *Canadian Social Policy: Issues and Perspectives.* Waterloo, ON: Wilfred Laurier Press.

Stanbury, W.T. 2003. "Low-Down and Dirty on Big Political Donations." *Hill Times online,* Ottawa, January 27.

Stanford, Jim. 2000. "Canadian Labour Market Developments in Inernational Context: Flexibility, Regulation, and Demand." *Canadian Public Policy* 26.

_____. 2001. "Social Democratic Policy and Economic Reality: the Canadian Experience." In P. Arestis and M.C. Sawyer (eds.), *The Economics of the Third Way: Experiences from Around the World.*

_____. 2003. "Does Growth Matter? GDP and the Wellbeing of Newfoundlanders." Presentation to NLFL Convention, Gander. At <powershow.com/view/69fde-NDZjM/Does_Growth_Matter_GDP_and_the_Wellbeing_of_Newfoundlanders_flash_ppt_presentation#.T-uxI64Q-PQ>.

_____. 2010. "The geography of auto globalization and the politics of auto bailouts." *Cambridge Journal of Regions, Economy and Society* 3.

Statistics Canada. 2006. *Canadian Economic Observer.* September.

_____. 2007a. "The Daily — Understanding Differences in Work Hours." *Statistics Canada.* Ottawa. At <http://www.statcan.gc.ca/daily-quotidien/070122/dq070122a-eng.htm>.

_____. 2007b. "National Income and Expenditure Accounts, Quarterly Estimates."

_____. 2008. "Labour Force Information."

_____. 2010. "Labour Force Survey Estimates (LFS), by North American Industry Classification System (NAICS), Sex and Age Group, Computed Annual Average (Persons x 1,000): Table 282-0008."

_____. 2011. "Quarterly Financial Statistics for Enterprises." *The Daily.* Ottawa. At <http://www.statcan.gc.ca/daily-quotidien/110223/dq110223a-eng.htm>.

Stinson, Jane, Nancy Pollak, and Marcy Cohen. 2005. *The Pains of Privatization: How Contracting Out Hurts Health Support Workers, Their Families, and Health Care.* Vancouver: Canadian Centre for Policy Alternatives B.C. Office.

Storey, Robert, and Eric Tucker. 2006. "All That Is Solid Melts Into Air: Worker Participation and Occupational Health and Safety Regulation in Ontario, 1970–2000." In V. Morgensen (ed.), *Worker Safety Under Siege: Labor, Capital, and the Politics of Workplace Safety in a Deregulated World.* Armonk: M.E. Sharpe.

Stout, John, and Jo-Anne Pickel. 2007. "The Walmart Waltz in Canada: Two Steps

Forward, One Step Back." *Connecticut Law Review* 39, 4.

Swift, Jamie, and Keith Stewart. 2005. "Union Power: the Charged Politics of Electricity in Ontario." *Just Labour: A Canadian Journal of Work and Society* 5 (Winter).

Tattersall, Amanda. 2010. *Power in Coalition: Strategies for Strong Unions and Social Change.* Ithaca, NY: Cornell University Press.

Telegram. 2002. "Jobless rate drops, still country's highest." St. John's, NL, August 10.

_____. 2008. "Unemployment Rate Expected to Dip: BMO." St. John's, NL, February 16.

Tremblay, Alain 2009. "La crise et le piratage de la Caisse de dépôt et placement." *Nouveaux Cahiers du socialisme* 2.

Trudeau, Pierre. 1962. "Economic Rights." *McGill Law Journal* 8, 2.

UNI Global Union. 2005. "Casino Workers Ratify First Contract and Great Blue Heron." At <http://union-network.org/ UNICasinos.nsf/0/ 4077ec5be6caa 599c1256ee50024d66d?OpenDocument>.

USW. 2004. *A Return to Fairness: Restoring the Right of Ontario's Employees to Unionize.* Toronto: United Steelworkers of America District 6. At <http://www.usw.ca/ admin/community/submissions/files/OLRA_04.pdf>.

_____. 2011. *Banning Replacement Workers. It Will Happen Eventually.* Toronto: United Steelworkers District 6. At <http://www.usw.ca/admin/district-6/news/files/ News6Apr11.pdf>.

Vongdouangchanh, Bea. 2011. "The Top 100 Lobbyists 2011." *Hill Times Online,* Ottawa, February 2.

Vosko, Leah (ed.). 2006a. *Understanding Labour Market Insecurity in Canada.* Montreal: McGill Queen's University Press.

_____. 2006b. *Precarious Employment: Understanding Labour Market Insecurity in Canada.* Kingston, ON, Montreal: McGill-Queen's University Press.

Vosko, Leah F., Martha MacDonald and Iain Campbell (eds.). 2009. *Gender and the Contours of Precarious Employment.* London: Routledge.

Walchuk, Bradley. 2009. "Ontario's Agriculture Workers and Collective Bargaining: A History of Struggle." *Just Labour: A Canadian Journal of Work and Society* 14 (Autumn).

Walkom, Thomas. 2010. "The Art of Reverse Class Resentment." *Toronto Star,* Feb 27.

Walters, David. 2000. "Worker Participation and the Management of Occupational Health and Safety: Reinforcing or Conflicting." In K. Frick, P.L. Jensen, M. Quinlan and T. Wilthagen (eds.), *Strategies, Systematic Occupational Health and Safety Management: Perspectives on an International Development.* Oxford: Pergamon Science.

Walters, Vivienne, Wayne Lewchuk, Jack Richardson, Lea Anne Moran, Ted Haines and Dave Verma. 1995. "Judgements of Legitimacy Regarding Occupational Health and Safety." In F. Pearce and L. Snider (eds.), *Corporate Crime: Contemporary Debates.* Toronto: University of Toronto Press.

Warnock, John. 2011. "Exploiting Saskatchewan's Potash: Who Benefits?" Regina SK. At <http://www.policyalternatives.ca>.

Warrian, Peter. 2010. "The Importance of Steel Manufacturing to Canada — A

Research Study." Toronto: *Munk Centre*. At <http://canadiansteel.ca/media/supporting_documentation/Warrian_Report_Final_Version.pdf>.

Western, Bruce. 1997. *Between Class and Market: Postwar Unionization in the Capitalist Democracies*. Princeton, NJ: Princeton University Press.

Western, Bruce, and Jake Rosenfeld. 2011. "Unions, Norms, and the Rise in American Wage Inequality." Cambridge, MA: Harvard University Paper. At <http://www.wjh.harvard.edu.>

Western Star. 2001. "CIBC Provincial Economic Outlooks." Corner Brook, NL, November 2.

_____. 2003. "Steady state: unemployment rate in province stayed the same in December as November." Corner Brook, NL, January 11.

Wildenthal, Bryan H. 2007. "Federal Labor Law, Indian Sovereignty, and the Canons of Construction." *Oregon Law Review* 86, 2.

Williams, Robert J., Yale D. Belanger and Jennifer N. Arthur. 2011. "Gambling in Alberta: History, Current Status and Socioeconomic Impacts." Edmonton: University of Lethbridge. At <http://hdl.handle.net/1880/48495>.

Williams, Robert J., Beverley L. West and Robert I. Simpson. 2007. *Prevention of Problem Gambling: A Comprehensive Review of the Evidence*. Guelph: Ontario Problem Gambling Research Centre.

Workers' Action Centre. 2007. "Working on the Edge." Workers' Action Centre. Toronto, ON. At <http://www.workersactioncentre.org/policy_and_research.html>.

WSIB (Workplace Safety and Insurance Board). 1997. *Statistical Supplement to the 1997 Annual Report. Toronto*. At <http://www.wsib.on.ca/files/Content/Downloadable%20File1997%20Statistical%20Supplement/Statseng.pdf>.

_____. 2009. *Statistical Supplement to the 2009 Annual Report*. Toronto. At <http://www.wsib.on.ca/files/Content/AnnualReports2009StatisticalSupplement/StatSupp09.pdf>.

Yalnizyan, Armine. 2004. "Paul Martin's Permanent Revolution." Ottawa: Canadian Centre for Policy Alternatives.

_____. 2010. "The Rise of Canada's Richest 1%." Ottawa: Canadian Centre for Policy Alternatives. At <http://www.policyalternatives.ca/publications/reports/rise-canadas-richest-1>.

Yates, Charlotte A.B. 1990. "The Internal Dynamics of Union Power: Explaining Canadian Autoworkers Militancy in the 1980s." *Studies in Political Economy* 31 (Spring).

_____. 2007. "Missed Opportunities and Forgotten Futures: Why Union Renewal in Canada has Stalled." In C. Phelan (ed.), *Trade Union Revitalisation: Trends and Prospects in 30 Nations*. Bern, SZ: Peter Lang Publishers.

ACKNOWLEDGEMENTS

Writing books is always a joint effort, but only when you have friends and colleagues happily pitch in is it an enjoyable experience. I could have never covered the vast and often complex topics in this book without the guidance and assistance of many.

My first debt is to David Mitchell, who has read, commented, and edited on all the chapters here, while also making innumerable valuable suggestions. Whether in Regina, Amsterdam, or London, David not only quickly turned around drafts, he just as deftly sharpened arguments and steered me away from many mistakes.

This book would also not have been possible without long conversations with union and labour activists and staff across the country, including Sam Gindin, Bill Murnighan, Mercedes Steedman, John Closs, and many others who wish to remain anonymous. And without the contributions of hundreds of Canadian scholars, journalists, and researchers who have their eyes and ears turned to what is happening across the country on a daily basis, this book would have been far poorer. I hope that the endnotes give at least a small indication of my (and the contributors') debt for their efforts. Leigha Bailey, my research assistant, very capably and without question managed putting the bibliography in order, while chasing down facts and citations.

Deep thanks as well to those to who read and commented on chapters. Stephen McBride, Larry Savage, Sam Gindin and David Fairey all quickly gave feedback when asked on short notice. Errol Sharpe of Fernwood has believed in our series on labour from the start and has been a steady guide throughout the process for this and our second volume, as he will — we are sure — in years to come. I am a grateful beneficiary of all these individuals' skill, professionalism, and goodwill.

A final note of thanks to Angela Carter, who offered both intellectual and personal support at every step and provided patience and empathy (as well as occasional editing) when yet another problem arose, all the while working on her own weighty project. Her curiosity about why things are the way they are (as well as her smile every morning) has made every day brighter and richer than they have any reason to be.

CONTRIBUTORS

Stephen R. Arnold is a business reporter with the *Hamilton Spectator*. He has written extensively about the steel and auto industries, labour, and economic change in Ontario. In 2010, he received the Labour Journalism Award from CEP Local 87M (which represents journalists working in the Southern Ontario Newsmedia Guild) for his coverage of the conflict between U.S. Steel and the United Steelworkers Local 1005.

Yale D. Belanger is an associate professor of Native American studies at the University of Lethbridge. He is the author of numerous articles and books, including *Gambling with the Future: The Evolution of Aboriginal Gaming in Canada* (Purich Publishing 2006), the first book-length treatment tracing the emergence of casino gaming among Canada's First Nations seeking improved economic development opportunities; and most recently, *First Nations Gaming and Gambling in Canada* (University of Manitoba Press 2011).

Regan Boychuk was Parkland Institute's public policy research manager in Calgary from 2009 to 2011. Regan has a long-time research interest in Alberta's oil and gas industry and is the author of *Misplaced Generosity: Extraordinary Profits in Alberta's Oil and Gas Industry* (Parkland 2010) and *Profits, Pressure, and Capitulation: Tory Energy Policy and Alberta's Natural Wealth* (Parkland 2010).

Sean T. Cadigan is professor and head of the Department of History, Memorial University. Previously, he was director of the Master of Employment Relations Program at Memorial. His book *Newfoundland and Labrador: A History* (Toronto 2009) won the J.W. Dafoe Book Prize in 2010. Cadigan's research focuses on the social, economic, and environmental history of fishing, forestry, and offshore oil and gas development in Newfoundland and Labrador.

Marlea Clarke is an assistant professor in political science at the University of Victoria and a research associate of the Labour and Enterprise Policy Research Group at the University of Cape Town.

Diana Gibson is the research director of the Parkland Institute in Edmonton. Her research examines Alberta's health-care system and economic policy. She is the author of *Access, Quality, and Affordability: Real Health Care Change for Albertans* (Parkland Institute 2010, with Colleen Fuller) and *The Spoils of the Boom: Income, Profits, and Poverty in Alberta* (Parkland Institute 2007).

David Fairey is a labour economist with the Trade Union Research Bureau and a research associate with the B.C. Office of the Canadian Centre for Policy Alternatives. He is the author of numerous reports on British Columbia labour market policy and labour market developments, including *Cultivating Farmworker*

Rights: Ending the Exploitation of Immigrant and Migrant Farmworkers in B.C. (Canadian Centre for Policy Alternatives 2008), *Negotiating Without a Floor: Unionized Worker Exclusion from B.C. Employment Standards* (Canadian Centre for Policy Alternatives 2007) and *Eroding Worker Protections: B.C.'s New "Flexible" Employment Standards* (Canadian Centre for Policy Alternatives 2005).

Peter Graefe is an associate professor of political science at McMaster University. His research deals with poverty in Ontario, Quebec politics, and federal-provincial relations in social policy. Recent publications include "The Politics of Social and Economic Development in Quebec" in (Stéphan Gervais (et al.) *Quebec Questions* (2011)); "The Gradual Defederalization of Canadian Health Policy" in (*Publius* (2009); and "State Restructuring and the Failure of Competitive Nationalism: Trying Times for Quebec Labour" in (Michael Murphy (ed.), *Quebec and Canada in the New Century: New Dynamics, New Opportunities* (Kingston: Institute of Intergovernmental Relations, 2007), 153–176.

Wayne Lewchuk is a professor in the School of Labour Studies and Department of Economics at McMaster University. Along with Marlea Clarke and Alice de Wolff he is the co-author of *Working Without Commitments: The Health Effects of Precarious Employment* (McGill-Queen's University Press 2011).

John Peters is an assistant professor of political science at Laurentian University. He is one of the editors of the *Labour in Canada* series with Fernwood Publishing. Recent publications include "Neoliberal Convergence in North America and Western Europe: Fiscal Austerity, Privatization, and Public Sector Reform" (*Review of International Political Economy* 2011), "The Rise of Finance and the Decline of Organized Labour in the Advanced Capitalist Countries" (*New Political Economy* 2011) and "Down in the Vale: Corporate Globalization, Unions on the Defensive, and the USW Local 6500 Strike in Sudbury, 2009–2010" (*Labour/Le Travail* 2010).

Tom Sandborn is a widely published freelance journalist, who covers labour and health policy beats for the *Tyee*, an online news journal in Vancouver, where some of the material in his chapter originally appeared. He also reviews fiction for the *Globe and Mail* and contributes political commentary and feature articles for the *Vancouver Courier*.

Alice de Wolff is a research coordinator who has managed projects and organizations related to equity, employment, adult education, and international development. She was a member of York University's Alliance on Contingent Employment.